Visual Studio 2013 and .NET 4.5 Expert Cookbook

Over 30 recipes to successfully mix the powerful capabilities of Visual Studio 2013 with .NET 4.5

Abhishek Sur

PUBLISHING

BIRMINGHAM - MUMBAI

Visual Studio 2013 and .NET 4.5 Expert Cookbook

First published: April 2013

Second edition: September 2014

Production reference: 1190914

Published by Packt Publishing Ltd.
Livery Place
35 Livery Street
Birmingham B3 2PB, UK.

ISBN 978-1-84968-972-4

www.packtpub.com

Cover image by Abhishek Pandey (abhishek.pandey1210@gmail.com)

Credits

Author
Abhishek Sur

Reviewers
Carlos Hulot

Darren Kopp

Sergey Kosivchenko

André Matos

Anand Narayanaswamy

Acquisition Editor
Kevin Colaco

Content Development Editor
Dayan Hyames

Project Coordinator
Venitha Cutinho

Technical Editors
Manan Badani

Shashank Desai

Dennis John

Copy Editors
Roshni Banerjee

Gladson Monteiro

Adithi Shetty

Proofreaders
Simran Bhogal

Maria Gould

Ameesha Green

Paul Hindle

Indexer
Hemangini Bari

Graphics
Sheetal Aute

Ronak Dhruv

Abhinash Sahu

Production Coordinator
Kyle Albuquerque

Cover Work
Kyle Albuquerque

About the Author

Abhishek Sur has been a Microsoft MVP since 2011. He is currently working as a Product Head with Insync Tech-Fin Solutions Pvt Ltd. He has profound theoretical insight and years of hands-on experience in different .NET products and languages. Over the years, he has helped developers throughout the world with his experience and knowledge. He owns a Microsoft User Group in Kolkata named Kolkata Geeks and regularly organizes events and seminars in various places to spread .NET awareness. A renowned public speaker, voracious reader, and technology buff, Abhishek's main interest lies in exploring the new realms of .NET technology and coming up with priceless write-ups on the unexplored domains of .NET. He is associated with Microsoft's Insider list on WPF and C# and stays in touch with Product Group teams. He holds a Master's degree in Computer Application along with various other certificates to his credit.

Abhishek is a freelance content producer, developer, and site administrator. His website `www.abhisheksur.com` guides both budding and experienced developers in understanding the details of languages and latest technologies. He has a huge fan following on social networks. You can reach him at `books@abhisheksur.com`, get online updates from his Facebook account, or follow him on Twitter `@abhi2434`.

About the Reviewers

Carlos Hulot has been working in the IT industry for more than 20 years in different capabilities, from software development and project management, to IT marketing / product development and management. He has worked for multinational companies such as Royal Philips Electronics, PricewaterhouseCoopers, and Microsoft. Currently, he is working as an independent IT consultant. Carlos is a Computer Science lecturer at two Brazilian universities and holds a PhD in Computer Science and Electronics from University of Southampton, UK, and a BSc degree in Physics from University of São Paulo, Brazil.

> I would like to thank my wife, Mylene Melly, for her continuous support. I would also like to thank my many colleagues over the years that have made it possible for me to learn what I know now about software development and the computer industry.

Darren Kopp is a father, husband, software engineer, and gamer. He started programming when creating a website for his clan in the game *Tribes* using ASP and then moved on to ASP.NET when .NET 1.1 was released.

Darren started professional development work with the golf industry, developing systems ranging from e-commerce solutions for golf shops to systems that tracked the swing profiles of golfers. He then moved on to the construction industry where he developed software that integrated payroll, human resources, service management, and project management.

Darren currently works for DevResults, which provide web-based solutions to the international development and humanitarian communities. When he isn't coding or spending time with his family, you can find him on Twitter making jokes and playing *Team Fortress 2* and *Battlefield 4*.

Sergey Kosivchenko is a 23-year-old software developer in the field of automation of business processes in manufacturing with about 5 years of experience. C#, WPF, and Entity Framework are some of the main tools used by Sergey to implement solutions. He spends most of his free time gaining new knowledge about software development and computer technologies.

For over 10 years, Sergey has been working in a company that develops web- and client-side applications and has now become one of the leaders in software development in the Southern Federal District of Russian Federation.

André Matos is a senior software engineer who discovered his passion for technology when he was a teenager. He got his first computer when he was 16, discovered the Internet a year later, and decided that he must know more about technology. He finished his MSc back in 2012 from a Portuguese university, Instituto Superior de Engenharia de Lisboa, specializing in Geographic Information Systems (GIS) and spatial data exploration.

André, now 27 years old, has experience in several technologies and platforms, starting his professional career back in 2008 with a mission to build a website for maps in Portugal to compete against Google Maps. There, he fell in love with JavaScript and GIS. He built the website and a GIS platform to support it and it was a huge success in Portugal.

Nowadays, André works for British Sky Broadcasting. His task is to build a video-on-demand service, which will run on multiple platforms. He is responsible for the backend infrastructure and service availability.

Apart from the frontend technologies, André is an open source enthusiast with several open source projects hosted on his GitHub repo (`http://github.com/apdmatos`), and has contributed to other projects, such as jQuery, Ninject, and Underscore.

Anand Narayanaswamy, an ASPInsider, works as a freelance writer based in Trivandrum, Kerala, India. He was a Microsoft Most Valuable Professional (MVP) from 2002 to 2011 and had worked as a Chief Technical Editor for www.ASPAlliance.com for a period of 5 years.

Anand has also worked as a technical editor for several popular publishers, such as Sams, Addison-Wesley Professional, Wrox, Deitel, Packt Publishing, and Manning. His technical editing skills helped the authors of *Sams Teach Yourself the C# Language in 21 Days, Sams*; *Core C# and .NET: The Complete and Comprehensive Developer's Guide to C# 2.0 and .NET 2.0, Prentice Hall*; *Professional ADO.NET 2 Programming with SQL Server 2005, Oracle and MySQL, Wrox*; *ASP.NET 2.0 Web Parts in Action: Building Dynamic Web Portals, Wrox*, and *Internet and World Wide Web (4th Edition), Deitel*, to fine-tune the content.

He also contributed articles to the Microsoft Knowledge Base, and sites such as www.c-sharpcorner.com, www.developer.com, and www.codeguru.com, and delivered podcast shows.

Anand runs his own blog at LearnXpress (www.learnxpress.com) and provides blog script installation services. He also hosts a video channel at http://tv.learnxpress.com, where you can watch free videos related to Windows, social media, and other related technologies. He is the author and publisher of free LearnXpress study guides that can be downloaded in PDF format directly from his blog.

Anand can be reached at visualanand@gmail.com and will smile if you follow him on Twitter @visualanand.

www.PacktPub.com

Support files, eBooks, discount offers, and more

For support files and downloads related to your book, please visit www.PacktPub.com.

Did you know that Packt offers eBook versions of every book published, with PDF and ePub files available? You can upgrade to the eBook version at www.PacktPub.com and as a print book customer, you are entitled to a discount on the eBook copy. Get in touch with us at service@packtpub.com for more details.

At www.PacktPub.com, you can also read a collection of free technical articles, sign up for a range of free newsletters and receive exclusive discounts and offers on Packt books and eBooks.

http://PacktLib.PacktPub.com

Do you need instant solutions to your IT questions? PacktLib is Packt's online digital book library. Here, you can search, access, and read Packt's entire library of books.

Why subscribe?

- ▸ Fully searchable across every book published by Packt
- ▸ Copy and paste, print, and bookmark content
- ▸ On demand and accessible via a web browser

Free access for Packt account holders

If you have an account with Packt at www.PacktPub.com, you can use this to access PacktLib today and view 9 entirely free books. Simply use your login credentials for immediate access.

Instant updates on new Packt books

Get notified! Find out when new books are published by following @PacktEnterprise on Twitter or the *Packt Enterprise* Facebook page.

Table of Contents

Preface

The world is changing and the software industry is no exception. The software that exists today will be obsolete very soon. Introduction of new devices requires newer software. The changes are gradually reflected not only in the devices, but also in every sphere of the software industry—starting from natural language processing, embedded technology, microchip level programming, and so on. The hardware revolution asks for language enhancements to support better hardware. A high number of releases of software changes has always been common news for any developer. As a developer, it is very hard to know everything when a new release occurs. Learning continuously and gaining knowledge is the only way to survive in this dynamic software industry.

This book focuses on giving you expert advice on how to deal with changes in the software industry. It provides you with easy steps to deal with complex software problems. It gives you as many details as possible, and covers most of the technological domains in the world of .NET. This book is written in the form of recipes with step-by-step tutorials on every topic, where the developer accompanies the author in this wonderful journey into the known and hitherto unknown realms of .NET. This book presents you, as a developer, with easy steps to solve complex problems and thereby gives you the most relevant associated information that you would require. There is a special section (*There's more...*) for each recipe, which focuses on giving you extra knowledge on things that you might have missed. By the time you come to the end of this journey, you will enjoy the confidence that a clear understanding of .NET gives you.

This is a practical handbook that effectively utilizes the time spent while reading the book for the knowledge gained. This book is suitable for people who require solutions to problems in quick time, while providing a clear understanding of the topics with relevant sample code blocks. The examples given in this book are simple, easy to understand, and they map the user to port the same code with a few changes in the production environment. If you want to utilize your busy schedule to explore some of the ongoing technologies in the market, this book is for you.

What this book covers

Chapter 1, A Guide to Debugging with Visual Studio, focuses on giving you a basic understanding of the different environments set up inside Visual Studio and deals with all the necessary tools present inside Visual Studio to help in debugging a source. This chapter clarifies the debugging procedures in detail, followed by quick and easy sample code to help find bugs.

Chapter 2, Enhancements to WCF 4.5, deals with the Service Oriented Architecture using WCF. This chapter gives you knowledge on common problems that a developer needs to know and provides you with sample recipes to deal with them. It also gives a clear understanding on all the new features that come along with new releases.

Chapter 3, Building a Touch-sensitive Device Application Using Windows Phone 8, provides a quick introduction on device application development with the Windows Phone environment. This chapter provides simple solutions to some of the common problems when developing a Windows Phone application.

Chapter 4, Working with Team Foundation Server, deals with the source control functionality using Visual Studio ALM. The chapter provides detailed, step-by-step recipes to deal with development issues using a Team Foundation Server with the configuration and easy implementation of a successful TFS.

Chapter 5, Testing Applications Using Visual Studio 2013, provides a deeper insight on testing a full-fledged application. This chapter provides all the relevant information that you need to know about testing inside Visual Studio, enabling you to write tests quickly in easy steps, and a clear understanding of what is going on under the hood.

Chapter 6, Extending the Visual Studio IDE, focuses on presenting interesting facts related to adding more functionalities in Visual Studio. The need to customize Visual Studio itself is sometimes necessary to allow a developer to customize the tools inside the integrated environment. This chapter provides you with points that will help in dealing with extensions on the Visual Studio IDE in easy steps.

Chapter 7, Understanding Cloud Computing with Windows Azure, demonstrates the Microsoft implementation of cloud computing, enabling you to quickly adapt Azure in your own solution in easy steps. This chapter gives recipes to help a developer port their existing on-premise applications to the cloud.

What you need for this book

The basic software requirements for this book are as follows:

- Microsoft .NET Framework 4.5 and higher
- Microsoft Visual Studio 2013
- Windows 8 operating system
- A Windows Phone to deploy Windows Phone apps
- Latest web browsers
- An account on Windows Azure

Who this book is for

The purpose of this book is to give you ready-made steps in the form of recipes to develop common tasks that, as a developer, you might often be required to access. This book utilizes its chapters skillfully to provide as much information as it can and also in as much detail as necessary to kick-start the operation. This book also delivers in-depth analysis of some advanced sections of the subject to get you to an expert's level. If you are a beginner in the development environment and want to gain expertise on the ongoing technologies in the market, this book is ideal for you. Even for architects and project managers, this book is a guide to enriching your existing knowledge.

This book uses C# and Visual Studio 2013 with Windows 8 (as the operating system) in the examples. Even though you do not require any knowledge of Visual Studio to start, you are expected to have some basic theoretical and practical overall experience on the subjects to understand the recipes. The book bridges the gap between a beginner and an advanced developer.

Conventions

In this book, you will find a number of styles of text that distinguish between different kinds of information. Here are some examples of these styles, and an explanation of their meaning.

Code words in text, database table names, folder names, filenames, file extensions, pathnames, dummy URLs, user input, and Twitter handles are shown as follows: "The program will pause during the first `Run` method."

A block of code is set as follows:

```
static void Main()
{
    Thread.CurrentThread.Name = "Main Thread";
    Thread t1 = new Thread(new ThreadStart(Run));
    t1.Name = "Thread 1";
    Thread t2 = new Thread(new ThreadStart(Run));
    t2.Name = "Thread 2";
    t1.Start();
    t2.Start();
    Run();
}
static void Run()
{
    Console.WriteLine("hello {0}!", Thread.CurrentThread.Name);
    Thread.Sleep(1000);
}
```

When we wish to draw your attention to a particular part of a code block, the relevant lines or items are set in bold:

```
// Type 'Abhishek' in 'txtInput' text box
uITxtInputEdit.Text = this.ReverseStringTestParams.
UITxtInputEditText;
```

Any command-line input or output is written as follows:

```
ALTER DATABASE MyDatabase MODIFY (EDITION='BUSINESS', MAXSIZE=100GB)
```

New terms and **important words** are shown in bold. Words that you see on the screen, in menus or dialog boxes for example, appear in the text like this: "You can declare a local variable using the **Watch** window and use it in the conditions."

Warnings or important notes appear in a box like this.

Tips and tricks appear like this.

Reader feedback

Feedback from our readers is always welcome. Let us know what you think about this book—what you liked or may have disliked. Reader feedback is important for us to develop titles that you really get the most out of.

To send us general feedback, simply send an e-mail to `feedback@packtpub.com`, and mention the book title via the subject of your message.

If there is a topic that you have expertise in and you are interested in either writing or contributing to a book, see our author guide on `www.packtpub.com/authors`.

Customer support

Now that you are the proud owner of a Packt book, we have a number of things to help you to get the most from your purchase.

Downloading the example code

You can download the example code files for all Packt books you have purchased from your account at `http://www.packtpub.com`. If you purchased this book elsewhere, you can visit `http://www.packtpub.com/support` and register to have the files e-mailed directly to you.

Errata

Although we have taken every care to ensure the accuracy of our content, mistakes do happen. If you find a mistake in one of our books—maybe a mistake in the text or the code—we would be grateful if you would report this to us. By doing so, you can save other readers from frustration and help us improve subsequent versions of this book. If you find any errata, please report them by visiting `http://www.packtpub.com/submit-errata`, selecting your book, clicking on the **errata submission form** link, and entering the details of your errata. Once your errata are verified, your submission will be accepted and the errata will be uploaded on our website, or added to any list of existing errata, under the Errata section of that title. Any existing errata can be viewed by selecting your title from `http://www.packtpub.com/support`.

Piracy

Piracy of copyright material on the Internet is an ongoing problem across all media. At Packt, we take the protection of our copyright and licenses very seriously. If you come across any illegal copies of our works, in any form, on the Internet, please provide us with the location address or website name immediately so that we can pursue a remedy.

Please contact us at `copyright@packtpub.com` with a link to the suspected pirated material.

We appreciate your help in protecting our authors, and our ability to bring you valuable content.

Questions

You can contact us at `questions@packtpub.com` if you are having a problem with any aspect of the book, and we will do our best to address it.

1

A Guide to Debugging with Visual Studio

In this chapter, we will cover the following recipes:

- ▶ Debugging source code using breakpoints
- ▶ Using DataTips during debugging
- ▶ Debugging a multithreaded program
- ▶ Exploring the Command and Immediate windows
- ▶ Making use of IntelliTrace in Visual Studio
- ▶ Debugging a .NET program using the framework library source
- ▶ Debugging a process that is already deployed

Introduction

Being one of the best IDEs available, it may often seem that our knowledge about Visual Studio falls short when some special circumstances appear. Visual Studio provides hundreds of tools inside it and also some tools as extensions to help programmers develop software in the best possible ways. It incorporates features such as refactoring, code analysis, clone code finder, and so on to let a developer write better code and have the best experience while inside the IDE. Visual Studio has been so popular that it is not constrained to just software development; some people use it to edit documents and images, or even to publish content. It is so user friendly and easy to use that anyone can work on it at a basic level.

Debugging is the most important part of any application development process. People like to start debugging a program while developing code. Debugging is a process that lets you have a quick look at the current state of a program by walking through your code step by step and letting you identify what exactly is happening while the program is running. Developers expect an IDE to give them as much information as possible during a certain state of the program. Visual Studio has taken every step to improve the debugging experience of the IDE and make small tools to let developers find better ways to quickly find the possible problems in code (if any).

After opening the IDE, it is often the case that people start typing some code. But, it is unlikely that developers will always finish writing the code before they start debugging. After some part of the development is done, they tend to start debugging it to have a better understanding of the logic and functionalities. Some people start debugging even before they have written a single line of code. So debugging is not just identifying bugs, it is determining the merits and demerits of the code as well. Debugging inside Visual Studio is perhaps the best selling point of the IDE.

Visual Studio separates the environment layout completely while debugging. After writing your code, when you press *F5* on the keyboard or go to **Debug** | **Start Debugging**, Visual Studio adjusts the whole layout of the window and creates an environment that is best suited for debugging; for instance, when you are in the debug mode, generally the **Solution Explorer**, **Toolbox**, the **Properties** window, and so on get hidden. Instead, windows such as **IntelliTrace**, **Autos**, **Locals**, **Watch**, and **Call Stack** automatically open inside the IDE and get docked/adjusted to the layout inside the IDE. The IDE is smart enough to store the layout information of all the opened windows inside it when the debugging session is closed by the user for a particular project. Therefore, when you start debugging again, the IDE provides you an environment that is exactly adjusted to the left-hand side when the previous debug session is closed.

In this chapter, we will try to demonstrate some of the important debugging tools available in the IDE. Let's start with a simple class that consists of a few properties and methods:

```
public class TestClass
{
  public int Start { get; set; }
  public int End { get; set; }

  public TestClass(int start, int end)
  {
    this.Start = start;
    this.End = end;
  }
  public int GetSum(int start, int end)
  {
    var sum = 0;
    for (var i = start; i <= end; i++)
      sum += i;
    return sum;
```

```csharp
        }

    public string GetMessage()
    {
      var sum = this.GetSum(this.Start, this.End);
      return string.Format("Sum of all numbers between {0} and {1}
  is {2}", this.Start, this.End, sum);
    }
    public void PrintMessage()
      {
        var message = this.GetMessage();
        Console.WriteLine(message);
        Console.ReadKey(true);
      }


    }
    class Program
    {
      static void Main(string[] args)
      {
        var tclass = new TestClass(20, 30);
        tclass.PrintMessage();
      }
    }
  }
```

The dummy code that we are using here has a `TestClass`, which takes two arguments and stores data in the data members `Start` and `End`. `GetSum` is a method that sums up all the integers between `Start` and `End`. The `GetMessage` returns a message after calling `Sum` with `Start` and `End`, and finally `PrintMessage` prints the message on the console.

The program creates an object of `TestClass` and calls `PrintMessage` with `20, 30`. If you run the program, it shows `275` on the console.

Debugging source code using breakpoints

Breakpoints are used to notify the debugger to pause execution of the program at a certain line. The debugger stores the information of the line number and source code file inside the PDB file (known as the program database). The program built in the debug mode will have more information in the PDB file than the one in the release mode. Visual Studio reads the PDB file and pauses/resumes debugging based on the `Halt` statement it finds during the execution of the program.

How to do it...

Now let's create our first source code and try out debugging for the first time:

1. Click on the left-hand sidebar of the code or press *F9* on the keyboard being on the line where you want to pause execution of the program. The whole line will be colored in a dark red border (in general) with a red circle on the sidebar.

2. Press *F5* on the keyboard to start the program in the debug mode.

3. As soon as the program gets started, it will break at the point where the breakpoint is hit. Let's suppose we put a breakpoint on the first line of the `Main` method where the `TestClass` is instantiated:

```
static void Main(string[] args)
{
    TestClass tclass = new TestClass(20, 30);
    tclass.PrintMessage();
}
```

In the preceding screenshot, the red dot on the left-hand sidebar shows the breakpoint. The yellow block indicates the hit of the breakpoint. When you put the breakpoint on a line, the line is turned red by the IDE, and the current line is marked using a yellow block as shown with a small arrow on the left-hand side pane.

4. Press *F10* to skip the line and move to the next line.

5. Press *F11* to initiate the `PrintMessage` method. Press *F11* a couple more times to move to the actual calculation.

6. Inspect each and every line of the code to identify your bug (if any).

7. To continue executing the program, press *F5* again; the program will continue executing the rest of the code until it either finds another breakpoint on the code during its execution path or the program finishes execution.

How it works...

The debugger is a tool attached with the Visual Studio IDE that works in the background and inspects execution of the program. It holds a database of all the debug-related information and stores it in a program database file. The Visual Studio debugger stores the checksum of the file associated with the debugger, its full path, the line number, and the number of characters of the file. When we create a breakpoint in the file, the information gets stored on the PDB file or sometimes in the memory, and this will get evaluated when the program is running under the debug mode.

The debugger cannot work in certain situations when the debug information related to the file is invalid (when file checksum fails) or does not exist. For instance, say you have compiled the executable in a different source other than the one you are debugging with. In this case, Visual Studio is capable of determining whether the source code and the process running are the same.

There's more...

Now let's look at how to take advantage of breakpoints in the Visual Studio IDE.

Changing the execution step while debugging

The Visual Studio debugger is very smart and capable of doing a lot of things. You can change the execution path directly inside the debugger by not executing a certain line of the code or executing a certain line more than once.

While you are at the breakpoint, you can right-click on any line inside the IDE and select **Set Next Statement** or use *Ctrl + Shift + F10* to move the debugger to that line, as shown in the following screenshot:

public TestClass(int
{
    this.Start = sta
    this.End = end;
}
public int GetSum(in
{
    int sum = 0;
    for (int i = sta
        sum += i;
    return sum;
}
Set Next Statement
Go To Disassembly
Cut
Copy
Paste
Outlining
Find Matching Clones in Solution
Ctrl+Shift+F10
Ctrl+X
Ctrl+C
Ctrl+V
control shifts to
the current line

You can also drag the cursor of the current line using the mouse to move the cursor to any line in the code.

If you choose **Run to Cursor** from the right-click menu instead of **Set Next Statement**, the debugger will execute the lines in between and stop at the line that you select. If the line you select does not belong to the following execution of code, it will finish execution in regular course.

Labeling a breakpoint

When working with a large project, there are situations when you need to label your breakpoints for better management and categorization such that you can enable/disable a certain group of breakpoints depending on your requirements. Let's put some breakpoints on the code and start debugging using *F5* from the keyboard. The program will stop at the line where the first breakpoint is set, as shown in the following screenshot. Navigate to **Debug | Windows | Breakpoints** or press *Ctrl + D + B*.

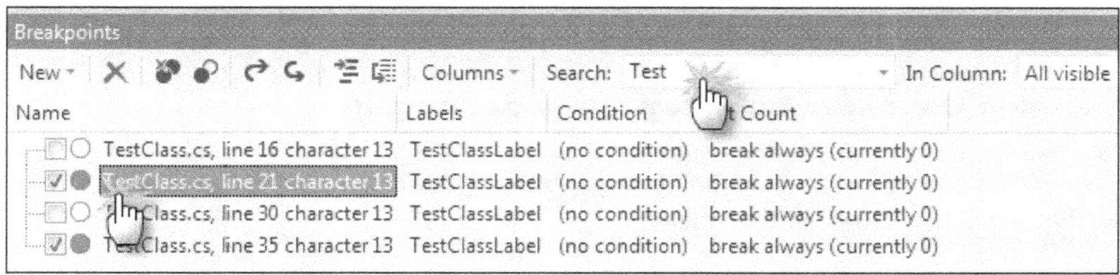

A window will appear that will show all the breakpoints you have set in the code. In the preceding screenshot, you can see **TestClassLabel**. Now, let us right-click either on the breakpoint in the code or in the **Tool** window and select **Edit labels**, as shown in the following screenshot:

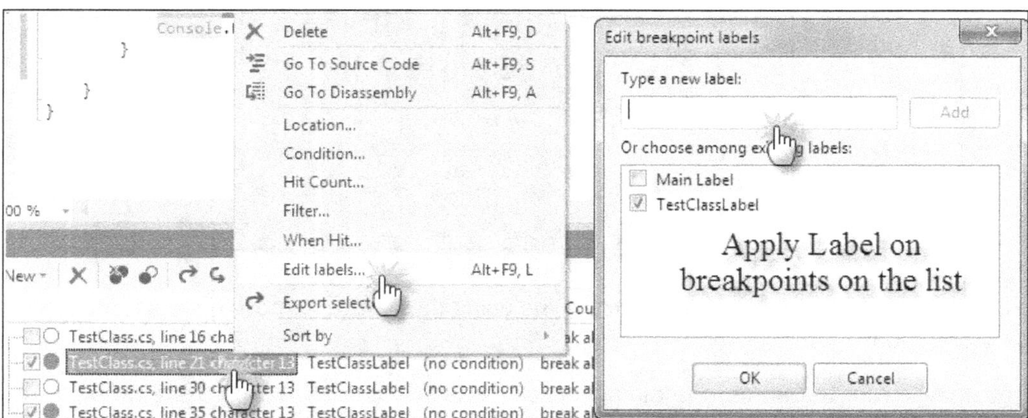

The command will pop up the **Edit breakpoint labels** dialog box, which lists all the labels and allows you to create a new label. Initially, it will be blank, but as you create more labels, the list will fill up. Once you have created the labels, you can choose any of the labels associated with the current breakpoint. You can also choose multiple breakpoints to select a label. Once you have selected the label for all the breakpoints individually, you can search in the **Search** box of the **Breakpoints** tool window to filter breakpoints from the list.

It is important to note that labels play a very important role in naming a breakpoint. When dealing with large projects, it will be really easy to manage breakpoints with labels to identify exactly which breakpoint it shows. The label is an alias to a breakpoint.

The breakpoint window also allows you to enable/disable an existing breakpoint. For instance, you can uncheck a breakpoint to disable the breakpoint in the actual code. Even though the breakpoint exists in the code, it is marked as disabled, and hence the program will not halt at that point.

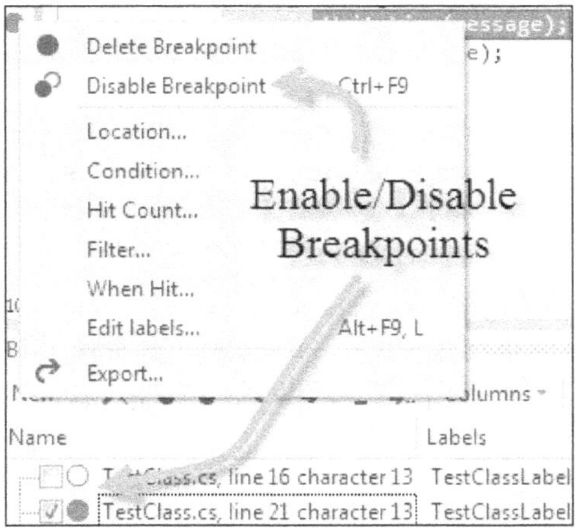

The preceding screenshot shows how to disable a breakpoint from the right-click menu. It can also be accessed using *Ctrl + F9*.

Adding a condition in breakpoints

Breakpoints can hold conditions and often come in handy when used in the iteration of a list or numeric value. Putting a halt inside an iteration means redundant breakpoints, and when the problem arises on a certain index of the loop, it is very hard to catch the exact value of the index. Conditions can help in putting a break only when a certain precondition is met. The conditional break allows placing an expression based on the current context and breaks only when the condition is met.

Right-click on the breakpoint either in the tool window or on the sidebar pane where the red breakpoint icon is shown and select a condition, as shown in the following screenshot:

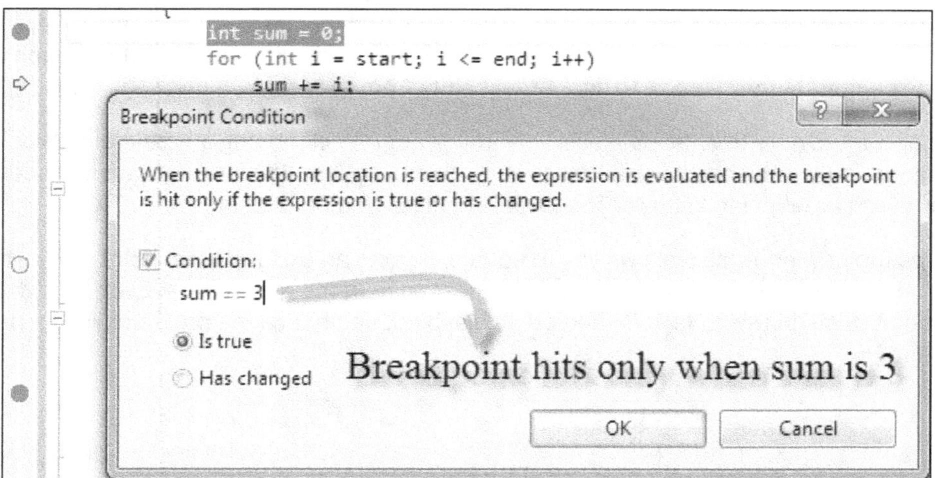

You can declare a local variable using the **Watch** window and use it in the conditions. The IDE validates the condition and stores it in the PDB file. The textbox that appears is also capable of showing the IntelliSense menu inside it to enhance condition writing.

The two radio buttons indicate what needs to be considered from the condition. If the condition returns a Boolean value, we choose the option **Is true**; otherwise, we choose **Has changed**, where the condition can be anything.

Note that after choosing a condition, the red breakpoint icon will show a plus symbol, which indicates that it is conditional.

Exporting breakpoints

Visual Studio allows you to import/export breakpoints. If many developers are working on the same code, you can share the breakpoints that you have created in one project with others or save it. So, if you have breakpoints organized with labels, everything is exported to a file that can be used later, as shown:

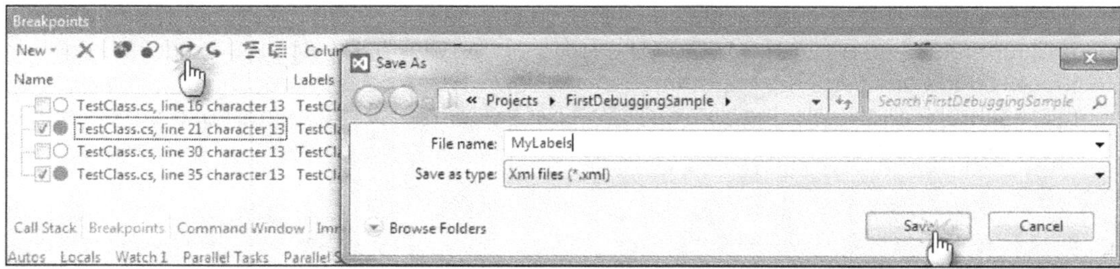

The file is actually an XML file, which produces XML content of all the breakpoints. A breakpoint, once exported, can be imported back again by choosing the **Import Breakpoint** button on the **Breakpoint** tool window.

Remember, breakpoints are created inside a `.suo` (**Solution User Option**) file, but the actual program halts are written inside the PDB file. Thus, while running the program from inside `vshost`, if PDB is not found, the file cannot hit the breakpoints even though the breakpoints exist on the IDE.

Breakpoint hit counters

A **breakpoint hit counter** is used to determine how many times a breakpoint has been hit on a particular line. Sometimes, it is needed to halt a program only when a certain number of breakpoints have already been hit. Consider a situation where you are iterating with a large number of loops. In these cases, we can configure the breakpoint to stop only when the number of hits it encounters reaches a threshold, as shown in the following screenshot:

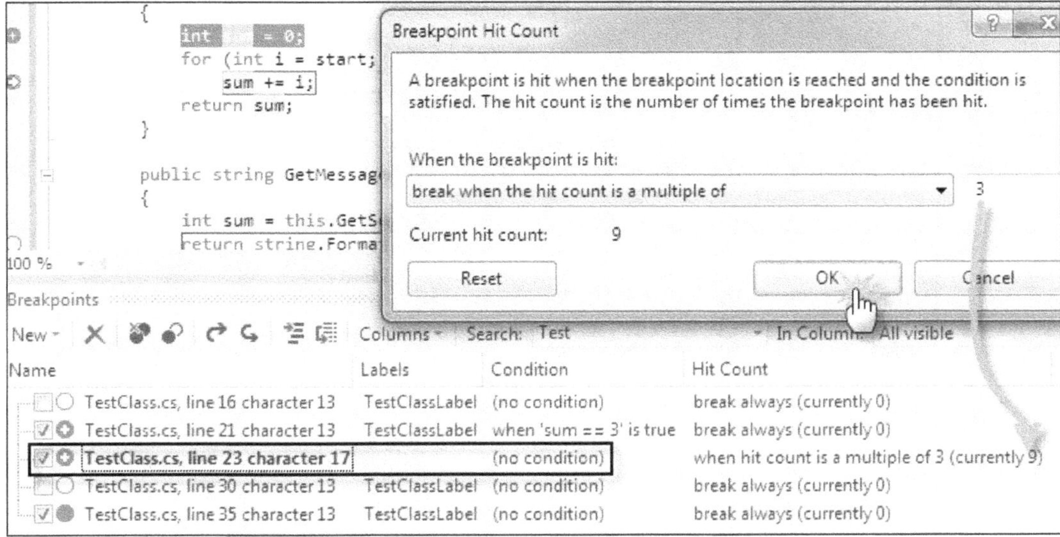

In the preceding screenshot, you can see the breakpoint hit count box, which is opened by right-clicking on the breakpoint and selecting **Hit Count**. The default setting is **Break always** but we can configure it to hit on a counter or a multiple of a counter, or even greater than equal to a counter.

Adding tracepoints while debugging

As a default, when a breakpoint is hit, it will halt the execution of the program and pause it until we run the program again. But when the application is pretty large, you may want to continue the program and either run a macro when the breakpoint is hit or invoke a trace method. The breakpoint in such cases is called a **tracepoint**. To open the tracepoint window, right-click on a breakpoint and select **When Hit**.

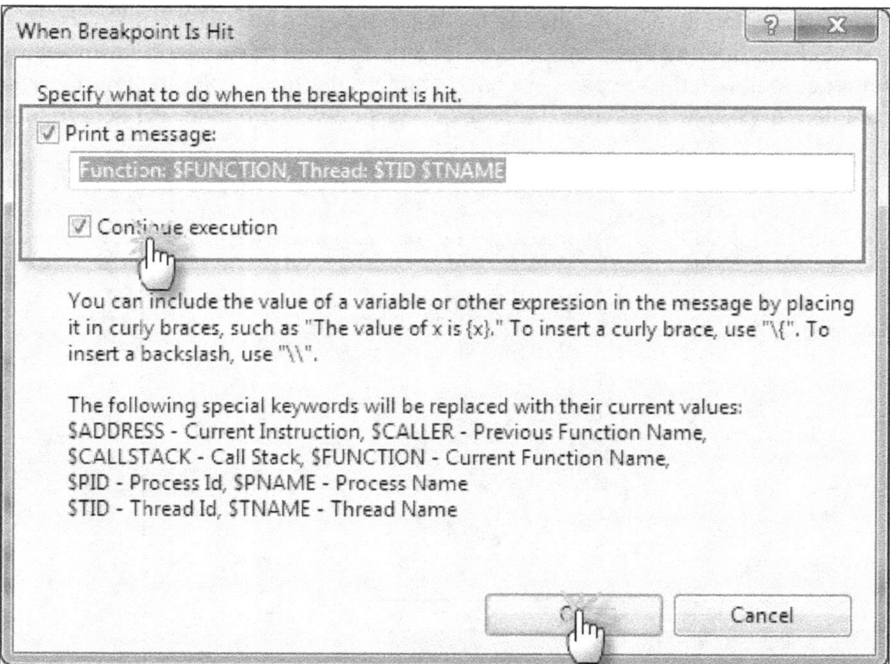

Notice that we print the function name, thread ID, and thread name when the breakpoint is hit. The tracepoints can print items on the output window based on the options listed on the window. Keywords such as **$ADDRESS, $CALLER**, and so on specified on the window provide macros that evaluate the specific context. After you place a tracepoint, the breakpoint identifier in the left-hand side of the screen will appear as a red diamond instead of a circle.

If you choose **Continue execution**, it means the macro that we selected will be executed without stopping the code execution.

Filtering breakpoints

Breakpoint filters allow you to specify any additional criteria of the breakpoint. With filters applied, you can specify the breakpoint to hit only for a specific machine, or a specific process or a thread. This is often required if you are executing your program several times with a different process ID each time and want to debug only on a certain process ID.

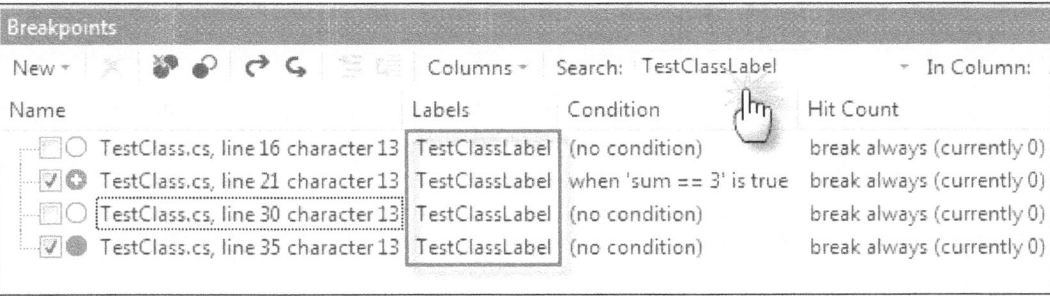

In the preceding screenshot, we filter the breakpoints based on the name of the computer and the process ID. The search box allows you to type in text and, based on the input, the window will filter all the breakpoints that match the labels of the searched string.

The information about the breakpoint is stored inside the `.suo` files in the IDE, but the implementation is produced when **MSBuild** builds the project. While debugging an application, if the source code isn't available but PDB is, the IDE opens the code disassembly to break.

Using DataTips during debugging

In this recipe, we will see how to work with DataTips during debugging. DataTips are individual data elements that can be seen on the editor when the program is debugged. They are advanced tooltip messages that can inspect objects and variables running in the current context.

How to do it...

Let's now see how to use DataTips with the following simple steps:

1. Place a breakpoint in the program and run it.

2. Hover over an object instance in the code or a variable to open a tooltip associated with the object.

3. A tooltip is a tree of members that can be expanded over the editor. You can toggle one object directly using the toggle button on the right-hand side of each object/value.

4. The pinned objects are placed on the screen and can be dragged inside the editor or you can even add comments on the toggled DataTips, as shown in the following screenshot:

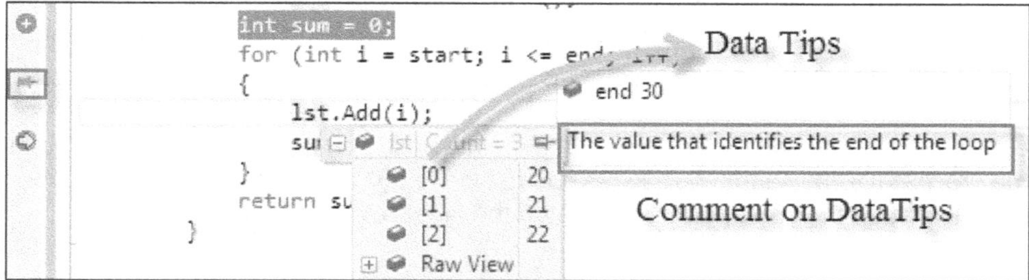

5. While debugging, the value changes to a contextual value while the last value is restored when the debug session is over. You can view the last value by hovering over the left-hand gutter, which leaves behind a blue-colored anchor pin.

How it works...

DataTips actually use the data type information about an object to display each value. Each object has a type associated with it. The debugger analyzes the type information about the object and recursively loads all the object information in the form of a hierarchical structure in the same way as we programmatically do using reflection APIs.

The IDE stores the DataTip information in persistent storage but not the data that represents the state of a program.

There's more...

Let's now explore some of the additional options that are available on DataTips for the IDE.

Importing/Exporting DataTips

DataTips can be imported or exported just like breakpoints. From the main menu, go to **Debug | Export DataTips**. It will show you a dialog box to store the DataTips in a file as shown in the following screenshot. Once the DataTips are stored in the file, you can open it to see its content. It's a SOAP-based XML file with all the information that is required to reload the DataTips again to a certain point. For instance, your comments or watched items will be kept intact in an XML file using tags such as **Comments** or **WatchItem#**. You can add any item as watch using the right-click context menu. The following screenshot shows the XML output on the right-hand side:

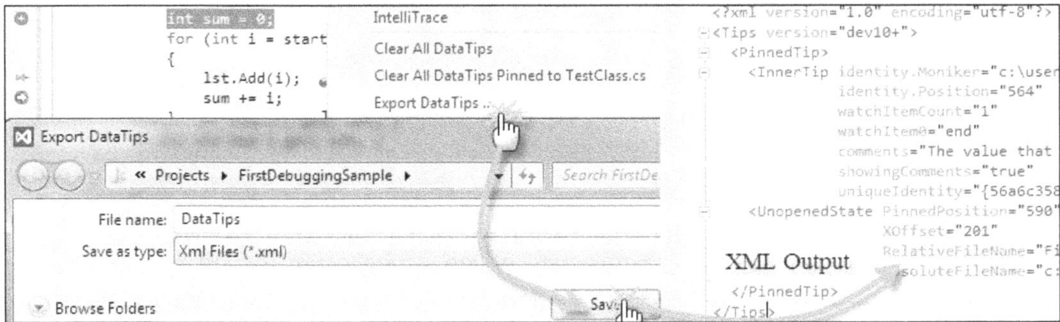

Once the file has been exported, Visual Studio can import the file in another Visual Studio IDE or in the same one and load the same environment of the DataTips when needed.

DataTips are really helpful for debugging and testing a large project.

Clearing DataTips

DataTips can be cleared either by dismissing each individual DataTip or using the **Debug** menu. You have the following two options:

- **Clear All DataTips**: This clears DataTips from all over the solution
- **Clear All DataTips pinned to [FileName]**: This clears DataTips associated only to the current file

Working with debugger visualizers

While debugging complex objects, the debugger is associated with a number of visualizers that help in displaying complex structures in better ways.

The visualizer creates a dialog box that appears on the Visual Studio IDE when an appropriate data type is loaded on the debugger. For instance, for a string instance, we generally have three visualizers associated. The **Text Visualizer** shows the string in the text format in a new window, as shown in the following screenshot. If the string content is XML, you can see the content in the associated XML visualizer and the HTML visualizer.

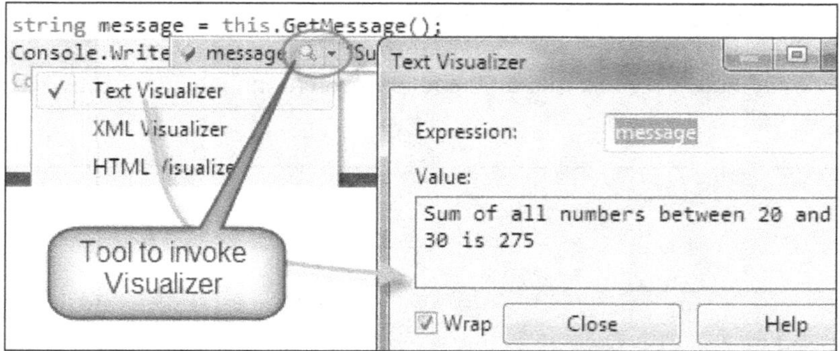

The debugger visualizer is associated with the data type of a class and is shown corresponding to either its loaded DataTips or in **Watch** windows. We can use a number of visualizers for a certain data type. We will see how to create a custom debugger visualizer later in this book.

Inspecting different Watch windows

Watch windows are places where you investigate objects just like DataTips. It is an alternative to DataTips. There are various types of Watch windows.

Autos

When the debugger hits a breakpoint, the **Autos** window shows all the objects and variables that are used in producing the current statement or items in context. Visual Studio automatically identifies the variables for you and shows them in this window. References are also listed inside **Autos** implicitly, as shown in the following screenshot:

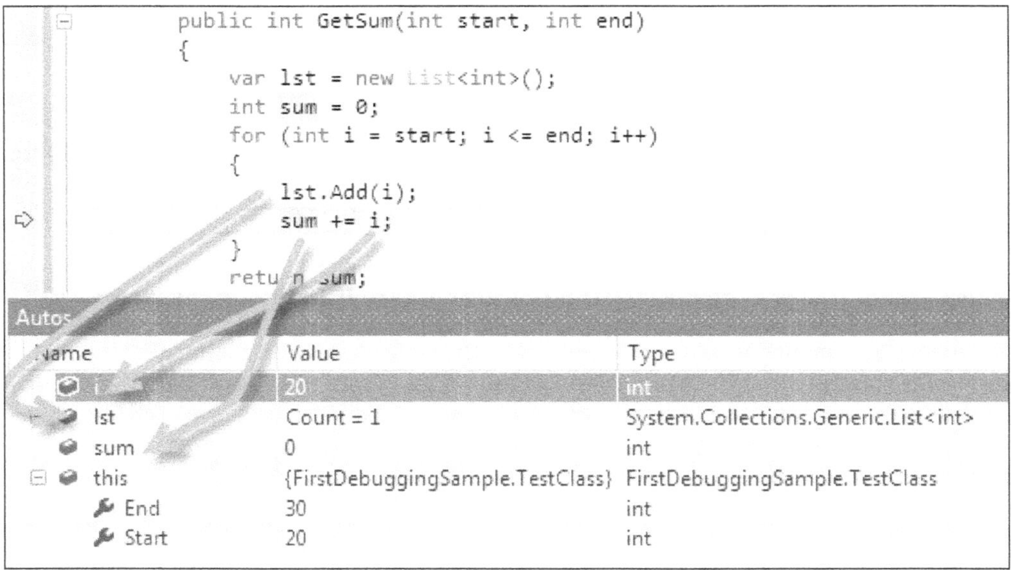

You can open the **Autos** windows using *Ctrl + D + A*.

Locals

Locals are variables that are local to the current context and thread of execution. You can view and modify the value of a variable in the break mode using Locals, as shown in the following screenshot. The **Locals** window updates its value when the program is in the break mode.

Watch windows

Watch windows are customized windows that show objects and variables based on what users customize. While in the break mode, you can right-click on any variable and select **Add to watch** to add the selected object in the **Watch** window. You can also drag-and-drop expressions in the **Watch** window. Notably, there are actually four **Watch** windows available in Visual Studio to separate variables from one another, and to ensure that you can group similar objects in a **Watch** window when dealing with a large number of variables at the same time.

Generally, when you right-click and select **Add to watch**, an object will always be added to the **Watch 1** window, but you can drag the expression from **Watch 1** to any of the **Watch** windows.

In the following screenshot, you can see four **Watch** windows; each of them capable of showing variables in sync. The **Watch** windows show a grid with the **Name**, **Value**, and **Type** of each expression. You can directly type the value of a variable inside the **Watch** windows to change the value of the watched variable. Watch windows are also capable of showing calculated values.

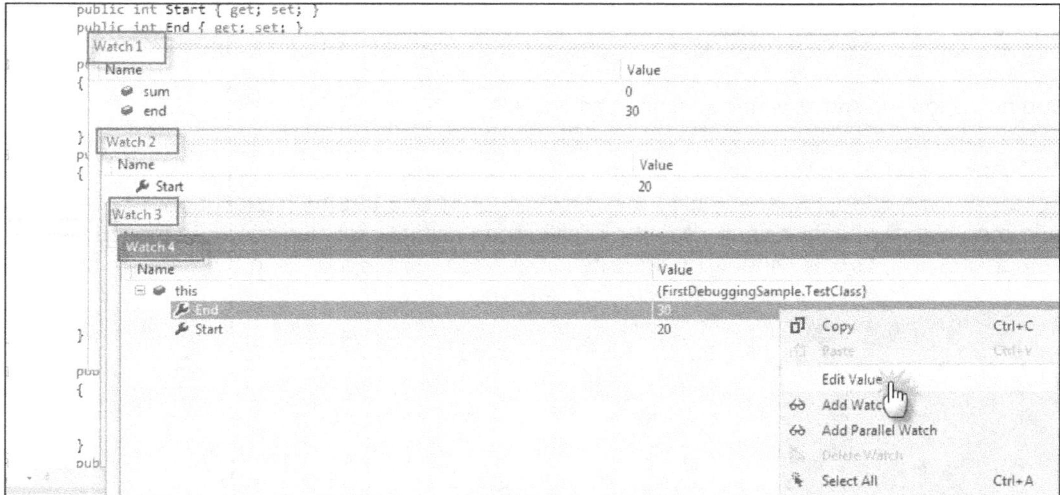

Like all other windows, Watch windows also show a tree when a complex object is loaded onto it. For instance, an object of a class in the preceding screenshot shows its properties inside a tree.

Creating an object ID

You can create an object ID of an object or variable from inside a Watch window as well. An object ID is an aliasing mechanism to edit the value of a variable using an identifier. Objects with object IDs can be accessed directly in all debugging tools (immediate window, command window, watch window, and so on). Right-click on any object in the **Watch** window and select **Make Object ID**, as shown in the following screenshot:

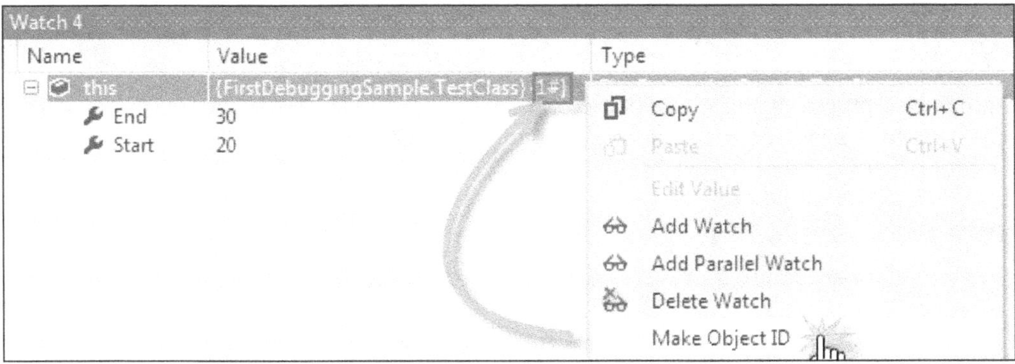

Once the object ID is created, Visual Studio puts a *n#* number corresponding to the variable that can be tracked easily by calling it later.

Working with the Error List window

Another important tool window that is most often required by any debugging session is the **Error List** window. After you build your project, this window appears automatically to show any errors, warnings, or information that you need to know. You can move the cursor to the exact location with details when we double-click on any record from the error list. The error list displays a description of the message, the file where the error occurred, column number, line number, and the project name.

You can toggle errors, warnings, and even messages. It also provides you with a search box to search in case the error list is pretty long, as shown in the following screenshot:

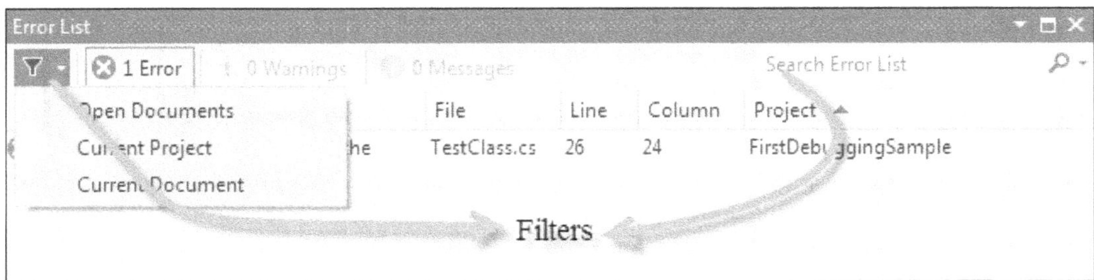

The **Error List** window also allows you to filter errors on **Open Documents**, **Current Project**, and even **Current Document**.

Debugging a multithreaded program

Multithreaded programming is one of the primary needs in modern day programming. In this recipe, let's take a look at how to debug a multithreaded program.

Getting ready

To test a multithreaded program, let's consider the following code:

```
static void Main()
{
  Thread.CurrentThread.Name = "Main Thread";
  Thread t1 = new Thread(new ThreadStart(Run));
  t1.Name = "Thread 1";
  Thread t2 = new Thread(new ThreadStart(Run));
  t2.Name = "Thread 2";
  t1.Start();
  t2.Start();
  Run();
}
static void Run()
{
  Console.WriteLine("hello {0}!", Thread.CurrentThread.Name);
  Thread.Sleep(1000);
}
```

Downloading the example code

You can download the example code files for all Packt books you have purchased from your account at `http://www.packtpub.com`. If you purchased this book elsewhere, you can visit `http://www.packtpub.com/support` and register to have the files e-mailed directly to you.

Here, we created two threads in parallel, each of them calling the `Run` method. We have given each thread a name to identify it in the editor.

How to do it...

Now, let's try debugging the concurrent program using Visual Studio with the following simple steps:

1. Place a breakpoint in the `Run` method and run the program by pressing *F5*.

2. The program will pause during the first `Run` method.

3. Open the **Threads** tool window by navigating to **Debug | Windows | Threads** or using *Ctrl + Alt + H*, as shown in the following screenshot:

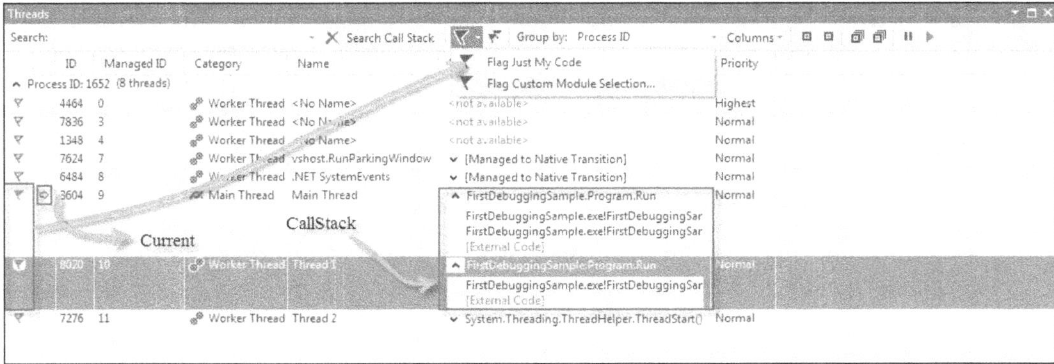

You can see in the preceding screenshot that the threads are listed in the window with their respective thread names and other information.

How it works...

A **Threads** window lists all the information about all the threads running in the current process. Other than a few default columns, you can add columns into the grid using **Columns**.

When we first run the program, the first call to the `Run` method is made. In the **Threads** window, it will show the current thread being executed using a yellow arrow sign. If you press *F5* again, the previous thread goes into a sleep, wait, or join mode. This means that the thread execution is either finished or the thread is in the sleep mode.

In our case, since we did not invoke a join or wait statement, the thread must have been destroyed after the complete execution, but as the process is still running, the thread object will still show up in the window until it is disposed. Obviously, the thread running is a background thread (`IsBackground = False`).

Note that you can also expand the thread location for any thread to get the call stack that is currently being executed. The call stack will remain open automatically during debugging, and double-clicking on the **Thread** pane will change the context of the current stack.

There's more...

Now let's discuss some of the other options that are available in the IDE that can help in our multithreaded programs. Let's explore them one by one.

How to Flag Just My Code

When running the sample code, there are two types of threads that are created inside the process. We created three threads from the user code, but you can find a few other threads that run with the user threads as well, for example, the Finalizer thread, which is set at the highest priority, Jitter, and so on. These threads should always be set aside.

It is sometimes important to identify the threads created by the user.

In the previous screenshot, you can select **Flag Just My Code** to flag threads that are created by the user code.

Debugging parallel programs

Another important technique is to debug parallel programs. Parallel programs are concurrent programs that may or may not induce a thread inside it. So, you cannot always handle a parallel program simply by using threads. The Visual Studio IDE comes with a number of additional tools that help in debugging parallel programs.

Let's consider the following code:

```
class Program
{
  static void Main(string[] args)
  {
    Task task_a = Task.Factory. StartNew(() => DoSomeWork(10000));
    Task task_b = Task.Factory.StartNew(() => DoSomeWork(5000));
    Task task_c = Task.Factory.StartNew(() => DoSomeWork(1000));

    Task.WaitAll(task_a, task_b, task_c);
  }

  static void DoSomeWork(int time)
  {
    Task.Delay(time);
  }
}
```

This is similar to the previously used code but using parallel asynchrony.

Similar to the **Thread** window, the parallel execution programs have **Parallel Stacks** and **Parallel Tasks** windows. Open them by navigating to **Debug | Windows**. Place a break point on `Task.Delay` and run the program, as shown in the following screenshot:

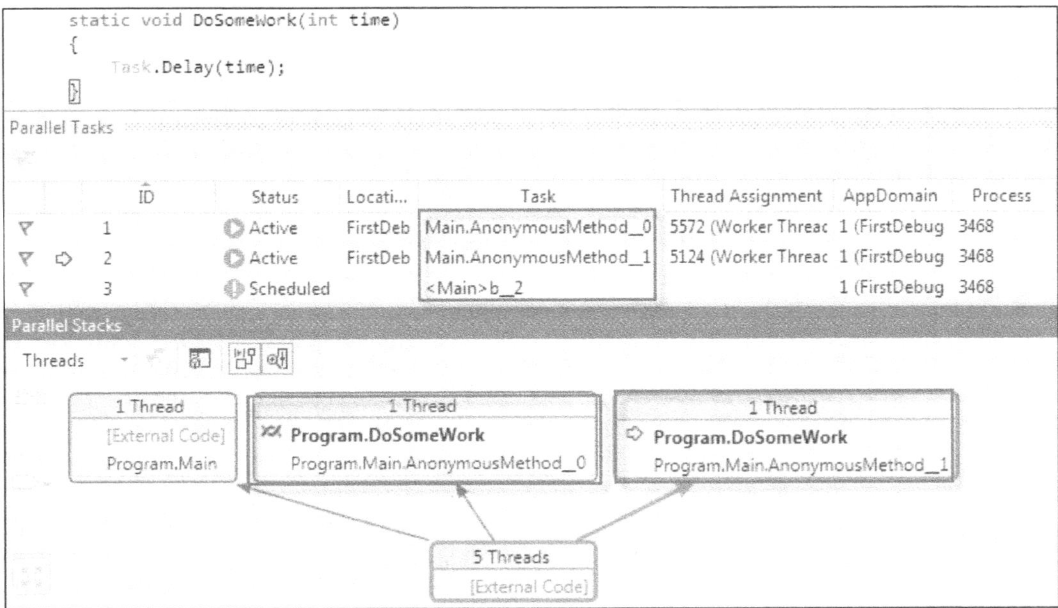

The **Parallel Tasks** window shows the different tasks that have been created for the program and the current status of each of the tasks. In the same way, **Parallel Stacks** shows the graphical view of all the task creations and how they are related to each other.

What are PDB files and what do they contain?

A debugger needs additional information about the project to work internally. The metadata information needs to be stored separately outside the actual executable such that the debugger can preload certain extent of the information prior to the execution of code; for instance, in Visual Studio, when you initiate a method or start debugging, the debugger automatically opens the appropriate files from the filesystem. This information is not available to the debugger inside the executable itself, but in a new type of file that coexists with the executable called program database files (PDB files). The basic schema of PDB files is:

- Addresses of all the methods that comprise the executable
- Name of the global variables and their addresses
- Source file names, checksum to determine the exact file content, line numbers, and so on
- Parameters, names of local variables, and the offset of them on the stack

Each PDB file is identified by a **globally unique identifier** (**GUID**). This GUID is stored in the header information of the file and it identifies the actual executable.

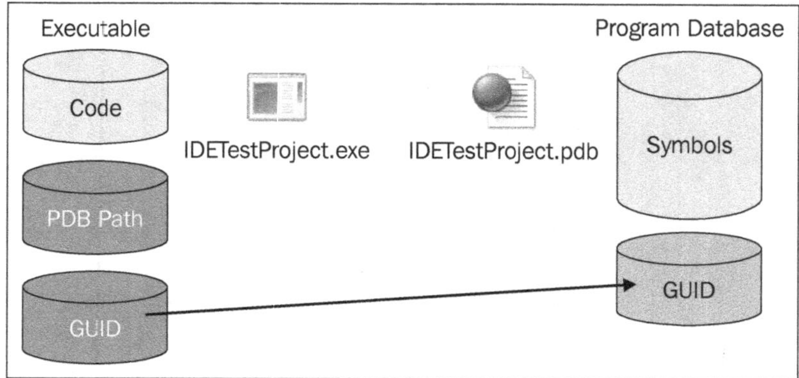

In the preceding figure, it is clear that the executable has the information about the source code file path and a GUID to uniquely identify itself. The PDB file holds this information as well. When the debugger loads the executable, it gets the PDB file path and loads the symbols from the file, if they are found. If the PDB files are not found, the debugger does not have any connection with the line the executable executes and the debug info on the same in the source file. Hence, the debugger cannot give you the flexibility of a line-by-line execution of a program.

The PDB files are generally much more important to the debugger than the source code itself. The PDB file loads the symbols into the vshost debugging environment and links the source code blocks with symbols. You can also maintain symbol servers to store the PDB files so that it is available to you while debugging.

See also

▸ You can learn more about parallel application debugging from `http://bit.ly/debugparallel`

Exploring the Command and Immediate windows

The **Command** window in the Visual Studio IDE is a special window that is useful to invoke commands inside Visual Studio; either those that are available through menu commands or that are hidden inside the IDE. You can use the **Command** window to edit, test, build, and debug applications. Instead of using the mouse to search commands, seasoned users of Visual Studio can save a considerable amount of time by using the **Command** window.

How to do it...

Being the most important part of the debugging tool, let's inspect how to use the Command and **Immediate** windows in the following steps:

1. To display the **Command** window, select **Other Windows** in the **View** menu and select **Command Window,** or simply press *Ctrl + Alt + A* on the keyboard.

2. When you are in the **Command** window, you will see a **>** symbol placed before every input. This is called a prompt.

3. The **Command** and **Immediate** windows are very powerful. Almost every commonly used command that you can invoke from the IDE is available as a command from these windows. Let's start operating the **Command** window by using `Build.Compile`.

   The very first thing that you will notice is the **IntelliSense** menu that pops up as you start typing. When you press enter to run the command, the project will be compiled. This is the same as pressing *F6*. Similarly, you can use `Debug.Start` to start debugging the application.

   The **Command** and **Immediate** windows can help with things that are hard to find and not just the items that you can easily find inside the IDE. Type `Debug.ListMemory` when you are in a breakpoint. You will see the list of memory used with the current line. You can explore the **Build** and **Debug** menus to find out more interesting commands such as these.

4. Let's look at some of the shortcuts available for the **Command** or **Immediate** windows:

   - `?`: This gives you the value of a variable (you can also use `Debug.Print` to do the same)
   - `??`: This sends the variable to the **Watch** window
   - `Locals`: This shows the **Locals** window
   - `Autos`: This shows the **Autos** window
   - `GotoLn`: This sets the cursor to a specific line
   - `bp`: This places a breakpoint to the current line

Similar to the **Command** window, the **Immediate** window lets you test the code without having to run it. The **Intermediate** window is used to evaluate, execute statements, or print variable values.

To open the **Immediate** window, navigate to **Debug | Windows** and select **Immediate**.

You can move back to the **Immediate** window by typing `immed` and to the **Command** window by typing the `cmd` command.

How it works...

Visual Studio is a huge environment with a lot of API support exposed from within it. Each of these sets of API commands are exposed through the **Command** window such that you can easily execute them by writing the command directly being within the IDE. Some of the commands that you can invoke through the **Command** window are still available to the IDE itself as visual tools, but there are a number of other commands that are not often used and are hidden from the normal users. They can be invoked only using commands. The **Command** window lets the user invoke commands on Visual Studio either in the debugging mode or in the normal mode. It would be good to specify some of the commands that are not available in the normal mode, for instance, `Debug.BuildSolution` or anything associated with the Debug interface. Some of the commands such as `Build.AttachtoProcess` or anything associated with the build interface are available only in the normal mode.

Immediate windows are generally used while debugging. It is the most popular tool to evaluate expressions at runtime, create variables on the fly, and/or print values.

Some of the commonly used commands in the Visual Studio IDE are associated with a command alias. For instance, if you use `?`, it is equivalent to `Debug.Print`, the `??` command is equivalent to `Debug.QuickWatch`, `addproj` is equivalent to `File.AddNewProject`, `tabify` is used to invoke `Edit.TabifySelection`, and so on. You can use interfaces in the **Command** window, such as **Debug**, **File**, **Edit**, **View**, **Tools**, and **Window**, each of which provides a lot of the associated commands.

There's more...

Now let's consider some of the other items that you need to know.

The differences between the Command and Immediate windows

Even though both the **Command** and **Immediate** windows can be used interchangeably while debugging an application, there is one basic difference between the use cases of these windows.

The **Command** window is used to execute commands or aliases directly from being within the IDE. You can execute almost all the commands that are either available in menus of the IDE or hidden somewhere. The **Command** window can load dlls or packages into the IDE as well.

The **Immediate** window, on the other hand, is solely used during debugging and is useful to execute statements, print values of a contextual variable, or even evaluate expressions. Generally, the **Immediate** window is quite capable of executing large expressions while being in the debugging mode in the same way as it does inside **Watch** windows.

 ▶ You can see `http://bit.ly/commandalias` to get a list of all the command
    aliases available

Making use of IntelliTrace in Visual Studio

IntelliTrace is another great feature of the Visual Studio IDE. IntelliTrace debugging is
sometimes called historical debugging. It operates in the background and records each and
every thing you do during debugging. IntelliTrace traces all the information for all the events
that occur during debugging and you can get information for all those tasks when required.

How to do it...

Let's demonstrate how to use IntelliTrace while debugging inside Visual Studio:

1. Once the debugger has started, open IntelliTrace in the **Debug** menu if you don't see
    it opened already.

2. After running a couple of steps in the code, you can see the debugger IntelliTrace logs
    in the **IntelliTrace** tool window.

3. Open each window to inspect each event status.

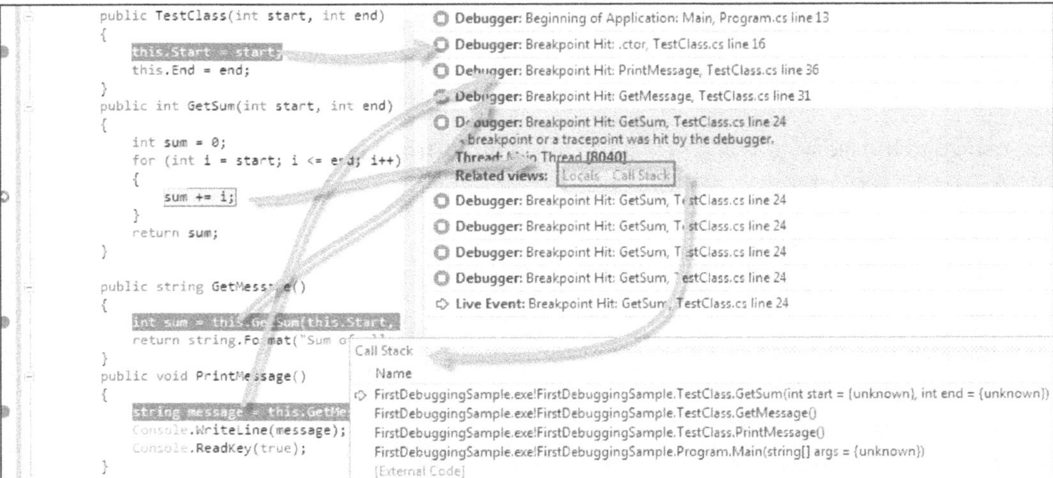

4. Each of the blocks contain **Call Stack** information and a **Locals** set, as shown in the preceding screenshot. The command opens its respective tool window with appropriate data. The editor also gets highlighted when a particular event is highlighted in IntelliTrace.

5. You can filter IntelliTrace logs by choosing the appropriate categories and threads.

How it works...

IntelliTrace traces each of the events that go on with the program during debugging and produces trace files of the `.itrace` extension. Debugging more will increase the size of the file. The IntelliTrace files are by default stored in your hard drive. To see where these files are stored, navigate to **Tools | Options | IntelliTrace | Advanced**, or simply type `IntelliTrace` and navigate to **IntelliTrace | Advanced**, as shown in the following screenshot:

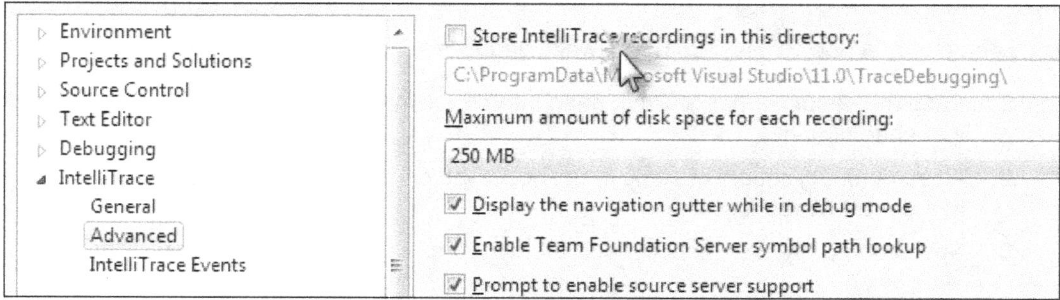

In this dialog box, you can configure how much IntelliTrace debug information needs to be stored. You can uncheck the option to stop storing the IntelliTrace debugger information.

You can go to the filesystem and select the **Store IntelliTrace in this directory** option to choose the `TraceDebugging` directory.

There's more...

Now let's look into some of the other interesting features of IntelliTrace that we may have missed.

Saving an IntelliTrace file

An IntelliTrace file can be saved directly to the hard drive (`.itrace`) by choosing the **Save** button from the tool window. When you choose the **Save** button, it prompts the location where you want to save the content. Once you save the content, you can double-click and reopen the content in Visual Studio to get the entire report of the debugging session.

In the report, it produces a neat graph of the complete execution of the application with all the modules that are loaded, the entire system info, exceptions occurred during execution (if any), test data (if any), and the threads. It also lists the web requests that are made from the application, as shown in the following screenshot:

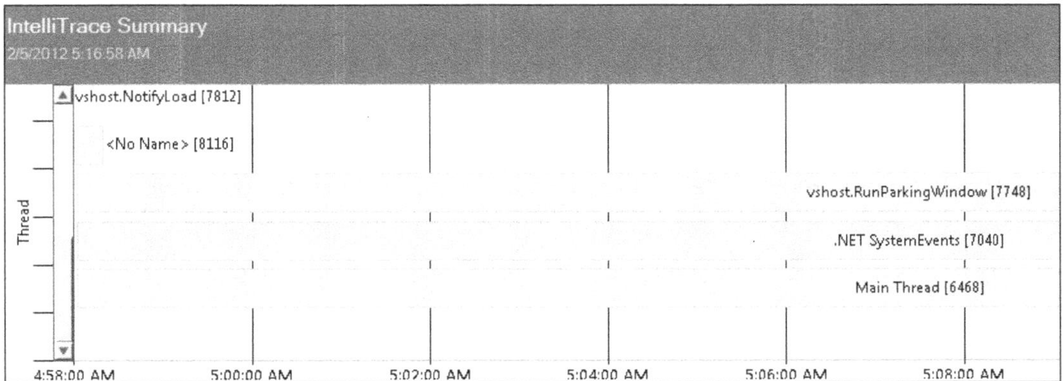

The IntelliTrace logs are so elaborate that the IDE can produce the same environment when you double-click on the any of the threads (or in particular, the main thread).

Reducing the size of trace files

As we can see, IntelliTrace files are considerable in size; we can filter them to log trace information only to the modules specific to our requirement. Go to **Tools | Options** and then **IntelliTrace | Modules**, or directly type `IntelliTrace` in the IDE search box and type `IntelliTrace` to open the following screen:

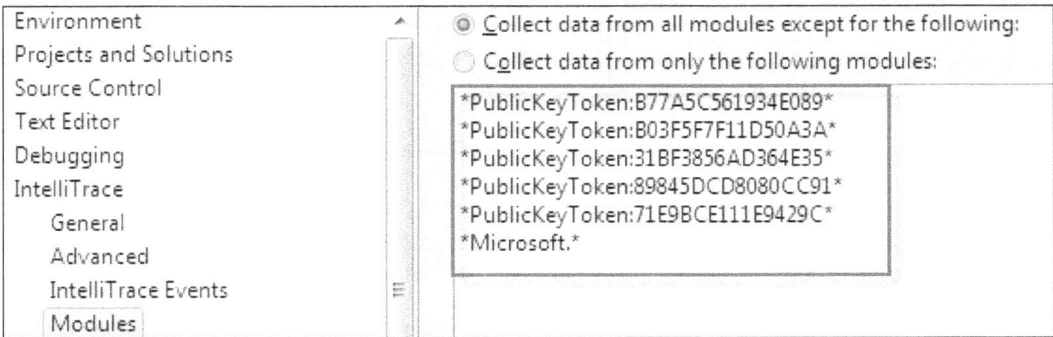

To capture data, you can choose either the modules you want except the listed modules or the reverse based on the radio button you choose. Generally, we bother only about our own code. Let's select the first radio button and then select the **Add** button. Specify the filename that you need to omit the IntelliTrace information from and select **OK**.

To test our application, we will create a new dll and write the name of the dll in the **Add a Pattern** dialog box. Now, when you debug the code, the detailed information for the calls to the dll will be missing.

Working with Debugger Canvas

Debugger Canvas is another interesting tool for advanced debugging. It is actually built on top of IntelliTrace and helps in getting all the information about debugging in one single instance.

To work with Debugger Canvas, you need to install it from the following location: `http://bit.ly/debuggercanvas`.

Once you install Debugger Canvas to the IDE, you can open a new canvas by navigating to **Debug | Debugger Canvas | Create New Canvas**. Now let's put a breakpoint in the code and run the program.

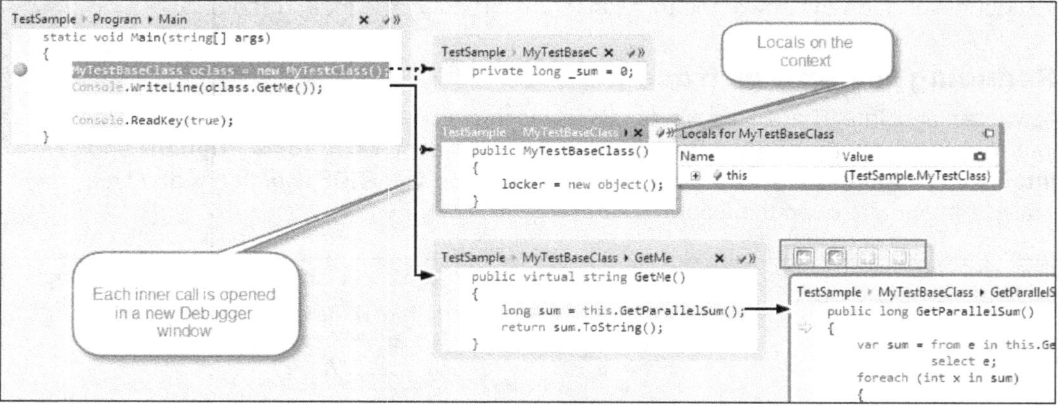

You can see that the code is now shown inside Debugger Canvas on the IDE. On choosing **Step Into** from the menu or pressing *F11*, it produces another box with the code where the cursor is moved to. There are navigation keys to move back and forth between these windows.

Debugger Canvas is helpful at times when you want to see the entire call stack of the code and easily move back from one call stack to another easily. Debugger Canvas also has an option in the right-hand side corner of each canvas element, which shows the locals of the current execution block as seen in the preceding screenshot.

Debugging a .NET program using the framework library source

The .NET library source code has already been released. This gives you a chance to locate and debug the actual source code that has been used to build the library that you are using. This is very useful as the code that has been downloaded from the server will contain a lot of comments, which will help you with the internals of the library that we are using.

How to do it...

Source code debugging is another technique for .NET library debugging. Let's take a look at how you can use Visual Studio to step into Microsoft Source for the .NET library:

1. To debug your code with the .NET library source code, you first need to go to **Tools** | **Options** and then navigate to **Debugging** | **General**.

2. Turn off **Enable Just My Code**.

3. Turn on **Enable source server support**, as shown in the following screenshot:

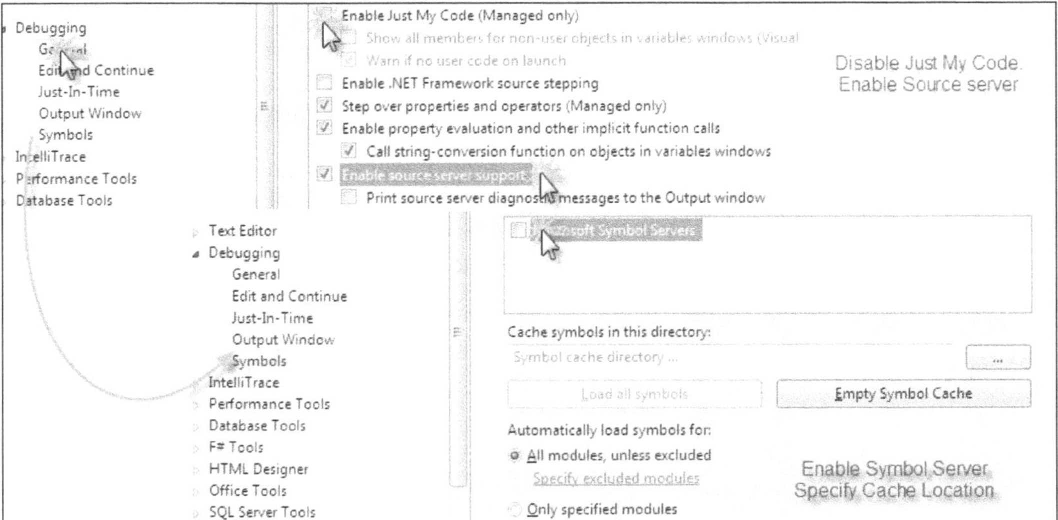

4. Now, in the **Symbols** tab of the window, you need to specify the cache server location where it can get the program debug information.

5. Set the symbol file location to `http://referencesource.microsoft.com/symbols`.

6. Set the cache location where the symbols will get downloaded as soon as you use it during debugging. You need to make sure that the location is accessible from your user account.

7. You can select a list of options for which the reference server will be connected to the symbols. For best results, we should select the modules that you need to load symbols to.

8. You can also load all the symbols once at this time and use them during debugging.

9. You can now start debugging.

How it works...

Microsoft actually maintains a number of servers that hold static files. These files are available based on the checksum. Once the symbols are loaded onto your machine, the reference server can be used to download the appropriate source file directly while you are debugging your application and press **Step Into** to a method that is defined in the .NET class library. As we already know, a program database (PDB) file holds all the information about line numbers, location, and even the checksum of the file. Visual Studio invokes a request to a file by sending this information available in the symbol files and downloads the appropriate file.

Let's start our sample application and place a breakpoint in the first line of the code. Now run the project until the breakpoint is hit. Open **Call Stack**, right-click on **MSCorlib**, and select **Load Symbols**. This will download the symbols of **MScorlib**, which will take a considerable amount of time. Once the symbols are downloaded, you can start debugging your application.

You can see that when the download is complete, the **Call Stack** frames turn dark because all the line numbers are now available. Now you can press *F11* to step into the library code, say, for instance, `Console.WriteLine`.

You will be prompted with a license agreement when you choose **Call Stack** for the first time. You can even use **Call Stack** to move back and forth to different call statements.

You cannot evaluate some of the variables and values while debugging as .NET bits that are shipped with the .NET framework are built in the optimized mode. Putting a break just above the line can show the content of the code.

Don't expect the source of all .NET dlls to be available. Most of the dlls are already made available and as time goes, it will increase the numbers. If you see that **Load Symbols** is disabled or the PDB isn't loading, then you should consider that the dll is not available.

Debugging a process that is already deployed

It is sometimes necessary to debug a process that is already running. This is necessary when building a Windows service or an application that cannot have a user interface or an entry point assigned to it. The debugging process helps the IDE to debug a running process from inside the IDE if the appropriate debug symbols are there within the IDE.

Getting ready

To debug a running process, you need to first run the program. You can either run the program on the current machine by going to the `bin` folder of the project and double-clicking on the `.exe` file, or you can host it in another computer on the network.

You should remember that when you want to debug your application from a remote machine, you need to have `MSVSMON.exe` or **Microsoft Visual Studio Remote Debugging Monitor** running.

How to do it...

Let's now take a look at debugging an already deployed process in the following simple steps:

1. To debug a process, you need to open the exact code that built the project to create the process.

2. Once you open the code, go to **Debug | Attach to Process**, where an IDE window will pop up, as shown in the following screenshot:

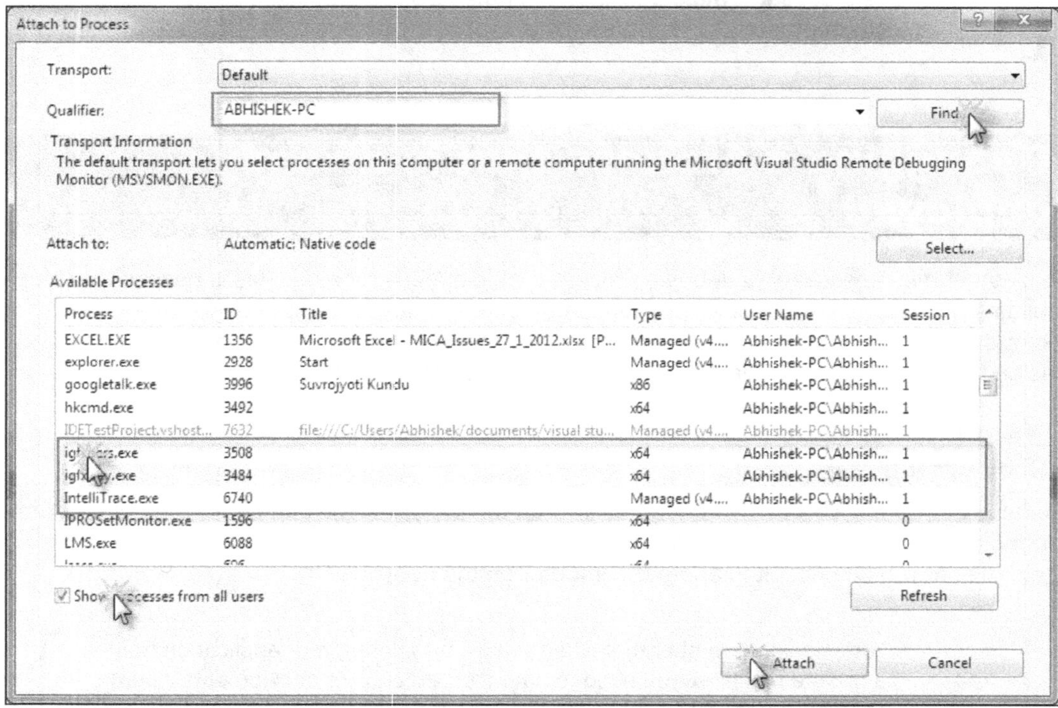

3. The **Attach to Process** dialog box allows you to either select a process from the list on your machine, or select a process running on the remote machine by either choosing the PC using the **Browse** button in the **Qualifier** or typing the IP address of the machine.

4. Once you select the machine, choose the process that you want to debug.

5. You can choose **Show process from all users** or **Show process from all sessions** to get a list of processes that are run by other users in other sessions too.

6. Once you find the process that you want to debug, select it and click on **Attach**.

7. If everything is fine, the process will get attached with the source code.

How it works...

To clarify how the **Attach to Process** feature works, you need to first understand how the debugger works inside Visual Studio. Visual Studio Debugger is a module running inside Visual Studio, which can inspect each IL instruction that is being executed by the process and matches the source code in the project. This mapping is done using a special file that holds information of each and every instruction, the file info, its checksum, and so on, called the PDB file. When the process gets executed, the actual mapping instruction set is also read from the PDB file by the debugger, and when it finds any halt or break or even an exception in the process, it automatically pauses the process inside Visual Studio and opens the source code corresponding to the IL statement just encountered. Visual Studio Debugger is also capable of displaying the local information and other related debugging information in the exact source code line.

In the case of remote debugging, one must run the Remote Debugging Monitor called `MSVSMon.exe` on the same machine where the remote process is running. This file comes free with your Visual Studio installation and you can run it directly from the Visual Studio command prompt. The remote debugging needs an exception of `MSVSMon` against the firewall.

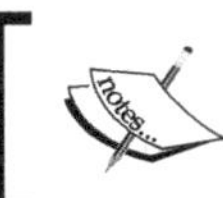

> To debug a process, it can be deployed in the debug mode; otherwise, the release mode process can also be attached with reduced debugging functionalities.

You must also run as an administrator or the same user who is running the process. Sometimes, it can ask for the user ID and password when logging in to a remote machine.

There's more...

Working with a debugger for a running process is very interesting and useful. Let's look at some of the other interesting debugging techniques that you might apply to improve the debugging experiences of a program.

Calling a debugger using code

For users who want to debug by writing, the .NET class library opens up some interesting debugger APIs that you can invoke from your source code to call the debugger manually.

From the very beginning, there is a `DEBUG` preprocessor variable that determines whether the project is built in the debug mode.

You can write the following:

```
#IF DEBUG
/// The code runs only in debug mode
#ENDIF
```

The preprocessor directives are actually evaluated during compile time, which means the code inside `#IF DEBUG` will only be compiled in the assembly when the symbol is included.

There are other options such as `Debug.Assert`, `Debug.Fail`, `Debug.Print`, and so on. All of them only work in the debug mode. In the release mode, these APIs won't get compiled.

You can also call the debugger attached with the process, if any, using `Debugger.Break()`, which will break the debugger in the current line. You can check `Debugger.IsAttached` to find whether the debugger is attached to the current process, as shown in the following screenshot:

We can also load and attach a process directly to the debugger using code by referencing the `EnvDTE` packages. We will discuss them later in this book.

> When you start debugging your code, Visual Studio launches the actual process and one in `.vshost` in its filename. Visual Studio enhances the experience of debugging by enabling partial trust debugging and improved *F5* experience using the `vshost` file. These files act specially in the background to attach the actual process with predefined AppDomain to experience flawless debugging. The `.vshost` files are solely used by the IDE and shouldn't be shipped in an actual project.

Visual Studio needs **Terminal Services** to run inside Visual Studio as it communicates with the process even when it is in the same machine using Terminal Services to maintain a seamless experience on both the normal and remote debugging of a process.

2

Enhancements to WCF 4.5

In this chapter, we will cover the following recipes:

- ▶ Understanding Windows Communication Foundation (WCF) by creating a basic application

- ▶ Hosting a WCF service in different hosting environments

- ▶ Streaming data over a network using a WCF service

- ▶ Writing a REST-based WCF service

- ▶ Creating a WCF service using the Open Data Protocol standards

- ▶ Extending a WCF service (service extensibility)

Introduction

In today's world, enterprise applications are the key to any enterprise. We are in the age of devices. People use one or multiple devices to be connected with the external world. Business processes need shared services, which can be consumed by these devices. Basically, an application can either consume data directly from the database tier or use loosely coupling models and get data from a hosted service. Most enterprises prefer to have a loose coupling on data so that their apps are maintained and also to sustain a clear separation of the application and business logic. Most of the big giants expose their data using standard compliant web-based services and the clients use them to consume data. Some of the services are also hosted behind the secure socket layer and require a secure encrypted connection between the host and the client to perform a data transfer.

Modern enterprises rely on standardized data points so heavily that many of them are now sharing public content through a common gateway enterprise in a format that is globally supported such that third-party clients can connect to their endpoint and consume their data services to represent information. The hype of ATOM, RSS, or other syndication standards is one of the reasons to support the most standard format. An enterprise exposes shared data in the form of RSS feeds, which can be consumed by a number of RSS-feed readers such that the data easily reaches the common mass.

Service-oriented architecture is a design principle that people follow to outline well-defined services that can be consumed by the external world using a common set of contracts, and each of the services can be individually modified independent of each other. They also need to provide a message-based communication approach based on open standards. As a technology giant, Microsoft has also implemented the SOA design principle and provided an easy way of implementation. Microsoft has named it **Windows Communication Foundation** (**WCF**). WCF makes it very easy to create and consume service-oriented business processes similar to point-to-point architectures. It is an architecture that has been moving forward in the .NET environment to address service-oriented architecture by providing a standard way to write services. WCF combines the existing technologies, such as TCP, named pipes, web services, sockets, and MSMQ and creates an easy way to implement a standard SOA representation. WCF has been widely accepted as a standard format to write web services with the support of multiple protocols and endpoints.

Simple Object Access Protocol (**SOAP**) is one of the preferred SOA models, where communication between the two parties is made using an XML representation of data. SOAP is an extensible message standard supported by W3C, which generally runs on the HTTP protocol under the request-response model, and communicates between two endpoints using standard messages with a predefined header information for each envelope.

Each service provides a WSDL that defines the definition of the public interfaces including the metadata, such as protocol bindings and message formats. Generally, WSDL is defined in an XML format such that it is clearly understood and can be used by devices on different platforms to invoke functionalities of the service. WSDL is similar to **Interface definition language** (**IDL**) for web services. The definition of WSDL is that it is typically used during design time to build proxy classes, which will be later used to send and receive responses from the server. The main advantage of the WSDL standard is that it is platform independent and easy to implement. Let's look into the architecture of WCF, as shown in the following figure:

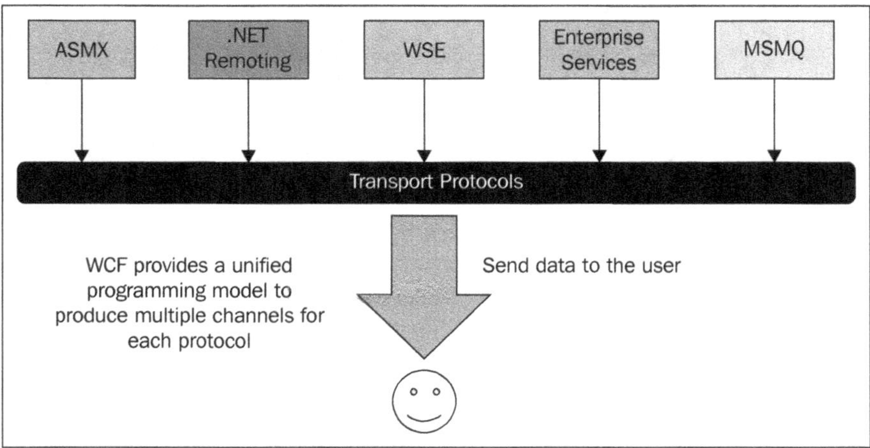

It is important to note that all distributed technologies are based on the same concept. However, each of them provides specific services unique to the product. For instance, ASMX is a traditional web service that provides a standard SOAP-based communication protocol. Remoting is used to provide remote access of two .NET-based applications. As a programmer, you are forced to learn each of these technologies one by one to make use of them. WCF provides a unified solution to all the distributed technologies. It provides a single programming model to leverage the features of any of the preceding distributed technologies. This means you can write one service once and expose different endpoints just by configuring WCF, and everything will work in the same way as it did for specific technologies.

In WCF, the three most important things that you need to remember (popularly termed as the ABCs of WCF) are as follows:

- **Address** (where): This represents a unique network URL that specifies the service and where messages can be sent. Generally, it is made up of the protocol, IP address of the network terminal, and service location.

- **Binding** (how): This represents how the client should communicate with the service. WCF supports a number of binding protocols that you can use to define the service, for example, `BasicHttpBinding`, `WSHttpBinding`, `MsmqIntegrationBinding`, `NetTcpBinding`, `NetNamedPipeBinding`, and so on.

- **Contract** (what): This defines what the messages should contain. The contract is generally a set of interfaces that the client needs to take care of to request the service.

Now, let's create the simplest WCF service to get a basic idea of how it works.

Understanding Windows Communication Foundation (WCF) by creating a basic application

WCF is easy and simple. A large number of APIs are built inside .NET, which provides an easy way to implement a WCF service. Visual Studio provides the appropriate tools to create proxy classes automatically when a service reference is taken into a project such that the user only needs to configure the service with a proper endpoint address and the service will start working. In this recipe, we are going to look at the internal details and the API that you need to consider to create and connect services. We are not going to use the tools of Visual Studio to build this service. We will later explain how to make use of Visual Studio to quickly create services in other recipes.

Getting ready

Building a service with Visual Studio is very easy and automatic but if we consider not using it, we will have to manually perform a lot of plumbing to ensure that everything works correctly. We will use a class library to define our WCF service and host the service in the server; we will then consume the same from the client in this recipe later such that after going through the recipe, you will have a clear idea of what happens underneath.

How to do it...

Now let's create an application using Visual Studio to demonstrate components:

1. Open Visual Studio and create a console application. We will name it `SampleFirstServiceServer`. This console project will be used to host a WCF Service.

2. Add a reference `System.ServiceModel.dll` file to the project. This `.dll` extension references all the important APIs that need to work with WCF.

3. Create an interface to define a method contract. We will define the most simple contract that takes a string and returns a string, and name it `MyFirstMethod`:

```
[ServiceContract]
    public interface IFirstWCF
    {
        [OperationContract]
        string MyFirstMethod(string inputText);
    }
```

4. Here, you can see that the contract has been annotated using the `ServiceContract` attribute. WCF internally uses attributes to find the contract of a service when it is called upon. The `ServiceContract` attribute defines the main type of contract that the service understands.

5. The `MyFirstMethod` contract has been annotated using `OperationContract`, which defines the contract to a particular operation. Hence, the interface forms a major contract between the client and the server.

6. Now, let's implement the interface into a concrete type as follows:

```
public class FirstSimpleWCF : IFirstWCF
{
    public string MyFirstMethod(string inputText)
    {
        Console.WriteLine("Message Received : {0}",
          inputText);
        Console.WriteLine(OperationContext.Current.RequestContext
    .RequestMessage.ToString());
        return string.Format("Message from server {0}",
          inputText);
    }
}
```

In the preceding code, we defined the body of `MyFirstMethod`. The method actually prints the message received by it and returns the same text with some extra content from the server.

It is important to note that the contextual `Request` object is available from `OperationContext.Current.RequestContext`. This object holds the entire message body that has been received by the server. The object also shows the header content, if any.

7. Here, `RequestMessage` will print the entire body of the XML content received by the server, which is parsed to call this method.

8. Now as our service is ready, we need to host it in our Console Application. WCF services generally need to be hosted somewhere. You have options to host a WCF service in a Console Application, a Windows Service, IIS, Windows Activation Service, and so on.

9. To host a service inside a Console Application, we are going to use the `ServiceHost` class present in the `ServiceModel` namespace. This class takes a URL and hosts the service on it such that any request received at the endpoint will be handled automatically by the server.

```
public static void Main()
{
    BasicHttpBinding binding = new BasicHttpBinding();

    Uri serviceUri = new Uri("http://localhost:8000");
    ServiceHost host = new ServiceHost(typeof(FirstSimpleWCF),
serviceUri);
    host.AddServiceEndpoint(typeof(IFirstWCF), binding,
       "OperationService");
    host.Open();

    Console.WriteLine("Service is hosted to the Server");
    Console.ReadLine();

    host.Close();
}
```

10. As already mentioned, we have to maintain the ABCs of any WCF service. Here, the address is specified using `serviceUri` such that we will host our service at port `8000`.

11. We also need to specify the binding for the service. Here, we use `BasicHttpBinding` (which is the same as traditional ASMX services). We add this endpoint to `ServiceHost`, which points to the actual implementation of the service. The `AddServiceEndpoint` option connects a binding with the service endpoint. We call our service endpoint `OperationService`.

12. Finally, we will call `Open` to start hosting the service.

13. If you start the service, you will see the message **Service is hosted on the server**, and that port `8000` is available for the service.

Remember that if you are using Visual Studio to run the service, it will require administrative permission to open a port from the console. Please restart Visual Studio using the **Run as administrator** link on the right-hand side of the screen, and then click on the context menu to run the console service host.

14. As the service is already hosted on the server, we now need a way to call the service from the client machines. Let's create another Console Application and call it `SampleFirstWCFClient`.

15. We will create a similar interface such as `IFirstWCF` in the Client Application too. The name of `ServiceContract` and `OperationContract` should be the same, as shown in the following code:

```
[ServiceContract]
public interface IFirstWCF
{
    [OperationContract]
    string MyFirstMethod(string inputText);
}
```

Here, both the contracts are matched using a common contract document. By the way, the mapping of the interface is only needed to correctly map the data during serialization/deserialization of the objects.

It is also worth mentioning that the serialization is not restricted to exactly match the property names in the classes. You can simply use the `DataContract` and `DataMember` attributes to assign the exact element names of data with your programmable objects. For example, say `OperationContract` looks like this:

```
string MyFirstMethod(Message Input);
[DataContract(Name="ServerMessage",
Namespace="http://schemas.com")]
public class Message
{
        [DataMember(Name="Message")]
        public string Text { get; set; }
}
```

In the preceding code, the `ServerMessage` element will be mapped to `Message`, and `Message` is mapped to `Text` on the client side. The `DataContract` and `DataMember` attributes are used during serialization/deserialization of a WCF communication.

16. We will then use this contract to pass data to the server and client. To connect to the service, we are going to use the `ChannelFactory` class as shown in the following code:

```
static void Main(string[] args)
{
    Console.WriteLine("Press Enter to call Server");
    string enteredString = Console.ReadLine();
    BasicHttpBinding binding = new BasicHttpBinding();
    ChannelFactory<IFirstWCF> factory = new
        ChannelFactory<IFirstWCF>(binding,
new EndpointAddress("http://localhost:8000/OperationService"));

    IFirstWCF proxy = factory.CreateChannel();
```

```
string methodFromServer = proxy.MyFirstMethod(enteredString);

Console.WriteLine(methodFromServer);

Console.ReadLine();
}
```

17. Here, the `ChannelFactory` class binds the client with the server using a service endpoint and a contract used to connect the service. The `CreateChannel` method automatically creates a proxy class that can be used to proxy data to the server.

18. If you run the client and post a message to the server, the server will return the same message to the client.

How it works...

The preceding example covers the basics of calling methods on a service via WCF, showing both the client and server code. According to the basic configuration, the service contains three main components: the address that states where the service is hosted, the binding that states how the messages need to be sent and received, and the contract that states what needs to be transferred.

In the entire process of hosting from the server side to client side, there are two main classes that I have used to initiate the whole service:

- `ServiceHost` (inside the server)
- `ChannelFactory` (inside the client)

A `ServiceHost` class is instantiated based on the type of service that you have implemented to host your service. This class maps the actual service contract with the binding and address. When the object of `ServiceHost` is available, you can do anything with the ABCs of the service. In the previous recipe, we used the `ServiceHost` class to configure our service to handle `BasicHttpBinding`, which means the transfer format will be XML- and SOAP-based. When a client calls the service, the `ServiceHost` class parses the messages, creates the context, and calls the service. It is important to note that on every call to the service, the `ServiceHost` class creates an object of `FirstSimpleWCF` and removes it from memory whenever the service completes execution. If you want your service object to be reused, you can add a `ServiceBehavior` option for this. For instance:

```
[ServiceBehavior(InstanceContextMode=InstanceContextMode.Single)]
public class FirstSimpleWCF : IFirstWCF
{
}
```

This `ServiceBehavior` option indicates that the instance of the service needs to be created only once and the object stays in the memory of `ServiceHost` until the whole service gets disposed. If there is a single service object, it is important to note that for every call to the service, `ServiceHost` creates a new execution context to handle the request. The execution context may use `SynchronizationContext` or IO threads or simply threads to support scalability. The object locking and synchronization on WCF is handled automatically.

The `ServiceHost` class is also capable of handling the metadata of the service from the configuration file. If you have specified a configuration section under `<system.serviceModel>` inside `app.config`, the `ServiceHost` class will automatically load the configuration and configure itself.

Name	Value	Type
⊟ 🌐 host	{System.ServiceModel.ServiceHost}	System
⊟ 🌐 base	{System.ServiceModel.ServiceHost}	System
⊞ 🌐 base	{System.ServiceModel.ServiceHost}	System
⊞ 🔧 Authentication	{System.ServiceModel.Description.ServiceAuthentica	System
⊞ 🔧 Authorization	{System.ServiceModel.Description.ServiceAuthorizat	System
⊟ 🔧 BaseAddresses	Count = 1	System
⊞ 🌐 [0]	{http://localhost:8000/}	System
⊞ 🌐 Raw View		
⊞ 🔧 ChannelDispatchers	{System.ServiceModel.Dispatcher.ChannelDispatche	System
⊞ 🔧 CloseTimeout	{00:00:10}	System
🔧 Credentials	null	System
⊟ 🔧 Description	ServiceType={FirstServiceLibrary.FirstSimpleWCF}	System
⊞ 🔧 Behaviors	Count = 5	System
🔧 ConfigurationName	"FirstServiceLibrary.FirstSimpleWCF"　🔍 ▾	string
⊟ 🔧 Endpoints	Count = 1	System
⊟ 🌐 [0]	Address={http://localhost:8000/OperationService}	System
⊞ 🔧 Address	{http://localhost:8000/OperationService}	System
⊞ 🔧 Behaviors	Count = 0	System
⊞ 🔧 Binding	{System.ServiceModel.BasicHttpBinding}	System
⊞ 🔧 Contract	Name={IFirstWCF}, Namespace="http://tempuri.org	System
⊞ 🔧 EndpointBehaviors	Count = 0	System
🔧 IsSystemEndpoint	false	bool
⊞ 🔧 ListenUri	{http://localhost:8000/OperationService}	System
🔧 ListenUriMode	Explicit	System
🔧 Name	"BasicHttpBinding_IFirstWCF"　🔍 ▾	string
⊞ 🌐 Non-Public members		
⊞ 🌐 Raw View		
🔧 Name	"FirstSimpleWCF"　🔍 ▾	string
🔧 Namespace	"http://tempuri.org/"　🔍 ▾	string
⊞ 🔧 ServiceType	{Name = "FirstSimpleWCF" FullName = "FirstService	System
⊞ 🌐 Non-Public members		
⊞ 🔧 Extensions	{System.ServiceModel.ExtensionCollection<System.{	System
🔧 ManualFlowControlLimit	2147483647	int
⊞ 🔧 OpenTimeout	{00:01:00}	System
⊞ 📑 Static members		
⊞ 🌐 Non-Public members		
🔧 SingletonInstance	null	object
⊞ 🌐 Non-Public members		

If you look at the whole `ServiceHost` object in the watch window, you will see that the object exposes a number of properties. It creates an object of `ServiceDescription`, which maintains the ABCs and different configuration elements of the service. The `ServiceHost` class also maintains a runtime socket listener that listens to the port created for the service as specified by `BaseAddress` for any incoming requests. When it receives any requests, it parses the whole message and calls the service object. If you specify the service object to be singleton, it places the initial object in the `SingletonInstance` property and reuses it every time the service is called. A special XML parser is also built in the `ServiceHost` class to parse incoming requests and deserialize it into objects.

Just like `ServiceHost`, for the client side we have instantiated an object of `ChannelFactory`. Even though the `ServiceHost` and `ChannelFactory` classes look almost similar, there is a basic difference between the two. The `ChannelFactory` class only maps with the contract but not with the actual implementation of the service. It then creates a proxy class that is used to call the service through `Listener`. The data we pass through the public interface is automatically serialized and sent through the channel. Just like `ServiceHost`, a `ChannelFactory` class reads the contracts defined inside the configuration and configures itself.

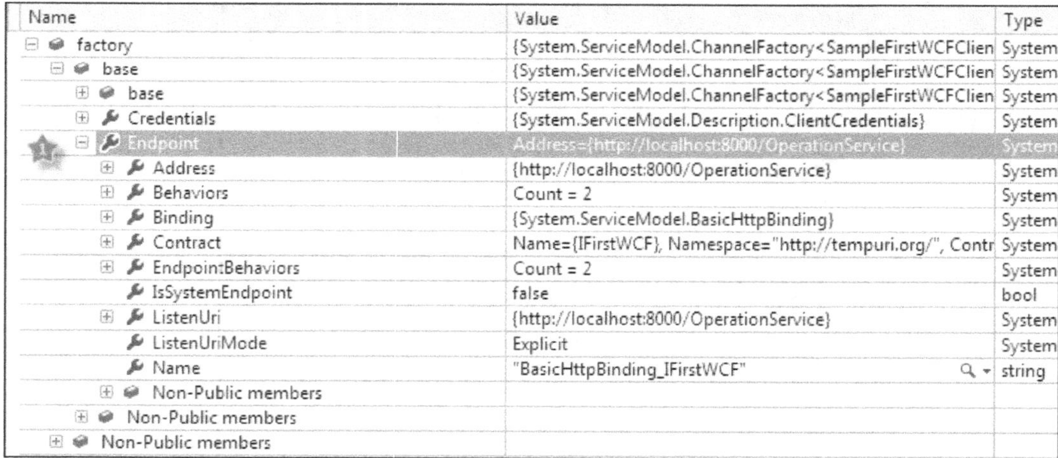

Name	Value	Type
⊟ ☁ factory	{System.ServiceModel.ChannelFactory<SampleFirstWCFClien	System
⊟ ☁ base	{System.ServiceModel.ChannelFactory<SampleFirstWCFClien	System
⊞ ☁ base	{System.ServiceModel.ChannelFactory<SampleFirstWCFClien	System
⊞ 🔑 Credentials	{System.ServiceModel.Description.ClientCredentials}	System
⊟ 🔑 Endpoint	Address={http://localhost:8000/OperationService}	System
⊞ 🔑 Address	{http://localhost:8000/OperationService}	System
⊞ 🔑 Behaviors	Count = 2	System
⊞ 🔑 Binding	{System.ServiceModel.BasicHttpBinding}	System
⊞ 🔑 Contract	Name={IFirstWCF}, Namespace="http://tempuri.org/", Contr	System
⊞ 🔑 EndpointBehaviors	Count = 2	System
🔑 IsSystemEndpoint	false	bool
⊞ 🔑 ListenUri	{http://localhost:8000/OperationService}	System
🔑 ListenUriMode	Explicit	System
🔑 Name	"BasicHttpBinding_IFirstWCF"	string
⊞ ☁ Non-Public members		
⊞ ☁ Non-Public members		
⊞ ☁ Non-Public members		

The `ChannelFactory` class only exposes the endpoint of the service with ABCs configured, and the credentials, if any, that are required to call the service.

One important thing to remember is that the proxy class, which is used to communicate between the client and the server, is based on the contract specified between the server and the client. The server side can contain more than one contract, but WCF does not force you to implement all of them when using the client.

To understand this, let's create another method inside the server interface with its implementation as shown in the following code:

```
[ServiceContract]
public interface IFirstWCF
{
    [OperationContract]
    string MyFirstMethod(string inputText);
    [OperationContract]
    string MySecondMethod(string inputText);
}
```

On the server side, we have a service method called `MySecondMethod` that we get without changing the `ServiceContract` service on the client side. Now, if you run the same application again, you will see that even though the client side `IFirstWCF` does not contain a definition of `MySecondMethod`, it can still call the existing interface `MyFirstMethod` from it. This is because the `ChannelFactory` class automatically serializes the request made from it to an XML request object and sends the request through the socket. It does not send the actual object to the server.

In the case of `BasicHttpBinding`, SOAP messages are transferred. The SOAP message contains a well-defined envelope with a header and body of the message inside it. On the server side, as we have printed out `RequestMessage`, we can see the actual structure of the envelope, which the `channelFactory` proxy object creates and sends through the channel. The following screenshot shows how the actual envelope is laid out when **Hi** is sent to the server using the proxy object. The proxy object creates a well-defined contract and sends it to the specified address. The **Action** option specifies the actual contract name (**IFirstWCF/MyFirstMethod**).

```
<s:Envelope xmlns:s="http://schemas.xmlsoap.org/soap/envelope/">
  <s:Header>
    <To s:mustUnderstand="1" xmlns="http://schemas.microsoft.com/ws/2005
essing/none">http://localhost:8000/OperationService</To>
    <Action s:mustUnderstand="1" xmlns="http://schemas.microsoft.com/ws/
addressing/none">http://tempuri.org/IFirstWCF/MyFirstMethod</Action>
  </s:Header>
  <s:Body>
    <MyFirstMethod xmlns="http://tempuri.org/">
      <inputText>Hi</inputText>
    </MyFirstMethod>
  </s:Body>
</s:Envelope>
```

There's more...

Now that we know the basics of WCF, let's evaluate a few more things that are worth remembering.

Understanding IMetadataExchange endpoint and adding it to the application

If you like your service endpoint to be discoverable to the external world, the `MetadataExchange` endpoint is useful. WCF uses the `IMetadataExchange` interface to return metadata about the service. The metadata can be a **Web Services Definition Language** (**WSDL**) document that describes all the methods and data types associated with the service.

A service with proper metadata can be discoverable and there are a number of tools that can automatically create contracts and types associated with the service using the metadata endpoint.

Let's now add a `mex` endpoint for the service such that the service can be discoverable from the outside:

```
BasicHttpBinding binding = new BasicHttpBinding();

Uri serviceUri = new Uri("http://localhost:8000");
ServiceHost host = new ServiceHost(typeof(FirstSimpleWCF),
    serviceUri);
host.AddServiceEndpoint(typeof(IFirstWCF), binding,
    "OperationService");

ServiceMetadataBehavior smb = new ServiceMetadataBehavior();
smb.HttpGetEnabled = true;
host.Description.Behaviors.Add(smb);
Binding mexBinding = MetadataExchangeBindings.CreateMexHttpBinding();
host.AddServiceEndpoint(typeof(IMetadataExchange), mexBinding,
    "mex");
host.Open();

Console.WriteLine("Service is hosted to the Server");
Console.ReadLine();

host.Close();
```

Here, `MetadataExchangeBindings.CreateMexHttpBinding` is an API to get a binding contract for the `IMetadataExchange` interface. When `ServiceEndpoint` is added to `IMetadataExchange`, the service provides a WSDL, which the tools can use to discover types.

After you run this code and open the server-side console, you can open a web browser and type `http://localhost:8000/?wsdl` to get the WSDL for the application. The `HttpGetEnabled` method needs to be enabled to ensure that the browser can request the WSDL using the `GET` request.

By the way, you need not define the endpoint configuration in code; the configuration can also be done using the configuration file (`app.config/web.config`). Let's see how the previous configuration can be defined in configuration files so that it can be modified easily without recompiling the project:

```xml
<system.serviceModel>
    <services>
      <service
          name="Microsoft.ServiceModel.Samples.CalculatorService">
        <host>
          <baseAddresses>
            <add baseAddress="http://localhost:8000/"/>
          </baseAddresses>
        </host>
        <endpoint address=""
                  binding="basicHttpBinding"
                  contract="IFirstWCF" />
        <endpoint address="mex"
                  binding="mexHttpBinding"
                  contract="IMetadataExchange" />
      </service>
    </services>
    <behaviors>
      <serviceBehaviors>
        <behavior>
          <serviceMetadata httpGetEnabled="True"/>
        </behavior>
      </serviceBehaviors>
    </behaviors>
  </system.serviceModel>
```

The previous XML can be placed in the configuration file and can be used later when defining `ServiceHost` in code.

Using DataContract in a service

In the simplest WCF service that we have created in this recipe, we didn't use many of the complex data types. But in real-world scenarios, people generally need complex data types to be transferred between the client and the server. The WCF proxy classes automatically serialize the complex types into XML and post them to the server. Similarly, when received, it desterilizes the content into the appropriate type.

To define a complex data type, we need to use the `DataContractAttribute` class to annotate the type, and each member that needs to be serialized during the transfer should be annotated using `DataMemberAttribute`:

```
[ServiceContract]
public interface IFirstWCF
{
    [OperationContract]
    string MyFirstMethod(string inputText);
    [OperationContract]
    Data MySecondMethod(Data inputText);
}
[DataContract]
public class Data
{
    [DataMember]
    public string Message { get; set; }
}
```

In the preceding `IFirstWCF` service, we used a complex data type called `Data`, passed it into `MySecondMethod`, and got back the same from the server. We then implemented `MySecondMethod` in the class and hosted the service. Once the service is hosted, you can check the WSDL for it. You can see that `DataContract` is now defined with `ComplexType`. You can get the type of the object from `http://localhost/?xsd=xsd2` if you have followed this procedure.

The XSD defines the schema of the message body that needs to be sent to the server to call `MySecondMethod`.

Now, if you run the client without changing the string request and response for the `MySecondMethod` interface, it will throw an error as the formatter cannot deserialize the string request to complex data (`Data`), which the server is expecting.

```
IFirstWCF proxy = factory.CreateChannel();
string methodFromServer = proxy.MySecondMethod(enteredString);

Console.WriteLine(methodFromServer);

Console.ReadLine();
}

[ServiceContract]
public interface IFirstWCF
{
    [OperationContract]
    string MyFirstMethod(string inputText);
    [OperationContract]
    string MySecondMethod(string inputText);
}
```

> **! ProtocolException was unhandled**
>
> The formatter threw an exception while trying to deserialize the message: There was an error while trying to deserialize parameter http://tempuri.org/:inputText. The InnerException message was 'Error in line 1 position 140. Expecting state 'Element'.. Encountered 'Text' with name '', namespace ''. '. Please see InnerException for more details.
>
> **Troubleshooting tips:**
>
> Get general help for this exception.

Now, we need to define the complex data type that reads the XSD, which is exposed through the WCF metadata. We need to make sure `ComplexType` is named `Data` and has a member called `Message` in it. The complex types can also be mapped to different element schemas using the properties in the `DataContract` and `DataMember` attributes.

Once we define the handwritten data type properly, you will see that the service runs smoothly.

Visual Studio's **Add Service Reference** creates the proxy classes properly on the client side; so if you are too lazy to create the proxy, you can use that option.

Using the svcutil tool to generate proxy classes

It would be cumbersome if the client needed to write all the complex types and proxy classes by hand. Think about a real-world business service. It could have hundreds of interfaces and thousands of complex types associated with it. Writing each of them manually would require a lot of effort from the client just to start using the service. Microsoft has built a tool called `svcutil`, which is shipped with Visual Studio. This tool creates a proxy by reading the metadata about the service that is passed into it. The tool uses a configuration file to get the configuration about the service. Let's define a configuration for the client as shown in the following code:

```
<system.serviceModel>
    <bindings>
        <basicHttpBinding>
            <binding name="BasicHttpBinding_IFirstWCF" />
        </basicHttpBinding>
    </bindings>
    <client>
        <endpoint address="http://localhost:8000/OperationService"
binding="basicHttpBinding"
            bindingConfiguration="BasicHttpBinding_IFirstWCF"
contract="IFirstWCF"
            name="BasicHttpBinding_IFirstWCF" />
    </client>
</system.serviceModel>
```

The client configuration defines the address, binding, and contract of the service. Let's try creating a file for the service that we have created. Open the Visual Studio 2012 developer console and run the following code:

```
svcutil /language:cs /out:generateProxy.cs /config:app.config http://
localhost:8000
```

If everything is fine and the `app.config` file is placed in the current directory, the `generateProxy.cs` file will be created from the service, which acts as a service proxy client. The following console shows the messages when the utility successfully creates the `generateProxy.cs` file. Similarly, you can also use the `svcutil` tool to generate classes for VB.NET.

```
C:\Users\buildfusion\Documents\Visual Studio 2012\Projects\FirstServiceLibrary\s
vcutilDemo>svcutil /language:cs /out:generateProxy.cs /config:app.config http://
localhost:8000/
Microsoft (R) Service Model Metadata Tool
[Microsoft (R) Windows (R) Communication Foundation, Version 4.0.30319.17929]
Copyright (c) Microsoft Corporation.  All rights reserved.

Attempting to download metadata from 'http://localhost:8000/' using WS-Metadata
Exchange or DISCO.
Generating files...
C:\Users\buildfusion\Documents\Visual Studio 2012\Projects\FirstServiceLibrary\s
vcutilDemo\generateProxy.cs
C:\Users\buildfusion\Documents\Visual Studio 2012\Projects\FirstServiceLibrary\s
vcutilDemo\app.config
```

See also

▸ Refer to the walkthrough on creating and consuming WCF services at `http://bit.ly/createwcf`

▸ Refer to the WCF tutorial at `http://bit.ly/wcftutorial`

Hosting a WCF service in different hosting environments

Hosting a service is an important part of any service. Coming from web services, WCF exposes more relevant APIs to handle different kinds of hosting environments. A WCF service can be hosted virtually anywhere, starting from a simple Console Application, a Windows Service, IIS, or even other hosting services such as Windows Activation Service. After the service is hosted on an environment, the service endpoint for a particular service gets exposed. When the host process runs, WCF will be available using the configured endpoints.

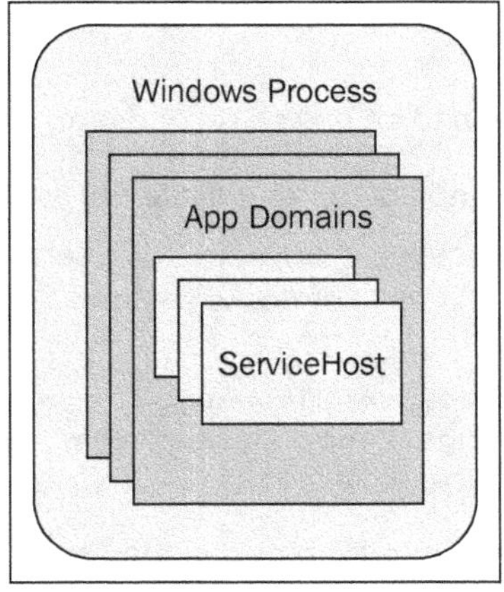

Any .NET application runs using a Windows process. Inside a process, you can host multiple .NET application domains. Each application domain logically separates the execution environment from another. WCF requires `ServiceHost` to host a worker process inside the application domain. Similarly, each application domain can host multiple worker processes. Each application represents service host-to-host multiple endpoints. In addition to that, WCF relies on the security and configuration features provided by an application domain. WCF, by default, uses the default identity of the process but you can impersonate the users too. Some of the hosting processes provide additional features. For instance, IIS provides automatic process recycling, resource throttling, logging, health indicators, and so on. Now, let's try out the different hosting environments in this recipe one by one to understand them further.

Getting ready

There are a number of ways to host a WCF service; one of them is in IIS. The latest version of IIS supports a number of endpoints, which can be used by the WCF service to host itself inside the IIS. As I have already mentioned, IIS gives you an edge while publishing your service inside it. Let's try IIS 7 to host our service.

IIS requires a physical file with a `.svc` extension to host the service properly. In our previous example, we already showed you how to host a service inside a console application using `ServiceHost`. The `ServiceHost` class is the class that creates the hosting environment for a service. If you are using IIS, you do not need to create an instance of `ServiceHost` because IIS automatically creates it for you. Let's create a web application and add a `.svc` file inside it.

How to do it...

Now let's create a WCF application to be hosted on different platforms:

1. Start a web application and add a `.svc` file to the project.

2. The SVC file template produces a `ServiceHost` server tag, which identifies that the IIS needs to create an object of `ServiceHost` and point to the appropriate service contract:

```
<%@ ServiceHost Language="C#" Debug="true"
  Service="SVCHostingProject.MySample"
    CodeBehind="MySample.svc.cs" %>
```

Here, the markup for the `.svc` file provides the `ServiceHost` implementation, which loads the service using the `ServiceHost` class automatically created by the ASP.NET pipeline inside IIS.

3. After the service has been implemented, we need to configure the `ServiceModel` element of `web.config` with all the bindings that the service needs to support:

```
<system.serviceModel>
    <services>
      <service name="SVCHostingProject.MySample">
        <endpoint name="basicHttpBinding"
                  address=""
                  binding="basicHttpBinding"
                  contract="SVCHostingProject.IMySample" />
        <endpoint name="mexHttpBinding"
                  contract="IMetadataExchange"
                  binding="mexHttpBinding"
                  address="mex" />
      </service>
    </services>
      <behaviors>
        <serviceBehaviors>
          <behavior name="">
            <serviceMetadata httpGetEnabled="true"
httpsGetEnabled="true" />
            <serviceDebug includeExceptionDetailInFaults="
false" />
          </behavior>
        </serviceBehaviors>
      </behaviors>
      <serviceHostingEnvironment aspNetCompatibilityEnabled="tru
e"
          multipleSiteBindingsEnabled="true" />
    </system.serviceModel>
```

The preceding configuration provided two endpoints for the service; one with `BasicHttpBinding`, which is the default binding for any web application, and the `mex` binding, which is the metadata exchange for the service. Please note that we have left the `Address` attribute blank for the endpoint. As WCF can be hosted inside a virtual directory, the address is automatically handled by the IIS itself and there is no need for an address definition in configuration.

4. Hosting a configuration also includes a special option to specify whether the service requires the ASP.NET compatibility mode. For instance, the service needing HTTP hosting may need the ASP.NET compatibility mode in configuration. To specify the ASP.NET compatibility mode for the service, we need to annotate the class with the `AspNetCompatibilityRequirements` attribute as follows:

```
[AspNetCompatibilityRequirements(RequirementsMode=
AspNetCompatibilityRequirementsMode.Required)]
public class MySample : IMySample
{

}
```

Marking the class with the `ASPNETCompatibilityRequirements` attribute will indicate that the class can run on ASP.NET compatibility.

5. Finally, you can publish this website inside IIS by pointing the published directory to a virtual directory.

6. If you are hosting inside `ConsoleApplication/Windows Application/Windows Service`, the only requirement that the application needs to make is to create an instance of the `ServiceHost` object.

7. The `ServiceHost` class automatically creates hosting environments taking reference from the service configuration for the process automatically, and hosts the service inside it:

```
ServiceHost host = new ServiceHost(typeof(MySample), new
  Uri("http://localhost:8080/MySample"));
host.Open();
```

Creating the host and opening it will host the service automatically inside the current application domain, and the `ServiceHost` class is capable of handling requests from the external environments. For any hosting environments, the host needs to be opened to start using the WCF service.

How it works...

The `ServiceHost` class is the primary type built inside the framework that hosts a WCF service. A WCF service is a contract-based model that is externally exposed using different types of endpoints supported by WCF. The `ServiceHost` class generally creates a `SocketListener` object inside it at a low-level to handle the requests from the external world. The call to open from `ServiceHost` is important as it opens up `Listener` on the port and the address specified for the service, and when any request is made to the address, it automatically spawns a new thread to handle the request.

The `ServiceHost` class automatically parses the incoming requests and dynamically creates the objects from the requests and calls the service logic. The `ServiceHost` class needs to call the `close` method when we want to release the service from memory.

There's more...

Let's consider a few more options for hosting.

What is Windows Process Activation Services (WAS)?

Hosting a WCF Service inside IIS is one of the most popular and well-accepted solutions worldwide. In IIS 5 or IIS 6, the solution of hosting a WCF service is strictly tied only to HTTP bindings. Even though WCF is very capable of hosting itself in other types of bindings that support a lower-level of interaction, there is no way to implement this in the previous version of IIS.

The WAS service enables hosting a service with any type of binding. IIS 7 implements a model called WAS, which takes on creating worker processes and providing generalized process activation and management.

Another important point to note is that even though WAS is a part of IIS 7, it can also be installed and configured separately. It is shipped with Windows Vista and Windows Server 2008.

When the first request comes for a service that is hosted on IIS 7, the listener adapter calls WAS to activate the worker process including the managed application domain for the specific application it is running on. As it does not matter whether the request is coming from ASP. NET or any other channel, once the process is activated for the current request, IIS handles the request automatically and retrieves the response and sends it back to the same channel. To start `ServiceHost` inside the application domain, the protocol handler calls the static method `EnsureServiceAvailable`, which will check and enable all service endpoints and transports.

To configure WAS for IIS, we need to edit the `applicationHost.config` file and add protocols for each binding element that needs to be supported:

```
<bindings>
<binding protocol="https" bindingInformation="*:443:" />
<binding protocol="http" bindingInformation="*:80:" />
<binding protocol="net.tcp" bindingInformation="808:*" />
<binding protocol="net.pipe" bindingInformation="*" />
<binding protocol="net.msmq" bindingInformation="localhost" />
<binding protocol="msmq.formatname" bindingInformation="localhost" />
</bindings>
```

You can also add the protocol bindings for a particular website using the `appcmd.exe` command.

See also

▶ Refer to the hosting WCF service at `http://bit.ly/wcfhosting`

Streaming data over a network using a WCF service

WCF is an easy way to implement a distributed application and also provides built-in functions to handle complex problems. Streaming is one of the most important problems we always need to consider while working over a network in distributed applications. Applications deployed over a cloud sometimes need download or upload capabilities. Downloading a large file over a network using a buffered read technique such as a SOAP-based response can really be a bottleneck to the system. Reading a very large file from the memory can terminate the server process with `OutofMemoryException`.

WCF allows you to send byte streams through the communication channel, or even allows you to implement a service that might take the stream start location from the service call and send the stream from a certain location. It allows you to use normal `HttpBinding` to support streams that have download or upload capabilities in the connected client-server architecture. Hence, there will be no timeouts to send or receive large files. In this recipe, I will show you how to use streaming to ensure your files are downloaded or uploaded correctly.

How to do it...

Let's create a streamed WCF application, which allows you to download/upload a stream resource to clients:

1. Create a service application and name it `WCFCommunicateService`.

2. The first thing that you need to do in order to create a service is `ServiceContract`. So once you create a service library, you need to delete the existing `Service1` and `IService1` files from the solution and add a new interface.

3. Create two methods inside the `ServiceContract` file; one for `FileDownload` and another for `FileUpload`. Let's see what the service definition looks like:

```
[ServiceContract]
public interface IFileTransferLibrary
{

    [OperationContract]
    void UploadFile(ResponseFile request);

    [OperationContract]
    ResponseFile DownloadFile(RequestFile request);
}
```

4. The contract defines the methods that are exposed outside. The `ServiceContract` attribute defines the interface that will have members available outside. The `OperationContract` attribute identifies the exposed members. In the preceding contract, `IFileTransferLibrary` has two methods: `UploadFile`, which takes an object of `ResponseFile`, and `DownloadFile`, which returns an object of `ResponseFile`. In the following code, you will see that we have used `MessageContract` instead of `DataContract`. The `DataContract` attribute is used to specify XML representation for the data that is transferred over the network, while `MessageContract` follows the SOAP standard to communicate data and therefore, this type of service can be accessed by any client that follows SOAP standards:

```
[MessageContract]
public class ResponseFile : IDisposable
{
    [MessageHeader]
    public string FileName;

    [MessageHeader]
    public long Length;

    [MessageBodyMember]
```

```csharp
    public System.IO.Stream FileByteStream;

    [MessageHeader]
    public long byteStart = 0;

    public void Dispose()
    {
        if (FileByteStream != null)
        {
            FileByteStream.Close();
            FileByteStream = null;
        }
    }
}

[MessageContract]
public class RequestFile
{
    [MessageBodyMember]
    public string FileName;

    [MessageHeaderMember]
    public long byteStart = 0;
}
```

The `RequestFile` and `ResponseFile` files are attributed with `MessageContract` instead of `DataContract` for the complex types. It is important to note that as we are going to send data using streaming, we need to break all of the data into a sequence of packages. The `DataContract` attribute sends the whole object at a time and is not capable of producing packet information about the data that is sent over the network. The `MessageContract` attribute on the other hand sends them as small messages and is capable of producing the packet data for the streams. Also, note that we have used a disposable pattern to ensure that the file gets closed when the client gets disconnected.

5. The `MessageBodyMember` attribute is added to the message body of the envelope it sends over the network. There can be only one body element for the whole message. The body holds the data that needs to be streamed. For every request, we have placed `byteStart`, which indicates where the download/upload should start from.

6. To download a file, we need to first open the file and return the `Stream` as the result. Let's see what the code will look like:

```
public ResponseFile DownloadFile(RequestFile request)
{
    ResponseFile result = new ResponseFile();

    FileStream stream =
  this.GetFileStream(Path.GetFullPath(request.FileName));
    stream.Seek(request.byteStart, SeekOrigin.Begin);
    result.FileName = request.FileName;
    result.Length = stream.Length;
    result.FileByteStream = stream;
    return result;

}
private FileStream GetFileStream(string filePath)
{
    FileInfo fileInfo = new FileInfo(filePath);

    if (!fileInfo.Exists)
        throw new FileNotFoundException("File not found");

    return new FileStream(filePath, FileMode.Open,
  FileAccess.Read);
}
```

You can see that we keep the `Stream` open for the file and seek the byte location from where the `Stream` needs to start. We set `FileByteStream` for the current `Stream` and let the response return to the client.

7. Similarly, in the case of `UploadFile`, we need to write the file to disk at a certain position as follows:

```
public void UploadFile(ResponseFile request)
{

    string filePath = Path.GetFullPath(request.FileName);

    int chunkSize = 2048;
    byte[] buffer = new byte[chunkSize];

    using (FileStream stream = new FileStream(filePath,
  FileMode.Append, FileAccess.Write))
      {
          do
          {
```

```
            int readbyte =
request.FileByteStream.Read(buffer, 0, chunkSize);
            if (readbyte == 0) break;

        stream.Write(buffer, 0, readbyte);
    } while (true);
        }
```

8. In the `UploadFile` method, we are actually using `Stream` to extract data from the client side. We are reading from `FileByteStream` and writing the bytes back to the server disk location. We should also remember that we need to close the stream after the write operation is completed. In the previous code, we are using a `Using` block to automatically call the `Dispose` method, releasing/closing `Stream`.

9. Let's now configure the service endpoint to support streaming:

```xml
<bindings>
    <basicHttpBinding>
      <binding name="FileTransferServicesBinding"
        transferMode="Streamed"
        messageEncoding="Mtom"
        sendTimeout="01:05:00"
        maxReceivedMessageSize="10067108864">
      </binding>
    </basicHttpBinding>
  </bindings>
```

Here, we have specified the `transferMode` binding called `Streamed` and the `messageEncoding` property called `Mtom`. The streamed `transferMode` ensures that the server sends the message response in streams and encoded to `Mtom`.

10. Finally, host the service using `ServiceHost`. We create a console application and use `ServiceHost` to host the service.

```
using (ServiceHost host = new ServiceHost(typeof(FileTransferLibra
ry)))
{
        host.Open();
        Console.WriteLine("Service Started!");
}
```

11. Now let's create the client application to download/upload files to the server. A client is actually a consumer of the service. The client can add a reference to the services and can produce the discovery files that will help you access the streamed services. It will also allow you to produce progress behavior for the file.

12. Add a service reference to the client so that you can call it. The service reference will automatically create the discovery files.

13. Use server methods directly to store or send stream or data:

```csharp
public void StartDownloading()
{
    Stream inputStream;
    try
    {
        string filePath = System.IO.Path.Combine("Download", this.
FileName);
        string fileName = this.FileName;
            long startlength = 0;
        FileInfo finfo = new FileInfo(filePath);
        if (finfo.Exists)
            startlength = finfo.Length; // If File exists
  we need to send the Start length to the server
        long length = this.Client.DownloadFile(ref
  fileName, ref startlength, out inputStream);
        using (FileStream writeStream = new System.
IO.FileStream(filePath, FileMode.OpenOrCreate,
  FileAccess.Write))
        {
            int chunkSize = 2048;
            byte[] buffer = new byte[chunkSize];
            do
            {
                int bytesRead = inputStream.Read(buffer, 0,
  chunkSize);
                if (bytesRead == 0) break;
                writeStream.Write(buffer, 0, bytesRead);
                this.ProgressValue = (int)(writeStream.Position *
100 / length);
            }
            while (true);
        }
    }
    catch
    {
//Log file errors here. Generally when file not found //or
  edited or Channel is faulted.
    }
    finally
    {
        if(inputStream != null)
            inputStream.Dispose();
    }
}
```

14. The code allows you to save the file to the disk. You can easily stop this operation by killing the thread that is downloading the file. The operation will be stopped and the file will remain in the disk until it is downloaded. When you resume, the process is called again. As in the function, we check the size of the file and send it back to the server. This will ensure that the server will start sending the file from a specific point.

How it works...

WCF communicates between two communication channels using sockets. Sockets are low-level implementations of communicating between two machines where one remains a `SocketListener`, which is stated here as the server side where the WCF service is hosted; another one is the socket client, which is used to connect to `SocketListener` and send/receive data. The sockets work at the TCP level and send serialized raw data between two communication channels.

WCF is a framework implemented on top of the socket API, which lets a programmer create contracts and based on it, the WCF API will understand how to serialize and communicate between the sockets.

Sockets support streaming internally. One can easily implement logic such that after sending a fixed set of bytes from one socket, it waits for acknowledgment from the other socket before the next set of bytes are sent. WCF implements this feature inside its API. It allows breaking the whole stream into a number of data packets that are defined as `MessageContract` and can be sent through a channel.

Writing a REST-based WCF service

The term **Representational State Transfer** (**REST**) was coined by Roy Fielding and is a design pattern for a networked system. In this pattern, the client invokes a web request using a URL, so the basic idea of a REST pattern is to generate a unique URI to represent data.

In Wikipedia, REST is quoted as:

> *"Representational State Transfer is intended to evoke an image of how a well-designed Web application behaves: a network of web pages (a virtual state-machine), where the user progresses through an application by selecting links (state transitions), resulting in the next page (representing the next state of the application) being transferred to the user and rendered for their use."*

This means REST is intended for web applications where the browser invokes each request by specifying a unique URI, as shown in the following figure:

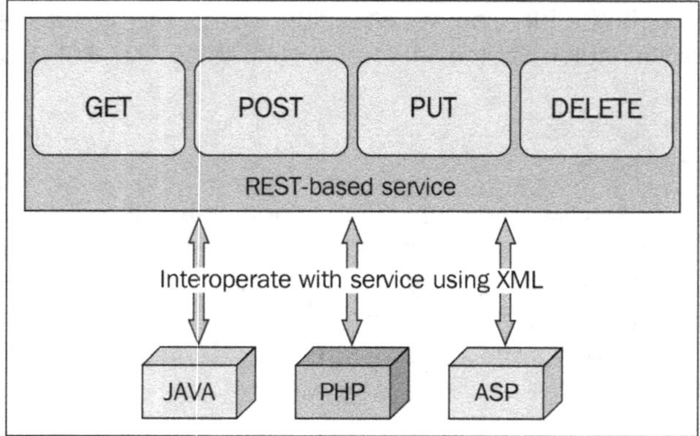

In the preceding figure, it is clear that any technology can easily call a REST-based service using basic HTTP requests.

There are a few basic thoughts behind the implementation of REST-based services. Let's look into them:

- Web is very simple and successful
- Web standards are fixed over time
- Web services should follow the standards of the Web

REST uses web verbs to communicate to services. Verbs such as `GET`, `POST`, `DELETE`, and `PUT` are major verbs for REST-based applications. If you consider Hi-REST for your application, you should be strict in choosing these verbs. The norms are as follows:

- `GET`: This is used to retrieve data
- `POST`: This is used to append data to the server
- `PUT`: This is used to insert and update data in the server
- `DELETE`: This is used to delete data from the server

REST services have a number of major advantages, which people are always inclined toward in order to implement:

- Less overhead on messages (no envelope required to warp every call).
- Very standardized. REST uses normal HTTP verbs to communicate with the server.
- REST is more user-friendly than others. It communicates using hierarchy with data where the URL defines what exactly the result is all about.

- The XML doesn't always need to be a medium of transport. You can also make use of JSON objects to communicate.
- REST uses predefined HTTP verbs.
- REST can take part in search engine optimizations as it is representational. The URL is the representation of data.

The features of REST-based services are never-ending. It is very popular nowadays not only because it is interoperable, but because it is easily consumed by the existing toolsets that support standard HTTP verbs.

How to do it...

Let's now create a REST-based WCF service using the following steps:

1. First, launch Visual Studio and use WCF Service Application to create a project. We will call it `ContactService`.

2. Delete the default files that have been created automatically from the project template (`IService1.cs` and `Service1.svc`), and add a new WCF Service to the solution. We will call it `ContactCRUD.svc`.

3. The project now includes two files with their template implementations. As we are going to implement a service that deals with contacts, we need to implement the `IContactCRUD` interface:

```
[ServiceContract]
public interface IContactCRUD
{
    [WebGet(UriTemplate = "contact/{roll}")]
    [OperationContract]
    Contact GetContact(string roll);

    [WebInvoke(Method = "POST", UriTemplate = "contacts")]
    [OperationContract]
    bool SaveContact(Contact currentContact);

    [WebInvoke(Method = "DELETE", UriTemplate = "contact/{roll}")]
    [OperationContract]
    bool RemoveContact(string roll);

    [WebInvoke(Method = "PUT", UriTemplate = "contact")]
    [OperationContract]
    bool UpdateContacts(Contact contact);

    [WebGet(UriTemplate = "contacts")]
```

```
        [OperationContract]
        List<Contact> GetAllContacts();
}


[DataContract]
public class Contact
{
        [DataMember]
        public int Roll { get; set; }

        [DataMember]
        public string Name { get; set; }

        [DataMember]
        public string Address { get; set; }

        [DataMember]
        public int Age { get; set; }
}
```

In the preceding code, we have specified the `WebInvoke` method to define the REST configuration for each interface. The `WebGet` method is used only for `GET` requests, while you can employ other methods easily using `WebInvoke`. Each of the attributes takes `UriTemplate`, which defines the routing URL that points to the service.

It is also worth mentioning that you can specify the request/response format for a particular interface as well. If you do not specify anything, it will take XML as a medium of transport. You can also specify JSON on either `WebInvoke` or `WebGet` as follows:

```
[WebGet(UriTemplate = "contacts", RequestFormat=
WebMessageFormat.Json, ResponseFormat=
WebMessageFormat.Json)]
```

4. The implementation of the class is very simple as well. We will create an in-memory list of contacts, which operates on the list such that the `GetContact` method will get an individual contact object from the list, the `SaveContact` method will put the contact on the list, the `DeleteContact` method will remove that particular contact from the list, and the `UpdateContact` method will update a contact element.

5. REST-based services require `webHttpBinding` as the binding. Let's consider configuring the service as shown in the following code:

```
<system.serviceModel>
  <services>
```

```xml
    <service name="ContactService.ContactCRUD"
behaviorConfiguration="httpBehavior">
        <endpoint address="" binding="webHttpBinding"
          contract="ContactService.IContactCRUD"
          behaviorConfiguration="httpEndpointBehavior">
        <identity>
          <dns value="localhost"/>
        </identity>
        </endpoint>
        <endpoint address="mex" binding="mexHttpBinding"
contract="IMetadataExchange"/>
      </service>
    </services>
    <behaviors>
      <serviceBehaviors>
        <behavior name="httpBehavior">
          <serviceMetadata httpGetEnabled="True"/>
          <serviceDebug includeExceptionDetailInFaults="False"/>
        </behavior>
      </serviceBehaviors>
      <endpointBehaviors>
        <behavior name="httpEndpointBehavior">
          <webHttp />
        </behavior>
      </endpointBehaviors>
    </behaviors>
    <serviceHostingEnvironment aspNetCompatibilityEnabled="true"
multipleSiteBindingsEnabled="true" />
  </system.serviceModel>
```

Here, the service is configured with `webHttpBinding` and a contract pointing to `ContactService.IContactCrud`. The service is getting hosted at port `8080`. Remember to specify `httpGetEnabled=true` to ensure that the application can invoke the GET request, which is required for REST-based services.

6. As our service is completed, let's try to examine it for each of the methods that we have specified for the service. Let's add `Testpage` on the project to invoke the requests. We are going to use `Jquery ajax` to request the service.

> By the way, you can also use any tool that can handle HTTP requests such as `PostMan` (a Chrome plugin) or Fiddler (from Telerik), but we are going to create a web page assuming you haven't used any of these tools before.

7. Let's add a jQuery library to the solution inside a `JS` folder and add a few buttons to handle each of these service interfaces. Our service is hosted as `ContactCRUD.svc` in IIS and we can call this URL to communicate with the service. Let's create a small UI with one table and a few textboxes to take values for the contact class. We created a few buttons and a table on the screen to show the data from the service, as shown in the following screenshot:

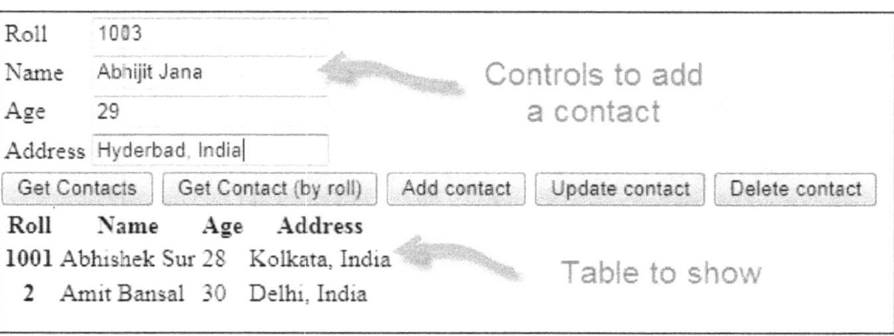

In the previous UI that we built, we placed a number of buttons, each of which pointed to a certain web service interface. We are going to call each service through these buttons and update the server. For instance, `GetContacts` will call `GetService` to get all contacts from the server, while `UpdateContact` calls the PUT service to update the existing contact information on the server.

8. The first service that we are going to look at is the `GET` service for `GetContact` and `GetContact` (by roll), as shown in the following code:

```
function returnContacts() {
    $.ajax({
        type: "GET",
        url: "ContactCRUD.svc/Contacts", success: function
(data) {
            updateTable(data);
        },
        error: function (msg) {
            alert(msg);
        }
    });
}
function returnContact() {
    var roll = $("#roll").val();
    $.ajax({
        type: "GET",
        url: "ContactCRUD.svc/contact/" + roll,
        success: function (data) {
            updateTable(data);
```

```
        },
        error: function (msg) {
            alert(msg);
        }
    });
}
function updateTable(data) {
    $("#output").find("tr:gt(0)").remove();
    $(data).find('Contact').each(function () {
        var roll = $(this).find('Roll').text();
        var name = $(this).find('Name').text();
        var age = $(this).find('Age').text();
        var address = $(this).find('Address').text();
        $('<tr></tr>').html('<th>' + roll + '</th><td>' +
name + '</td><td>' + age + '</td><td>' + address +
'</td>').appendTo('#output');
    });
}
```

In the preceding code, we made a `GET` request to the server. The first one is the request for all contacts without any parameters while the second one is for contacts with parameters. The `$.ajax` function is an API to call the server side. The AJAX requests receive an XML response, which is then appended to the table with the ID output using the `updateTable` function.

9. In the case of the `POST` request, the data needs to be sent inside the body of the AJAX object. jQuery provides a data property, which can be used to set the data that needs to be posted to the service:

```
function postContact() {
    var postObj = "<Contact><Address>" + $("#address").val() + "</
Address><Age>" + $("#age").val() +
"</Age><Name>" + $("#name").val() + "</Name><Roll>" +
$("#roll").val() + "</Roll></Contact>";
    $.ajax({
        type: "POST",
        url: "ContactCRUD.svc/contacts",
        contentType: "application/xml; charset=utf-8",
        data: postObj,
        success: function (data) {
            returnContacts();
            $(":text").val('');
        },
        error: function (msg) {
            alert(msg);
        }
    });
}
```

In the preceding code, we are posting an XML contact element to the service. The `contentType` method here is essential to let the service know that the data that sent is actually XML content.

10. Similar to `POST`, the `PUT` request also sends data inside the body of an AJAX call. The `PUT` request is used to update data on the server:

```
function putContact() {
    var postObj = "<Contact><Address>" + $("#address").val() + "</
Address><Age>" + $("#age").val() +
"</Age><Name>" + $("#name").val() + "</Name><Roll>" +
$("#roll").val() + "</Roll></Contact>";
    $.ajax({
        type: "PUT",
        url: "ContactCRUD.svc/contact",
        contentType: "application/xml; charset=utf-8",
        data: postObj,
        success: function (data) {
            returnContacts();
        },
        error: function (msg) {
            alert(msg);
        }
    });
}
```

Similar to the `POST` request, the `PUT` request also posts data into the body, while the type specified as `PUT` and the service URL are changed.

11. The `DELETE` statement is used to delete content from the server:

```
function deleteContact() {
    var roll = $("#roll").val();
    $.ajax({
        type: "DELETE",
        url: "ContactCRUD.svc/contact/" + roll,
        success: function (data) {
            returnContacts();
        },
        error: function (msg) {
            alert(msg);
        }
    });
}
```

The preceding AJAX call invokes a `DELETE` statement on the server. The `DELETE` statement works in a similar way to the `GET` request, where the URL itself identifies the data.

How it works...

REST is a new design pattern that has been put forward in the SOA architectures and has been widely used by enterprises because it uses the very old W3C HTTP request standards to manipulate data. Some leading social media giants, such as Twitter and Facebook, use REST to work with its services.

Internally, REST uses the routing API. The data that is passed using the REST URI is parsed by the .NET routing API, which then calls the appropriate function on the server. The main advantage of REST is that it is representational and data is in human-readable format.

A WCF Service method can be made REST-based by specifying an attribute `WebInvoke` to it. The `WebInvoke` attribute specifies the following properties:

- `BodyStyle`: This specifies the body style of messages that are sent to and from the service. The `BodyStyle` property can be bare (which means the body is not wrapped inside anything) or wrapped (`WrappedRequest` or `WrappedResponse`).

- `Method`: This specifies the HTTP method that is used to send the request for the WCF interface. The `WebGet` service can be used to specify `GET` requests for a service as well.

- `RequestFormat`: You are free to specify either the XML or JSON format of the request using this property.

- `ResponseFormat`: You can use this property to specify the response format of the WCF service.

- `UriTemplate`: This specifies the routing URL that needs to be parsed from the request URL to call a method.

Once the WCF service is configured properly, the `REST` methods for the server are enabled based on the configuration you have specified.

There's more...

Let's take this further with some additional topics.

Working with WebSockets in WCF

With the introduction of HTML5, WebSocket is one of the burning features that WCF needed badly. WCF 4.5 introduced WebSocket, which enables the browser sockets to communicate directly with the server WCF services, including the implementation of two-way communication channels directly from the browser.

Ever since web services came into being, developers have always tried to leverage their time to implement message formats in a way that makes the application run faster. The implementation of REST and JSON can be seen speeding up as we are trying to reduce the size of the data that is sent over the network, but we are still moving and parsing text to make it in a standard format, which is the slowest data transfer mechanism. Binary data gives the best output. However, as we communicate using the HTTP protocol, there is always an overhead while working over the Web.

Performance is not the only issue; HTTP is tied to the request/response cycle too. Even for asynchronous AJAX-based services, the request has to wait for a certain interval until the server can process the initial request and return the response. The browser then needs to parse the response body to generate the document object. This is a slower approach of communication.

A far better arrangement would be for a client to submit its request in a "fire and forget" kind of arrangement and then the service calls the client back with some data.

WebSockets addresses all these issues and also goes through the process of standardization. It uses TCP to communicate, giving you the benefit of a faster protocol as it works at a lower level than HTTP without additional HTTP header information. WebSockets also supports sending both binary and text formats. The best part of WebSockets is the two-way communication between the browser and the server.

To use WebSockets, the service needs to be configured with `NetHttpBinding`. Let's create `DuplexContract` for the WebSocket as follows:

```
[ServiceContract(CallbackContract=typeof(IDuplexCallbackContract))
]
public interface IDuplexContract
{
    [OperationContract]
    string GreetMeDuplex(string name);
}


[ServiceContract]
public interface IDuplexCallbackContract
{
    [OperationContract]
    void GreetingMe(string message);
}
```

In the preceding code, we implemented two contracts: one is the original duplex contract and the other is used as a callback. Here, the notion of execution is that the client calls `GreetMeDuplex` with a name and `GreetMe` from `IDuplexCallbackContract` will automatically call the client with a message.

The service implementation is as follows:

```
[ServiceBehavior(ConcurrencyMode = ConcurrencyMode.Reentrant)]
public class WebSocketSampleService : IRegularContract,
IDuplexContract
{
    public string GreetMeDuplex(string name)
    {
        OperationContext.Current.
            GetCallbackChannel<IDuplexCallbackContract>().
GreetintMe("Hello "
+ name + " by WebSockets");
        return "Hello " + name;
    }
}
```

So in the implementation, we call the callback with a message and return the name. The callback will call the client itself directly with the message and also return a string response from the service.

To configure a `WebSocket` endpoint, we specify the endpoint binding as `netHttpBinding` as follows:

```
<service name="WebSocketSampleService">
<endpoint address="http://localhost:8083"
          binding="netHttpBinding"
          contract="Contracts.IDuplexContract"/>
</service>
<bindings>
  <netHttpBinding>
    <binding name="TextOverWebSockets" messageEncoding="Text"/>
  </netHttpBinding>
</bindings>
```

By specifying `messageEncoding`, we indicate that the service only supports text formats here. You can also set binary message encoding when required.

Finally, to consume the WebSocket service, we just add a reference to the service on a Console Application and call the service as follows:

```
WebSockets.IDuplexContract duplexProxy;
duplexProxy = new WebSockets.DuplexContractClient(
    callbackContext,
    "DuplexContract");
Console.WriteLine("Calling the duplex contract:");
Console.WriteLine(duplexProxy.GreetMeDuplex("ido"));

// Or use a DuplexChannelFactory
DuplexChannelFactory<WebSockets.IDuplexContract> dchf =
    new DuplexChannelFactory<WebSockets.IDuplexContract>(
        callbackContext,
        new NetHttpBinding(),
        new EndpointAddress("http://localhost:8083/"));
duplexProxy = dchf.CreateChannel();
Console.WriteLine("Calling the duplex contract using text encoded
messages:");
Console.WriteLine(duplexProxy.GreetMeDuplex("ido"));
```

In this way, `callbackContext` automatically gets called from the duplex WebSocket. Most of the modern browsers are capable of invoking a call, and WebSockets can directly call this service from it.

See also

 ▸ Refer to the REST and WCF services at `http://bit.ly/wcfrestful`

Creating a WCF service using the Open Data Protocol standards

The current trend of the software industry is moving towards Open Data Protocols. One of the most interesting and popular data protocols that have sprung into existence recently is Open Data Protocol or OData. OData is a web-based protocol used to query and/or update data. OData uses standard web technologies, such as HTTP, Atom Publishing Protocol, XML, and JSON to communicate and provide access to the information present on the server to the external world.

Even though OData is not the only way to enable representational-relational data from the server, it brings a standardization on how the data should be represented using a unique URI, which allows the data to be filtered, queried, manipulated, and so on. OData can be thought of as a tap from the ecosystem that exposes the dataset or a tap into the ecosystem of developers who can build applications very easily, as the way in which OData API works is easily understood by them.

In the Microsoft .NET platform, the ODATA services are encapsulated in WCF Data Services (which was formerly known as ADO.NET data services). These services are easy to use and come in handy for developers in the Microsoft world. .NET also provides a superior client library that makes it very easy to create tools that can consume the OData services.

Getting ready

Before we try to expose an OData service, it is important to create a database with some tables that might be useful to expose. Let's create three tables inside our SQL Server database:

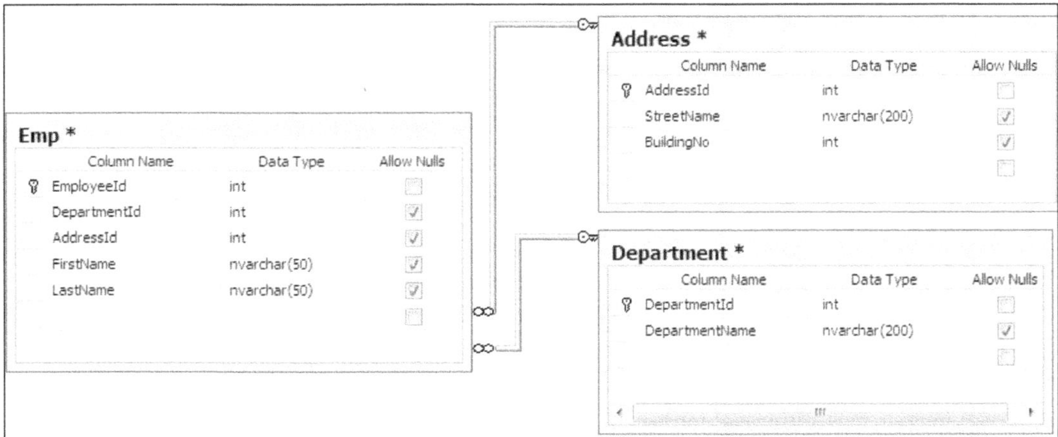

In the preceding screenshot, we created three tables. We created the relationships between the three tables so that we can generate the relationship inside our mode.

How to do it...

Now, let's create an OData service from Visual Studio:

1. Launch Visual Studio and create an ASP.NET web application. Create the web application to host the WCF data service.

2. Add an ADO.NET data model to the project and point it to the database that is created. We are going to use the Entity Framework to communicate with the database. Once it is successfully created, the entity data model will look like the following screenshot:

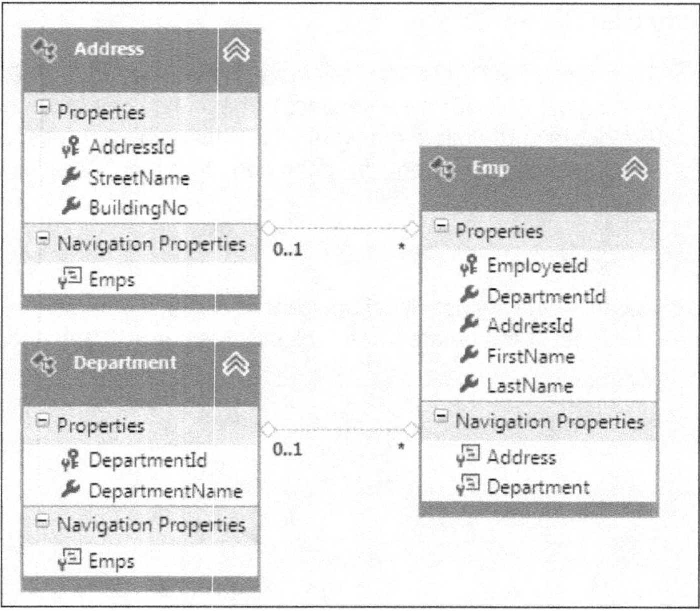

3. Now add a new WCF Data Service to the web application; we will call it `EmployeeDataService`.

4. After the WCF Data Service is added to the solution, replace the `/*Todo: put your data source class name here */` path with `ODataDbEntities`, which is the database context created from the Entity Framework.

5. Generally, OData services are restrictive in nature. If you do not set a proper permission to objects, either read or write, the objects are not exposed to the external world. Let's now configure the service with a set of rules as follows:

```
public static void InitializeService(DataServiceConfiguration config)
{
```

```
config.SetEntitySetAccessRule("*", EntitySetRights.AllRead);

//Set paging
config.SetEntitySetPageSize("*", 25);

config.DataServiceBehavior.MaxProtocolVersion =
DataServiceProtocolVersion.V3;
}
```

The preceding specification defines that the service exposes all the entities for `Read` with a custom pagination of 25 items per page.

6. The OData framework doesn't mean exposing everything from the database out on the Web. It means exposing specific entities with as much or as little granularity as you like. The OData framework provides you with support on intercepting queries, making custom behaviors, making custom service operations, and so on. For every request, the OData framework calls `OnStartProcessingRequest`, which you can intercept to add various cache headers:

```
protected override void OnStartProcessingRequest(ProcessRequestAr
gs args)
{
    base.OnStartProcessingRequest(args);
    HttpContext context = HttpContext.Current;
    HttpCachePolicy c = HttpContext.Current.Response.Cache;
    c.SetCacheability(HttpCacheability.ServerAndPrivate);
    c.SetExpires(HttpContext.Current.Timestamp.AddSeconds(60));
    c.VaryByHeaders["Accept"] = true;
    c.VaryByHeaders["Accept-Charset"] = true;
    c.VaryByHeaders["Accept-Encoding"] = true;
    c.VaryByParams["*"] = true;
}
```

In the preceding code, we have added the `HttpCache` header on every request that passes through the OData handler.

7. You can also use built-in interceptors such as `QueryInterceptor` or `ChangeInterceptor` to ensure that the OData service hooks itself to the custom logic specified on those methods before the object is returned:

```
[QueryInterceptor("Emp")]
public Expression<Func<Emp, bool>> OnQueryEmployee()
{
    //ToDo : Write your custom logic here.

    return e => true;

}
```

```
[ChangeInterceptor("Emp")]
public void OnChangeEmployee(Emp emp, UpdateOperations operation)
{
    if (operation == UpdateOperations.Add)
    {
        throw new DataServiceException(401, "We do not allow to
add new employees");
    }
}
```

8. In the preceding code, you can see that the `OnQueryEmployee` function is called when `Emp` is called from the client. You can write your own custom logic to filter data. The `OnChangeEmployee` function is called whenever any client tries to make changes to the data on the server. WCF Data Service will automatically hook itself onto the method and pass the `Emp` object with the operation.

9. Finally, the service can be hosted on IIS and the service URL can be called to get a reference for the service.

How it works...

WCF Data Service is a new implementation of Microsoft to support Open Data Protocol standards. It provides an easy way to expose objects based on the REST-based design principle. It uses its runtime serializers to convert data objects into standard formats of data such that they can be consumed by applications that support Open Data Protocol standards. The support for standard `AtomPub` APIs included in the services makes it even better.

From the programming perspective, there is not much to write to expose items. The API is made simple enough and a large set of APIs is used automatically to generate the standard API formats and sent as a response.

There's more...

As we have already seen how to create OData services, let's consider some things that we haven't covered yet.

Consuming OData services

Consuming OData services is easy. Let's take an example of an online OData service to show how we can consume it. We take the reference of the NuGet public API, which lists the packages that are supported by NuGet. NuGet is a free, open source public developer package management system. It helps a developer integrate a number of online .NET projects inside it by using its library hosted on the cloud. Now, let's connect to the OData service hosted by NuGet and take a reference to find the packages available on it. To connect to the NuGet package service, we add a reference of the following link to our project using the service reference at `http://packages.nuget.org/v1/FeedService.svc/`, as shown in the following screenshot:

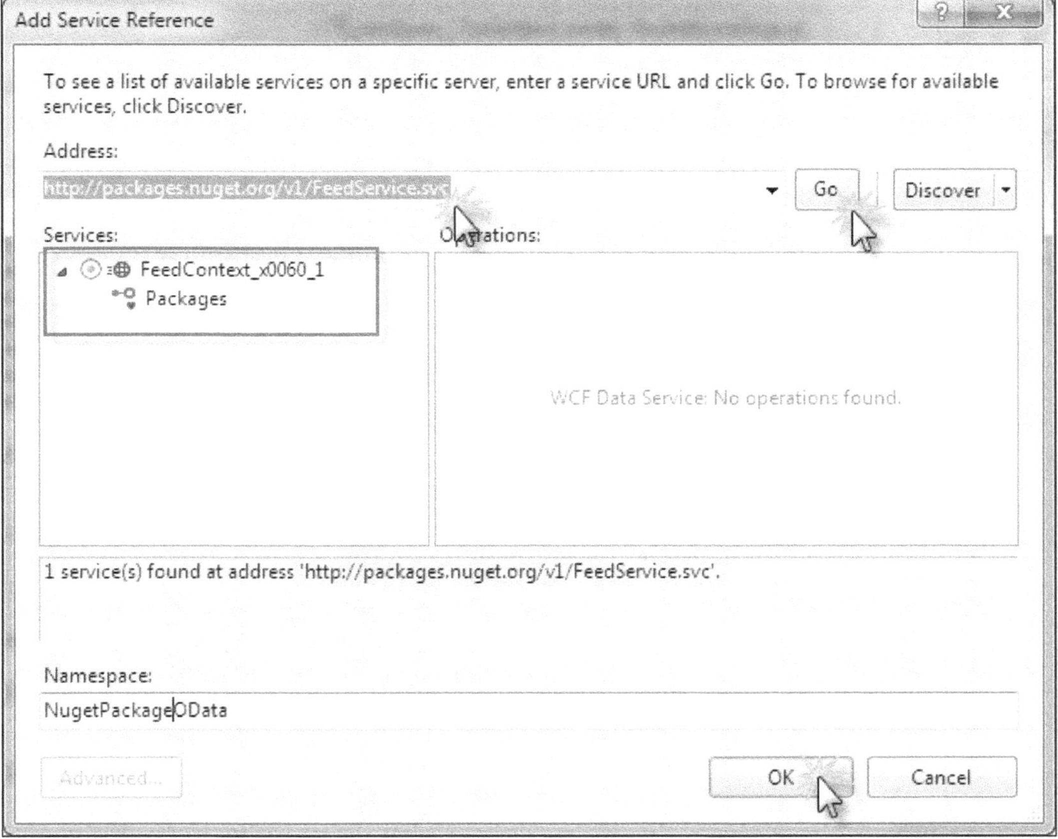

Here, when you add a reference to the NuGet `PackageOData` service, it will show you a public service that has a public interface called packages. The public API is freely available to everyone to keep a track of all the packages that are available with NuGet. We call the `Namespace` service `NugetPackageOData`.

After taking a reference from the public NuGet package API, let's create a new WPF application and a UI. The UI has a `TextBox` class, a `ListBox` class, and a `Button` class such that when the button is clicked, the query text from the `Textbox` class is searched on the `NugetPackage` service and the list is shown in the **List** section on the screen.

```xml
<DockPanel LastChildFill="True">
        <Grid DockPanel.Dock="Top">
            <Grid.ColumnDefinitions>
                <ColumnDefinition Width="80" />
                <ColumnDefinition Width="*" />
                <ColumnDefinition Width="100" />
            </Grid.ColumnDefinitions>
            <TextBlock Grid.Column="0" Text="Query:"
                    Margin="5" />
            <TextBox Name="txtQuery" Grid.Column="1"
                    Margin="5" />
            <Button Name="btnQuery" Grid.Column="2"
                Content="Query"
                Margin="5"
                Click="btnQuery_Click" />
        </Grid>
        <Separator Margin="5" />
        <ListBox Name="lstPackages" ItemsSource="{Binding}">
            <ListBox.ItemTemplate>
                <DataTemplate>
                    <Grid>
                        <Grid.ColumnDefinitions>
                            <ColumnDefinition Width="3*" />
                            <ColumnDefinition Width="0.5*" />
                            <ColumnDefinition Width="1.5*" />
                            <ColumnDefinition Width="2*" />
                            <ColumnDefinition Width="1*" />
                        </Grid.ColumnDefinitions>
                        <TextBlock Text="{Binding Id}"
Grid.Column="0" />

                        <TextBlock Text="{Binding Version}"
Grid.Column="1" />
```

```xml
                        <TextBlock Text="{Binding Authors}" Grid.
Column="2" />
                        <TextBlock Text="{Binding Dependencies}"
Grid.Column="3" />
                        <TextBlock Text="{Binding Created}"
Grid.Column="4" />
                    </Grid>
                </DataTemplate>
            </ListBox.ItemTemplate>
        </ListBox>
    </DockPanel>
```

In the preceding XAML, we create `DockPanel`, which hosts one grid and one list. The grid shows the top-panel to query the package and the list shows a list of packages returned by the service. We create an appropriate `DataTemplate` binding to ensure that the service package contract is maintained.

In the preceding code, we create an object of the `NugetOData` packager client and call its package API to get all the public APIs. We use the query sent from the textbox to load only the items that contain the key in their title:

```csharp
IEnumerable<V1FeedPackage> QueryNuGetPackage(string query)
{
    var client = new FeedContext_x0060_1(this.clientUri);
    var returnedPackages = client.Packages.Where(e =>
e.Title.ToUpper().Contains(query.ToUpper()));

    return returnedPackages;
}


private void btnQuery_Click(object sender, RoutedEventArgs e)
{
    if (string.IsNullOrWhiteSpace(txtQuery.Text))
        return;

    this.lstPackages.DataContext = this.QueryNuGetPackage(txtQuery.
Text);
}
```

The preceding code gets all the packages that are returned from the package OData public API and filters the returned data by the query text.

Securing the OData application behind a valid authentication

Authentication is an important consideration when dealing with OData services. The OData services exposes data using REST-based URLs and is available to the external world. In some cases, these data blocks need to be secured behind valid credentials. If we need to map using a Windows account, the IIS manager provides an ASP.NET Windows authentication automatically just by configuring the website, as shown in the following screenshot:

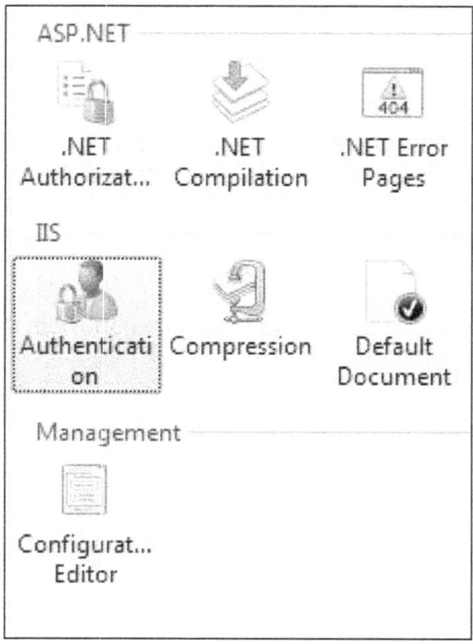

Double-click on the authentication icon of IIS to load the authentication, disable **Anonymous Authentication** for the website, and enable the **Basic Authentication** option. After the application is configured, the **Authentication** tab will look like the following screenshot:

Name	Status	Response Type
Anonymous Authentication	Disabled	
ASP.NET Impersonation	Disabled	
Basic Authentication	Enabled	HTTP 401 Challenge
Forms Authentication	Disabled	HTTP 302 Login/Redirect
Windows Authentication	Disabled	HTTP 401 Challenge

Once the **Basic Authentication** option is set for the site, the site will require the user to specify the Windows authentication credentials to log in.

On the other hand, if the service requires authenticating using custom credentials, you need to disable the **Basic Authentication** option and re-enable **Anonymous Authentication**. The web application can specify a custom HTTP module to pull the username and password from the request headers and perform the validation. Let's add an `IHttpModule` to the web application to initiate an authentication for the service.

Let's define `BasicAuthenticationModule`, which will ensure the following aspects:

- The service is called in the SSL for authentication
- The service has an `Authorization` header block on its request header
- The `AuthorizationHeader` provides a `base64` representation of a valid user's credentials as follows:

```
public class BasicAuthModule : IHttpModule
{
    public void Init(HttpApplication app)
    {
        app.AuthenticateRequest += new
EventHandler(app_AuthenticateRequest);
    }
    void app_AuthenticateRequest(object sender, EventArgs
e)
    {
        HttpApplication app = (HttpApplication)sender;
        if (!app.Request.IsSecureConnection)
        {
            BasicAuthModule.GenerateAutenticationFailedResponse(a
pp,
403, 4, "Please connect the service using HTTPS");
            app.CompleteRequest();
        }
        else if (!app.Request.Headers.AllKeys.
Contains("Authorization"))
        {
            BasicAuthModule.GenerateAutenticationFailedResponse(a
pp,
401, 1,
                "Please provide Authorization headers with
your request.");
            app.CompleteRequest();
        }
        else if (!BasicAuthProvider.Authenticate(app.Context))
        {
```

```
                BasicAuthModule.GenerateAutenticationFailedResponse(a
pp,
401, 1, "Logon failed.");
                app.CompleteRequest();
            }
        }
    private static void GenerateAutenticationFailedResponse(HttpAp
plication app,
int code, int subCode, string description)
        {
            HttpResponse response = app.Context.Response;
            response.StatusCode = code;
            response.SubStatusCode = subCode;
            response.StatusDescription = description;
            response.AppendHeader("WWW-Authenticate", "Basic");
        }
        public void Dispose()
        {
        }
    }
```

The preceding code defines `HttpModule`, which will be called automatically when a request needs authentication. The module checks whether the service is called using SSL and it also checks for the authorization header component. If everything is correct, it validates the user ID and password sent through the authorization header parsing the values using the `BasicAuthProvider` class.

The `BasicAuthProvider` class is like an `AuthenticationProvider` class, whose job is to validate the user ID and password that is sent in the authorization header block and return the credentials whether they are valid or not, as shown in the following code:

```
public class BasicAuthProvider
{
    public static bool Authenticate(HttpContext context)
    {
        string authHeader =
context.Request.Headers["Authorization"];
        IPrincipal principal;
        if (TryGetPrincipal(authHeader, out principal))
        {
            HttpContext.Current.User = principal;
            return true;
        }
        return false;
    }
}
```

The idea of authenticating the `BasicAuthProvider` class is to acquire the value of the authorization header and generate an `IPrincipal` object when authorization succeeds. The authentication calls the `TryGetPrincipal` object to authenticate the user and generate the `Principal` object, as shown in the following code:

```
private static bool TryGetPrincipal(string authHeader, out
IPrincipal principal)
    {
        string user;
        string password;
        if (TryParseAuthorizationHeader(authHeader, out user, out
password))
        {
            return TryAuthenticate(user, password, out principal);
        }
        principal = null;
        return false;
    }
```

In the preceding code, we try to parse the authorization header string that is passed by the client, and get the user ID and password from the Base64 encoded string in the authorization header block. The logic of parsing can be anything and depending on that, the client needs to send it.

```
private static bool TryParseAuthorizationHeader(string authHeader,
out string user, out string password)
    {
        user = "";
        password = "";
        if (string.IsNullOrEmpty(authHeader) ||
!authHeader.StartsWith("Basic"))
        {
            return false;
        }
        string base64EncodedCreds = authHeader.Substring(6);
        string[] creds =
Encoding.ASCII.GetString(Convert.FromBase64String(base64EncodedCre
ds)).Split(new char[] { ':' });
        if (creds.Length != 2 || string.IsNullOrEmpty(creds[0]) ||
string.IsNullOrEmpty(creds[1]))
        {
            return false;
        }
        user = creds[0];
        password = creds[1];
        return true;
    }
```

In the preceding code, we parsed the string inside the authorization header. Note that, in our case, the authorization header starts with the basic, and the username and password are split using `:`. The entire string is also Base64 encoded to ensure that we do not pass illegal characters.

```
private static bool TryAuthenticate(string user, string password,
out IPrincipal principal)
    {

        //Todo : Authenticate from database and generate the User
Identity here.
        if (user.ToLower().Equals("admin") && password.
Equals("myadminaccount"))
        {
            principal = new GenericPrincipal(
                new GenericIdentity(user), new string[] { "Users"
});
            return true;
        }
        else
        {
            principal = null;
            return false;
        }
    }
```

The `TryAuthenticate` function gets the user ID and password and returns a `genericPrincipal` object. The `principal` object is transferred into the context, which can be used later on when generating the output. Using this block, you can use any authentication technique to validate the user ID and password and specify respective permissions to the user. If you are using the ASP.NET membership and roles, the `GenericPrincipal` function constructor will allow you to specify roles for the identity.

```
principal = new GenericPrincipal(new GenericIdentity(user), Roles.
GetRolesForUser(user));
```

The preceding code generates the principle for the membership API.

Now, to configure the application to use the authentication module, we add the module to `Web.config` of the site as follows:

```
<system.webServer>
    <modules runAllManagedModulesForAllRequests="true">
      <add name="BasicAuthModule" type="WCFDataServiceApplication.
BasicAuthModule"/>
    </modules>
  </system.webServer>
```

The OData service itself supports query interceptors that let you allow/disallow an object to be sent to the client. Based on the interceptor, you can also filter your data.

The `QueryInterceptor` attribute intercepts any requests made by the client and you can set your logic to ensure whether the query is successful or not, as shown in the following code:

```
[QueryInterceptor("Emp")]
public Expression<Func<Emp, bool>> OnQueryEmployee()
{
    var user = HttpContext.Current.User;
    if (user.IsInRole("Administrators"))
        return e => true;
    else
        return e => false;
}
[ChangeInterceptor("Emp")]
public void OnChangeEmployee(Emp emp, UpdateOperations operation)
{
    if (operation == UpdateOperations.Add || operation ==
UpdateOperations.Change)
    {
        var user = HttpContext.Current.User;
        if (!user.IsInRole("Administrators"))
            throw new DataServiceException(401, "User do not have
permission to change employee credentials");
    }
}
```

In the preceding code, the `QueryInterceptor` attribute is used to ensure that `CurrentUser` is validated when the `emp` table is fetched. The OData environment will automatically call the `OnQueryEmployee` method and check whether the administrator role is set for the current user before letting it retrieve the employee information.

The `ChangeInterceptor` attribute is called when any DML operation is performed on the data. When the client requests to add or change or even delete this method, `OnChangeEmployee` gets called and it checks whether the user is in the administrator role; otherwise, it throws an exception down the pipeline.

Consuming the OData service

We have seen how to consume the OData service. If the service needs to pass request headers to be authenticated, you can pass it inside the `SendingRequest` event handler, as shown in the following code:

```
Uri serviceRootUri = new Uri(
                "https://localhost:8000/WCFDataServiceApplication/");
WCFDataServiceClient client =
    new WCFDataServiceClient(serviceRootUri);
```

```
client.SendingRequest += (o, requestEventArgs) =>
{
    var creds = username + ":" + password;
    var encodedCreds =
                Convert.ToBase64String(Encoding.ASCII.
GetBytes(creds));
    requestEventArgs.RequestHeaders.Add(
                "Authorization", "Basic " + encodedCreds);
};
var res = client.Emp.FirstOrDefault();
```

In the preceding code, the `WCFDataServiceClient` service is called. The `SendingRequest` event is handled to intercept the user ID and password for every call to the service to get the employee's information or any other objects. Please note the specific format of the authorization header.

See also

> ▸ Refer to WCF OData with ASP.NET at `http://bit.ly/wcfodata`

Extending a WCF service (service extensibility)

Extensibility is one of the most important concerns for any programming world. While developing a framework, a good architect always creates hooks, which lets the user explore these hooks and modify the way the framework behaves. WCF, being a powerful and simple tool to create services, also has a lot of hooks on its runtime, which will enable developers to write their own code and modify the way WCF behaves in certain scenarios. There are a great number of hooks available as interfaces in WCF, which allow you to change either the description or runtime of the WCF service.

The description of a service means all the things that are needed to start a service under the WCF environment. It includes:

- ▸ All aspects that WCF needs to start a service
- ▸ Endpoints (address, binding, and contract)
- ▸ Local behaviors

After `ServiceHost` is opened, we cannot change the description of the service until it is closed and restarted. When the `ServiceHost` service is opened, the WCF runtime is initialized and all the socket listeners are started. In this situation, the `ServiceDescription` service is frozen and any attempt to change the service description will be ignored.

There are a number of extensibility options available in WCF, which allow hooking and changing the default operation of the service. The options are as follows:

- Extending behaviors
- Extending serialization
- Extending metadata
- Extending security
- Extending channel system
- Extending the service host

Getting ready

Let's create a service and host the service in a Console Application as follows:

```
[ServiceContract]
    public interface ISecureTestService
    {
        [OperationContract]
        string MyDummyOperation(string name, string password);
    }


    public class MySecureTestService : ISecureTestService
    {
        public string MyDummyOperation(string name, string
          password)
        {
            return "Doing inside dummy service";
        }
    }
```

In the preceding code, we just defined a `ServiceContract` service and an operation called `MyDummyOperation`. We also defined the `ServiceHost` service to host our service directly inside our Console Application, as shown in the following code:

```
static void Main(string[] args)
{
    ServiceHost host = new ServiceHost(typeof(MySecureTestService));
    host.Open();
    Console.WriteLine("Secure service is running");
    Console.ReadKey(true);
}
```

Also, we configured the service with address and contract as follows:

```xml
<services>
    <service name="ServiceExtensibility.MySecureTestService"
behaviorConfiguration="Metadata">
        <host>
          <baseAddresses>
            <add baseAddress="http://localhost:8140/Service"/>
            <add baseAddress="https://localhost:8883/Service"/>
          </baseAddresses>
        </host>
        <endpoint address=""
                binding="basicHttpBinding"
                contract="ServiceExtensibility.ISecureTestService"/>
    </service>
  </services>
  <behaviors>
    <serviceBehaviors>
      <behavior name="Metadata">
        <serviceMetadata httpGetEnabled="true" />
      </behavior>
    </serviceBehaviors>
  </behaviors>
```

This is a simple service where we host our service in more than one scheme at different ports on the same machine. We also got `httpGet` enabled for metadata.

If we try to override the default behaviors of the WCF, we have four options to change the default behaviors of the service. They are as follows:

- Service behavior
- Endpoint behavior
- Contract behavior
- Operation behavior

In this recipe, let's look at how we can change each of these behaviors of the service.

How to do it...

Now, let's take steps to extend the WCF service with various schemes:

1. Let's say we want our `MyDummyOperation` to only be called using the HTTPS scheme, and when we call the service using HTTP, the operation fails. To do this, we create a class and implement it from `IServiceBehavior` as follows:

```
class RequireHttpsBehavior : Attribute, IServiceBehavior
{
    public void AddBindingParameters(ServiceDescription
serviceDescription, ServiceHostBase serviceHostBase,
System.Collections.ObjectModel.Collection<ServiceEndpoint>
endpoints,
System.ServiceModel.Channels.BindingParameterCollection
bindingParameters)
    {
    }


    public void ApplyDispatchBehavior(ServiceDescription
serviceDescription, ServiceHostBase serviceHostBase)
    {
    }


    public void Validate(ServiceDescription
serviceDescription, ServiceHostBase serviceHostBase)
    {
        foreach (var endpoint in
serviceDescription.Endpoints)
        {
            if (endpoint.Binding.Scheme !=
Uri.UriSchemeHttps)
                throw new InvalidOperationException("This
service requires HTTPS");
        }
    }
}
```

In the preceding code, inside the `Validate` method, we check all the endpoints associated with the service and we throw an `InvalidOperationException` when we find an endpoint other than the HTTPS scheme.

2. We then add the `ServiceBehavior` service either in the form of an attribute on the `ServiceContract` class (for that we need to inherit from the `Attribute` class), or we can directly add an object of this behavior in the `ServiceHost` object.

```
host.Description.Behaviors.Add(new RequireHttpsBehavior());
```

Now if I run the project, it will give an exception saying the service requires HTTPS.

3. The `EndpointBehavior` service can also be tweaked using the interface `IEndpointBehavior` as follows:

```
class LoggingEndpointBehavior : IEndpointBehavior
{

    public void AddBindingParameters(ServiceEndpoint
endpoint, System.ServiceModel.Channels.BindingParameterCollection
bindingParameters)
    {
    }

    public void ApplyClientBehavior(ServiceEndpoint
endpoint, System.ServiceModel.Dispatcher.ClientRuntime
clientRuntime)
    {
        clientRuntime.ClientMessageInspectors.Add(new
LoggingInspector());
    }

    public void ApplyDispatchBehavior(ServiceEndpoint
endpoint, System.ServiceModel.Dispatcher.EndpointDispatcher
endpointDispatcher)
    {

    }

    public void Validate(ServiceEndpoint endpoint)
    {
    }
}
```

4. Here, we have added `EndpointBehavior` such that it logs messages on the screen. We have added the `LoggingInspector` class, which inspects any requests and logs the data in the console.

5. To intercept `ContractBehavior`, we need to implement the `IContractBehavior` class. Let's define a contract behavior such that we use `BinaryEncoder` for the service rather than the textual encoders:

```
class BinaryEncoderContractBehavior : Attribute,
IContractBehavior
```

```
        {
            public void AddBindingParameters(ContractDescription
    contractDescription, ServiceEndpoint endpoint,
    System.ServiceModel.Channels.BindingParameterCollection
    bindingParameters)
                {
                    if (endpoint.Binding.CreateBindingElements().
    Find<MessageEncod
    ingBindingElement>() == null)
                        {
                            bindingParameters.Add(new
    BinaryMessageEncodingBindingElement());
                        }
                }
```

6. Here, we are changing the binding encoder to binary. We use `BinaryMessageEncodingBindingElement` as the binding for the contract such that when messages are sent or received, it uses the binary encoding rather than the text encoding. Remember, we generally use this tweak when we create `CustomBinding` for an operation. Before adding an encoder to the binding, it is also important to check whether there is already any binding associated. The `ContractBehavior` service can be added as an attribute to the `ServiceContract` class.

7. Operation behaviors are used to tweak values for an application. The `WebGet` or `WebInvoke` methods are operation behaviors that specify the actual `URITemplate` for the operation, and tweak the request to connect to an operation. Let's define an operation that will change the negative value to a positive value:

```
    class NonNegativeOperationBehavior : Attribute,
    IOperationBehavior
        {
            public void
    ApplyDispatchBehavior(OperationDescription
    operationDescription,
    System.ServiceModel.Dispatcher.DispatchOperation
    dispatchOperation)
                {
                    var originalInvoker =
    dispatchOperation.Invoker;
                    dispatchOperation.Invoker = new
    NoNegativeInvoker(originalInvoker);
                }

            public void Validate(OperationDescription
    operationDescription)
                {
```

```
            if (operationDescription.Messages.Count < 2 ||
operationDescription.Messages[1].Body.ReturnValue.Type !=
typeof(dcuble))
            {
                throw new InvalidOperationException("This
behavior can only be applied on operation which returns
double");
            }
        }
    }
```

Here, we have checked whether the operation that was invoked returns a double value. We check `ReturnValue` of the second message on `OperationDescription` as WCF returns two messages for an operation. We also create a new `OperationInvoker` to manipulate the value received when the operation is invoked.

8. To write the invoker, we pass the `OriginalInvoker` class as a wrapper, so that we return `OriginalInvoker` in places where we do not need to tweak, and we also do not need to rewrite the whole invoker as follows:

```
class NoNegativeInvoker : IOperationInvoker
{
    public NoNegativeInvoker(IOperationInvoker originalInvoker)
    {
        this.OriginalInvoker = originalInvoker;
    }

    public IOperationInvoker OriginalInvoker { get; set; }

    public object[] AllocateInputs()
    {
        return OriginalInvoker.AllocateInputs();
    }

    public object Invoke(object instance, object[] inputs, out
object[] outputs)
    {
        var result= OriginalInvoker.Invoke(instance, inputs, out
outputs);
        result = Math.Abs((double)result);
        return result;
    }

    public IAsyncResult InvokeBegin(object instance, object[]
inputs, AsyncCallback callback, object state)
    {
```

```csharp
        return OriginalInvoker.InvokeBegin(instance, inputs,
callback, state);
    }

    public object InvokeEnd(object instance, out object[] outputs,
IAsyncResult result)
    {
        var oresult= OriginalInvoker.InvokeEnd(instance, out
outputs, result);
        oresult = Math.Abs((double)oresult);
        return oresult;
    }

    public bool IsSynchronous
    {
        get { return OriginalInvoker.IsSynchronous; }
    }
}
```

In `NoNegativeInvoker`, we store `OriginalInvoker` as a property as it is passed in its constructor, and we return the values from `OriginalInvoker` wherever required. To tweak the behavior, we get the results of the invoke from `OriginalInvoker` and change it to an absolute value. We also need to do the same thing to `InvokeEnd` for async operations.

9. After adding `NonNegativeOperationBehavior` as an attribute for an operation that returns a double value, we ensure that it does not generate a negative value.

How it works...

The behaviors are one of the primary key elements for WCF programming. While defining a service endpoint, you can configure it so that the service behavior calls your own code rather than already predefined behaviors associated with the WCF API. In this recipe, we have covered how you can use interface hooks to define your own `ServiceBehavior`, `EndPointBehavior`, `ContractBehavior`, and `OperationBehavior` classes. As we go down the line, the WCF supports a lot of other enhancements, such as runtime extensibility, `ServiceModel` extensibility, WCF channel extensibility, and serialization extensibility.

3

Building a Touch-sensitive Device Application Using Windows Phone 8

In this chapter, we will cover the following recipes:

- Building your first Windows Phone 8 application following the MVVM pattern
- Working with Launchers and Choosers in Windows Phone
- Working with relational databases and persistent storage
- Working with notifications in Windows Phone

Introduction

Windows Phones are the newest smart device that has come to the market and host the Windows operating system from Microsoft. The new operating system that was introduced to the market significantly differs from the previous Windows mobile operating system. Microsoft has shifted gears on producing a consumer-oriented phone rather than an enterprise mobile environment. The operating system is stylish and focused on the consumer. It was built keeping a few principles in mind:

- Simple and light, with focus on completing primary tasks quickly
- Distinct typography (Segoe WP) for all its UI
- Smart and predefined animation for the UI

- Focus on content, not chrome (the whole screen is available to the application for use)
- Honesty in design

Unlike the previous Windows Phone operating system, Windows Phone 8 is built on the same core on which Windows PC is now running. The shared core indicates that the Windows core system includes the same Windows OS, including NT Kernel, NT filesystem, and networking stack. Above the core, there is a Mobile Core specific to mobile devices, which includes components such as **Multimedia**, **Core CLR**, and **IE Trident**, as shown in the following screenshot:

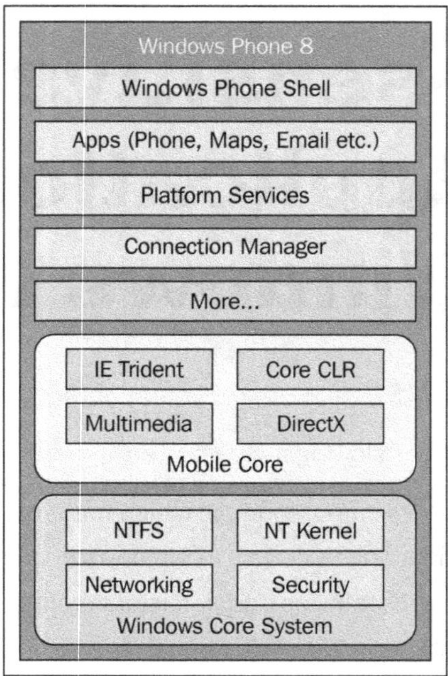

In the preceding screenshot, the Windows Phone architecture has been depicted. The **Windows Core System** is shared between the desktop and mobile devices. The Mobile Core is specific to mobile devices that run Windows Phone Shell, all the apps, and platform services such as background downloader/uploader and scheduler.

It is important to note that even though both Windows 8 and Windows Phone 8 share the same core and most of the APIs, the implementation of APIs is different from one another. The Windows 8 APIs are considered **WinRT**, while Windows Phone 8 APIs are considered **Windows Phone Runtime** (**WinPRT**).

Building your first Windows Phone 8 application following the MVVM pattern

Windows Phone applications are generally created using either HTML5 or Silverlight. Most of the people still use the Silverlight approach as it has a full flavor of backend languages such as C# and also the JavaScript library is still in its infancy. With Silverlight or XAML, the architecture that always comes into the developer's mind is MVVM. Like all XAML-based development, Windows 8 Silverlight apps also inherently support MVVM models and hence, people tend to adopt it more often when developing Windows Phone apps. In this recipe, we are going to take a quick look at how you can use the MVVM pattern to implement an application.

Getting ready

Before starting to develop an application, you first need to set up your machine with the appropriate SDK, which lets you develop a Windows Phone application and also gives you an emulator to debug the application without a device. The SDK for Windows Phone 8 apps can be downloaded from Windows Phone Dev Center at `http://dev.windowsphone.com`. The Windows Phone SDK includes the following:

- Microsoft Visual Studio 2012 Express for Windows Phone
- Microsoft Blend 2012 Express for Windows Phone
- The Windows Phone Device Emulator
- Project templates, reference assemblies, and headers/libraries
- A Windows 8 PC to run Visual Studio 2012 for Windows Phone

After everything has been set up for application development, you can open Visual Studio and create a Windows Phone app. When you create the project, it will first ask the target platform; choose **Windows Phone 8** as the default and select **OK**. You need to name and create the project.

How to do it...

Now that the template is created, let's follow these steps to demonstrate how we can start creating an application:

1. By default, the project template that is loaded will display a split view with the Visual Studio Designer on the left-hand side and an XAML markup on the right-hand side. The `MainPage.xaml` file should already be loaded with a lot of initial adjustments to support Windows Phone with factors. Microsoft makes sure that they give the best layout to the developer to start with. So the important thing that you need to look at is defining the content inside the `ContentPanel` property, which represents the workspace area of the page.

> The Visual Studio template for Windows Phone 8 already gives you a lot of hints on how to start writing your first app. The comments indicate where to start and how the project template behaves on the code edits in XAML.

2. Now let's define some XAML designs for the page. We will create a small page and use MVVM to connect to the data. For simplicity, we use dummy data to show on screen. Let's create a login screen for the application to start with.

3. Add a new page, call it `Login.xaml`, and add the following code in `ContentPanel` defined inside the page:

```xml
<Grid x:Name="ContentPanel" Grid.Row="1" Margin="12,0,12,0"
VerticalAlignment="Center">
            <Grid.RowDefinitions>
                <RowDefinition Height="Auto"/>
                <RowDefinition Height="Auto" />
                <RowDefinition Height="Auto" />
            </Grid.RowDefinitions>
            <Grid.ColumnDefinitions>
                <ColumnDefinition />
                <ColumnDefinition />
            </Grid.ColumnDefinitions>

            <TextBlock Text="UserId" Grid.Row="0"
Grid.Column="0" HorizontalAlignment="Right"
VerticalAlignment="Center"/>
            <TextBox Text="{Binding UserId, Mode=TwoWay}"
Grid.Row="0" Grid.Column="1" InputScope="Text"/>
            <TextBlock Text="Password" Grid.Row="1"
Grid.Column="0" HorizontalAlignment="Right"
VerticalAlignment="Center"/>
            <PasswordBox x:Name="txtPassword" Grid.Row="1"
Grid.Column="1" PasswordChanged="txtPassword_PasswordChanged"/>
            <Button Command="{Binding LoginCommand}"
Content="Login" Grid.Row="2" Grid.Column="0" />
            <Button Command="{Binding ClearCommand}"
Content="Clear" Grid.Row="2" Grid.Column="1" />
        </Grid>
```

In the preceding UI Design, we added a `TextBox` and a `PasswordBox` inside `ContentPanel`. Each `TextBox` has an `InputScope` property, which you can define to specify the behavior of the input. We define it as `Text`, which specifies that the `TextBox` can have any textual data. The `PasswordBox` takes any input from the user, but shows asterisks (*) instead of the actual data. The actual data is stored in an encrypted format inside the control and can only be recovered using its `Password` property.

4. We are going to follow the MVVM pattern to design the application. We create a folder named `Model` in the solution and put a `LoginDataContext` class in it. This class is used to generate and validate the login of the UI.

5. Inherit the class from `INotifyPropertyChanged`, which indicates that the properties can act by binding with the corresponding `DependencyProperty` that exists in the control, thereby interacting to and fro with the UI.

6. We create properties for `UserName`, `Password`, and `Status`, as shown in the following code:

```
private string userid;
public string UserId
{
    get { return userid; }
    set
    {
        UserId = value;
        this.OnPropertyChanged("UserId");
    }
}

private string password;
public string Password
{
    get { return password; }
    set { password = value; this.
OnPropertyChanged("Password"); }
    }
 public bool Status { get; set; }
```

You can see in the preceding code that the property setter invokes an `OnPropertyChanged` event. This ensures that the update on the properties is reflected in the UI control:

```
public ICommand LoginCommand
    {
        get
        {
            return new RelayCommand((e) =>
```

```
                {
                        this.Status = this.UserId == "Abhishek"
        && this.Password == "winphone";

                        if (this.Status)
                        {
                                var rootframe =
        App.Current.RootVisual as PhoneApplicationFrame;
                                rootframe.Navigate(new Uri(string.
        Format("/FirstPhoneApp;component/MainPage.xaml?
        name={0}", this.UserId), UriKind.Relative));
                        }
                });
            }
        }
        public ICommand ClearCommand
        {
            get
            {
                return new RelayCommand((e) =>
                {
                    this.UserId = this.Password =
        string.Empty;
                });
            }
        }
```

We also define two more properties of type `ICommand`. The UI button control
implements the command pattern and uses an `ICommand` interface to invoke a
command. The `RelayCommand` used on the code is an implementation of the
`ICommand` interface, which could be used to invoke some action.

7. Now let's bind the `Text` property of the `TextBox` in XAML with the `UserId`
    property, and make it a `TwoWay` binding. The binder automatically subscribes
    to the `PropertyChanged` event. When the `UserId` property is set and the
    `PropertyChanged` event is invoked, the UI automatically receives the invoke
    request of code, which updates the text in the UI.

8. Similarly, we add two buttons and name them `Login` and `Clear` and bind them with
    the properties `LoginCommand` and `ClearCommand`, as shown in the following code:

```
<Button Command="{Binding LoginCommand}" Content="Login" Grid.
Row="2" Grid.Column="0" />
<Button Command="{Binding ClearCommand}" Content="Clear" Grid.
Row="2" Grid.Column="1" />
```

In the preceding XAML, we defined the two buttons and specified a command for
each of them.

9. We create another page so that when the login is successful, we can navigate the **Login** page to somewhere else. Let's make use of the existing `MainPage.xaml` file as follows:

```
<StackPanel x:Name="TitlePanel" Grid.Row="0"
Margin="12,17,0,28">
            <TextBlock Text="MY APPLICATION"
x:Name="txtApplicationDescription" Style="{StaticResource
PhoneTextNormalStyle}" Margin="12,0"/>
            <TextBlock Text="Enter Details" Margin="9,-
7,0,0" Style="{StaticResource PhoneTextTitle1Style}"/>
        </StackPanel>
```

    We add the preceding XAML to show the message that is passed from the **Login** screen.

10. We create another class and named it `MainDataContext`. We define a property that will hold the data to be displayed on the screen.

11. We go to `Login.xaml.cs` created as a code-behind of `Login.xaml`, create an instance of `LoginDataContext`, and assign it to `DataContext` of the page. We assign this inside the `InitializeComponent` method of the class, as shown in the following code:

```
this.DataContext = new LoginDataContext();
```

12. Now, go to **Properties** in the **Solution Explorer** pane, open the `WMAppManifest` file, and specify `Login.xaml` as the **Navigation** page. Once this is done, if you run the application now in any of the emulators available with Visual Studio, you will see what is shown in the following screenshot:

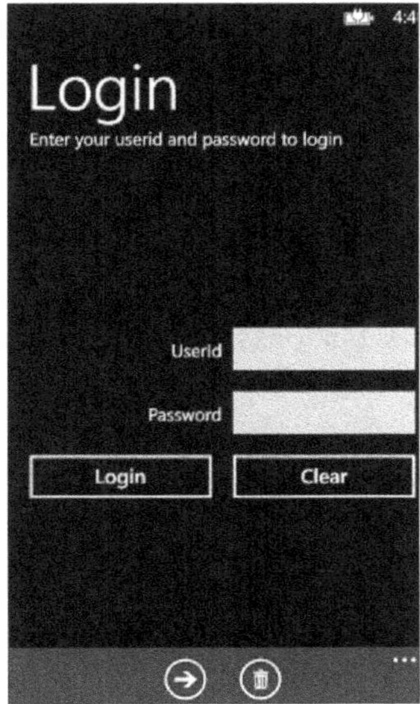

You can enter data in the **UserId** and **Password** fields and click on **Login**, but nothing happens.

13. Put a breakpoint on `LoginCommand` and press **Login** again with the credentials, and you will see that the `Password` property is never set to anything and evaluates to null. Note that, `PasswordBox` in XAML does not support binding to its properties. To deal with this, we define a `PasswordChanged` event on `PasswordBox` and specify the following code:

```
private void txtPassword_PasswordChanged(object sender,
RoutedEventArgs e)
{
        this.logindataContext.Password = txtPassword.Password;
}
```

The preceding code will ensure that the password goes properly to the `ViewModel`.

14. Finally, clicking on **Login**, you will see **Status** is set to `true`.

15. However, our idea is to the page from the **Login** screen to `MainPage.xaml`. To do this, we change the `LoginCommand` property to navigate the page, as shown in the following code:

```
if (this.Status)
{
        var rootframe = App.Current.RootVisual as
PhoneApplicationFrame;
        rootframe.Navigate(new Uri(string.Format("/
FirstPhoneApp;component/MainPage.xaml?
name={0}", this.UserId), UriKind.Relative));
}
```

Each WPF app contains an `ApplicationFrame` class that is used to show the UI. The application frame can use the `navigate` method to navigate from one page to another. The `navigate` method uses `NavigationService` to redirect the page to the URL provided. Here in the code, after authentication, we pass `UserId` as `querystring` to `MainPage`.

16. We design the `MainPage.xaml` file to include a pivot control. A pivot control is just like traditional tab controls, but looks awesome in a phone environment. Let's add the following code:

```
<phone:Pivot>
                <phone:PivotItem Header="Main">
                    <StackPanel Orientation="Vertical">
                        <TextBlock Text="Choose your
avatar" />
                        <Image x:Name="imgSelection"
Source="{Binding AvatarImage}"/>
```

```
                        <Button x:Name="btnChoosePhoto"
ClickMode="Release" Content="Choose Photo"
Command="{Binding ChoosePhoto}" />
                    </StackPanel>
                </phone:PivotItem>
                <phone:PivotItem Header="Task">
                    <StackPanel>
                        <phone:LongListSelector
ItemsSource="{Binding LongList}" />
                    </StackPanel>
                </phone:PivotItem>
            </phone:Pivot>
```

17. The `phone` tag is referred to a namespace that has been added automatically in the header where the `Pivot` class exists. In the previously defined `Pivot` class, there are two `PivotItem` with headers `Main` and `Task`. When `Main` is selected, it allows you to choose a photo from `MediaLibrary` and the image is displayed on **Image Control**. The `ChoosePhoto` command defined inside `MainDataContext` sets the image to its source, as shown in the following code:

```
public ICommand ChoosePhoto
{
    get
    {
        return new RelayCommand((e) =>
        {
            PhotoChooserTask pTask = new PhotoChooserTask();
            pTask.Completed += pTask_Completed;
            pTask.Show();

        });
    }
}
void pTask_Completed(object sender, PhotoResult e)
{
    if (e.TaskResult == TaskResult.OK)
    {
        var bitmap = new BitmapImage();
        bitmap.SetSource(e.ChosenPhoto);
        this.AvatarImage = bitmap;
    }
}
```

In the preceding code, the `RelayCommand` that is invoked when the button is clicked uses `PhotoChooserTask` to select an image from `MediaLibrary` and that image is shown on the `AvatarImage` property bound to the image source.

18. On the other hand, the other `PivotItem` shows `LongList` where the `ItemsSource` is bound to a long list of strings, as shown in the following code:

```
public List<string> LongList
        {
            get
            {
                this.longList = this.longList ??
this.LoadList();
                return this.longList;
            }
        }
```

The long list can be anything, a long list that is needed to be shown in the `ListBox` class.

How it works...

Windows Phone, being an XAML-based technology, uses Silverlight to generate UI and controls supporting the **Model-View-ViewModel** (**MVVM**) pattern. Each of the controls present in the Windows Phone environment implements a number of `DependencyProperties`. The `DependencyProperty` is a special type of property that supports `DataBinding`. When bound to another CLR object, these properties try to find the `INotifyPropertyChanged` interface and subscribe to the `PropertyChanged` event. When the data is modified in the controls, the actual bound object gets modified automatically by the dependency property system, and vice versa.

Similar to normal `DependencyProperties`, there is a `Command` property that allows you to call a method. Just like the normal property, `Command` implements the `ICommand` interface and has a return type `Action` that maps to `Command`. The `RelayCommand` here is an implementation of `ICommand` interfaces, which can be bound to the `Command` property of `Button`.

There's more...

Now let's talk about some other options, or possibly some pieces of general information that are relevant to this task.

Using ApplicationBar on the app

Just like any of the modern smartphones, Windows Phones also provides a standard way of communicating with the environment. Each application can have a standard set of icons at the bottom of the application, which enable the user to perform some actions on the application. The `ApplicationBar` class is present at the bottom of any application across the operating system and hence, people tend to expect commands to be placed on `ApplicationBar` rather than on the application itself, as shown in the following screenshot. The `ApplicationBar` class accepts 72 pixels of height, which cannot be modified by code.

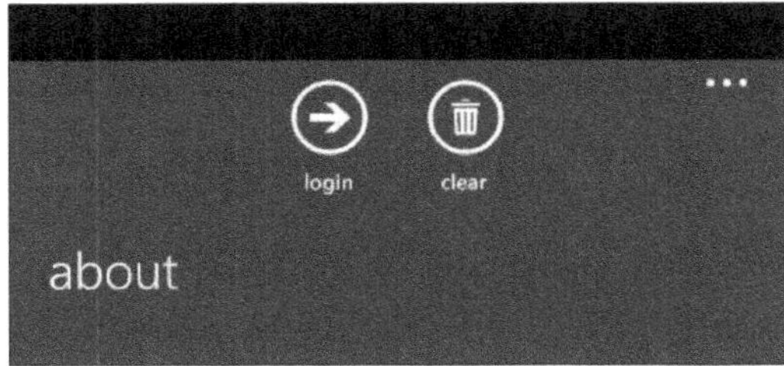

When an application is open, the application bar is shown at the bottom of the screen. The preceding screenshot shows how the `ApplicationBar` class is laid out with two buttons, **login** and **clear**. Each `ApplicationBar` class can also associate a number of menu items for additional commands. The menu could be opened by clicking on the **...** button in the left-hand side of `ApplicationBar`.

The page of Windows Phone allows you to define one application bar. There is a property called `ApplicationBar` on `PhoneApplicationPage` that lets you define the `ApplicationBar` class of that particular page, as shown in the following screenshot:

```
<phone:PhoneApplicationPage.ApplicationBar>
    <shell:ApplicationBar>
        <shell:ApplicationBarIconButton
Click="ApplicationBarIconButton_Click" Text="Login"
IconUri="/Assets/next.png"/>
        <shell:ApplicationBarIconButton Click="ApplicationBarIconB
uttonSave_Click" Text="clear"
IconUri="/Assets/delete.png"/>
        <shell:ApplicationBar.MenuItems>
            <shell:ApplicationBarMenuItem Click="about_Click"
Text="about" />
        </shell:ApplicationBar.MenuItems>
    </shell:ApplicationBar>
</phone:PhoneApplicationPage.ApplicationBar>
```

In the preceding code, we defined two `ApplicationBarIconButton` classes. Each of them defines the `Command` items placed on the `ApplicationBar` class. The `ApplicationBar.MenuItems` method allows us to add menu items to the application. There can be a maximum of four application bar buttons and four menus per page. The `ApplicationBar` button also follows a special type of icon. There are a number of these icons added with the SDK, which could be used for the application. They can be found at `DriveName\Program Files\Microsoft SDKs \Windows Phone\v8.0\Icons`.

There are separate folders for both dark and light themes. It should be noted that `ApplicationBar` buttons do not allow command bindings.

Tombstoning

When dealing with Windows Phone applications, there are some special things to consider. When a user navigates out of the application, the application is transferred to a dormant state, where all the pages and state of the pages are still in memory but their execution is totally stopped. When the user navigates back to the application again, the state of the application is resumed and the application is again activated. Sometimes, it might also be possible that the app gets tombstoned after the user navigates away from the app. In this case, the app is not preserved in memory, but some information of the app is stored. Once the user comes back to the app, the application needs to be restored, and the application needs to resume in such a way that the user gets the same state as he or she left it. In the following figure, you can see the entire process:

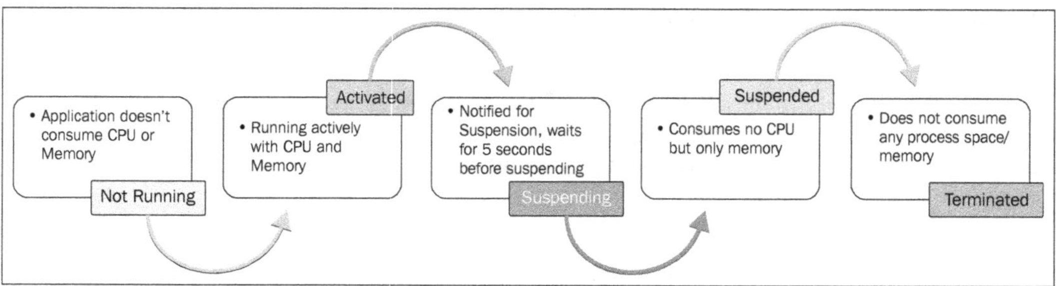

There are four states defined, the first one is the **Not Running** state where there is no existence of the process in memory. The **Activated** state is when the app is tapped by the user. When the user moves out of the app, it goes from **Suspending** to **Suspended**. It can be reactivated or it will be terminated after a certain time automatically.

Let's look at the **Login** screen, where you might sometimes tombstone the login page while entering the user ID and password. To deal with storing the user state data before tombstoning, we use `PhoneApplicationPage`. The idea is to serialize the whole `DataModel` once the user navigates away from the page and retrieves the page state again when it navigates back.

Let's annotate the `UserId` and `Password` of the `LoginDataContext` with `DataMember` and `LoginDataContext` with `DataContract`, as shown in the following code:

```
[DataContract]
    public class LoginDataContext : PropertyBase
    {
        private string userid;
        [DataMember]
        public string UserId
        {
            get { return userid; }
            set
            {
```

```
            UserId = value;
            this.OnPropertyChanged("UserId");
        }
    }

    private string password;
    [DataMember]
    public string Password
    {
        get { return password; }
        set { password = value; this.
OnPropertyChanged("Password"); }
    }
}
```

The `DataMember` property will indicate that the properties are capable of serializing. As the user types into these properties, the properties get filled with data so that when the user navigates away, the model will always have the latest data present.

In `LoginPage`, we define a property called `_isNewPageInstance` and set it to `false`, and in constructor, we set it to `true`. This will indicate that only when the page is instantiated, `_isNewPageInstance` is set to `true`.

Now, when the user navigates away from the page, `OnNavigatedFrom` gets called. If the user navigates from the page, we save `ViewModel` into `State` as shown in the following code:

```
protected override void OnNavigatedFrom(NavigationEventArgs e)
{
    base.OnNavigatedFrom(e);

    if (e.NavigationMode != System.Windows.Navigation.NavigationMode.
Back)
    {
        // Save the ViewModel variable in the page''s State
dictionary.
        State[""ViewModel""] = logindataContext;
    }
}
```

Once `DataModel` is saved in the `State` object, it is persistent and can be retrieved later on when the application is resumed as follows:

```
protected override void OnNavigatedTo(NavigationEventArgs e)
{
    base.OnNavigatedTo(e);
    if (_isNewPageInstance)
    {
```

```
        if (this.logindataContext == null)
        {
            if (State.Count > 0)
            {
                this.logindataContext = (LoginDataContext)
State[""ViewModel""];
            }
            else
            {
                this.logindataContext = new LoginDataContext();
            }
        }
        DataContext = this.logindataContext;
    }
    _isNewPageInstance = false;
}
```

When the application is resumed from tombstoning, it calls `OnNavigatedTo` and retrieves `DataModel` back from the state.

Working with Launchers and Choosers in Windows Phone

When creating an application for a phone, keep in mind that the application needs to interact with the phone environment. For instance, if you are building a contact list, you might sometimes import data from an existing contact list in the phone or you might also want to send an SMS or directly call a contact. These operations are interacting with the actual phone operating system from the application.

You can use Launchers and Choosers in your Windows Phone application to enable a user to perform common tasks on the phone environment. The Launcher and Chooser APIs invoke distinct built-in applications that replace the currently running application and when the actual operation is performed, the built-in application is again replaced by the application running on background with a callback, thus giving a seamless experience to the end users.

Getting ready

In this recipe, we are going to add a basic Launchers and Choosers task. Let's create a new project and add some buttons for some basic-level Launchers and Choosers.

To use **launchers** and **choosers**, we need to follow some basic steps:

1. Create an instance of the task.

2. Set the parameters and callback (if any).

3. Call the `show` method to invoke the task.

Let's create an UI to try some of the Launchers and Choosers. We use panorama to show the two tabs for **launchers** and **choosers**, as shown in the following screenshot:

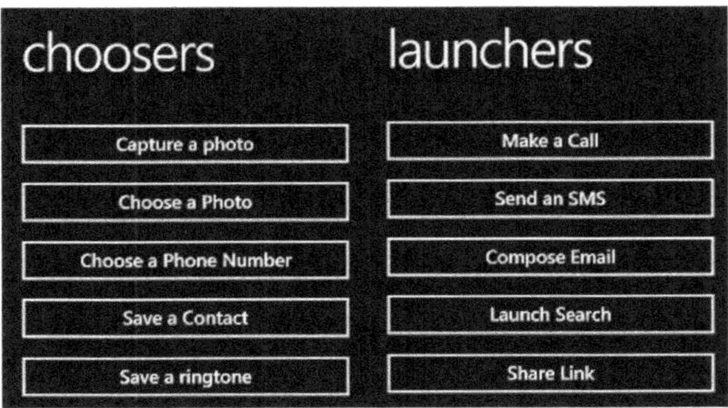

The preceding screenshot shows how the UI is laid out once we are complete with the XAML design. Let's now take a look at how the XAML looks:

```xml
<phone:Panorama Title="Launchers And Choosers">
    <phone:PanoramaItem Header="launchers">
        <StackPanel Orientation="Vertical">
                <Button Content="Make a Call" x:Name="btnCall"
Click="btnCall_Click" />
            <Button Content="Send an SMS" x:Name="btnSMS"
Click="btnSMS_Click"/>
            <Button Content="Compose Email" x:Name="btnEmail"
Click="btnEmail_Click" />
            <Button Content="Launch Search" x:Name="btnSearch"
Click="btnSearch_Click" />
            <Button Content="Share Link" x:Name="btnLink"
Click="btnLink_Click" />
            <Button Content="Share Status" x:Name="btnStatus"
Click="btnStatus_Click" />
        </StackPanel>
    </phone:PanoramaItem>
    <phone:PanoramaItem Header="choosers">
        <StackPanel Orientation="Vertical">
```

```xml
          <Button Content="Capture a photo" x:Name="btnCapturePhoto"
Click="btnCapturePhoto_Click" />
          <Button Content="Choose a Photo" x:Name="btnPhoto"
Click="btnPhoto_Click" />
          <Button Content="Choose a Phone Number"
x:Name="btnPhone" Click="btnPhone_Click" />
          <Button Content="Save a Contact" x:Name="btnContact"
Click="btnContact_Click" />
          <Button Content="Save a ringtone" x:Name="btnringtone"
Click="btnringtone_Click" />

          <Button Content="Save Email Address" x:Name="btnsaveEmail"
Click="btnsaveEmail_Click" />
        </StackPanel>
      </phone:PanoramaItem>
    </phone:Panorama>
```

We used the panorama control to define the two interfaces for Launchers and Choosers.
Now let's write code for these buttons.

How to do it...

Working with Launchers and Choosers is pretty straightforward. We need to just call the
appropriate class to invoke it. The steps are as follows:

1. Let's try some Launchers. To make a call, we need to use `PhoneCallTask`:

   ```csharp
   PhoneCallTask pcall = new PhoneCallTask();
   pcall.DisplayName = "Abhishek";
   pcall.PhoneNumber = "9999999999";
   pcall.Show();
   ```

   In the preceding code, `"Abhishek"` is called to his number.

2. We use `SmsComposeTask` to create an SMS:

   ```csharp
   SmsComposeTask stask = new SmsComposeTask();
   stask.Body = "This is test sms";
   stask.To = "99999999";
   stask.Show();
   ```

   There could be the `To` and `Body` properties for an SMS.

3. To send an e-mail, we use `EmailComposeTask`:

```
EmailComposeTask etask = new EmailComposeTask();
etask.Body = "This is test Email";
etask.Subject = "This is test subject";
etask.To = "contact@abhisheksur.com";
etask.Cc = "abhi2434@gmail.com";
etask.Bcc = "abhi2434@hotmail.com";
etask.Show();
```

   In the case of e-mails, you can use comma-separated entries of e-mail ID and send the e-mail from your configured e-mail client in Windows Phone.

4. To search a text in the built-in Bing search, we use `SearchTask`:

```
SearchTask stask = new SearchTask();
stask.SearchQuery = "abhishek";
stask.Show();
```

5. To share a status, we can use `ShareStatusTask`:

```
ShareStatusTask stask = new ShareStatusTask();
stask.Status = "This is a status sent from Windows Phone";
stask.Show();
```

6. To share a link, we can use `ShareLinkTask`:

```
ShareLinkTask sLink = new ShareLinkTask();
sLink.LinkUri = new Uri("http://www.abhisheksur.com");
sLink.Message = "See my website";
sLink.Title = "Abhisheks new Website";
sLink.Show();
```

   Here, the link would be shared with the configured social media channels configured on the phone.

7. In case of Choosers, the task will return a callback; when the task is finished, the `Completed` event gets fired. To capture an image from a camera, we use `CameraCaptureTask` or we use `PhotoChooserTask` to choose from `MediaLibrary`, as shown in the following code:

```
CameraCaptureTask cTask = new CameraCaptureTask();
cTask.Completed += (s, evt) =>
{
    if (evt.Error == null && evt.TaskResult ==
TaskResult.OK)
    {
```

```
            BitmapImage bmpImage = new BitmapImage();
            bmpImage.SetSource(evt.ChosenPhoto);
            image.Source = bmpImage;
        }
    };
    cTask.Show();
```

For `CameraCapture/PhotoChooserTask`, we need to add the
`ID_CAP_MEDIALIB_PHOTO` and `ID_CAP_ISV_CAMERA` capabilities.

8. For phone number selection task, we can use `PhoneNumberChooserTask`,
   as shown in the following code:

```
PhoneNumberChooserTask task = new PhoneNumberChooserTask();
task.Completed += (s, evt) =>
{
    if (evt.Error == null && evt.TaskResult ==
TaskResult.OK)
    {
        MessageBox.Show(evt.PhoneNumber + " phone number
selected.");
    }
};
task.Show();
```

This task requires the `ID_CAP_CONTACTS` capabilities. When the Chooser finishes its
execution, the `Completed` event returns `PhoneNumber`.

9. We can save `RingTone` to the Windows Phone environment using
   `SaveRingtoneTask`, as shown in the following code:

```
SaveRingtoneTask ringtonetask = new SaveRingtoneTask();
ringtonetask.Source = new Uri("appdata:/Assets/Ring-BlackIce.
wma");
ringtonetask.DisplayName = "My custom ringtone";
ringtonetask.Completed += (s, evt) =>
{
    if (evt.TaskResult == TaskResult.OK)
        MessageBox.Show("Ringtone saved");
};
ringtonetask.Show();
```

The ringtone source could be either `appdata:/` or `isostore:/`.

10. To save an e-mail to the contact, we can use `SaveEmailAddressTask` as shown in the following code:

```
SaveEmailAddressTask eaddr = new SaveEmailAddressTask();
eaddr.Email = "contact@abhisheksur.com";
eaddr.Completed += (s, evt) =>
{
    if (evt.TaskResult == TaskResult.OK)
        MessageBox.Show("Email address saved");
};
eaddr.Show();
```

The `SaveEmailAddressTask` function requires the `ID_CAP_CONTACTS` capabilities.

How it works...

Launchers and Choosers are special names used to communicate with the built-in applications present in the Windows Phone applications. The Windows Phone API provides a range of these Launchers and Choosers so that the application developer can use specialized classes to invoke the properties present on the phone.

For each task, there is an associated `ApplicationId` class. The Launcher and Chooser classes use this `ApplicationId` class to call the specific application of the phone with the configuration sent from the application.

You should also remember that Launchers are separate application launched from the application, so there is every chance that the actual application will get suspended or even terminated during the process. So, before using Launcher and Choosers, tombstoning could also be required.

There's more...

After looking at some of the basic Launchers and Choosers, there is always a notion of something more. Here are some of the items that are worth mentioning.

Adding Windows Phone toolkit to the solution

To add a NuGet Package, we go to the **Library Package Manager** option in the **TOOLS** tab and choose **Manage NuGet Packages for Solution**, as shown in the following screenshot:

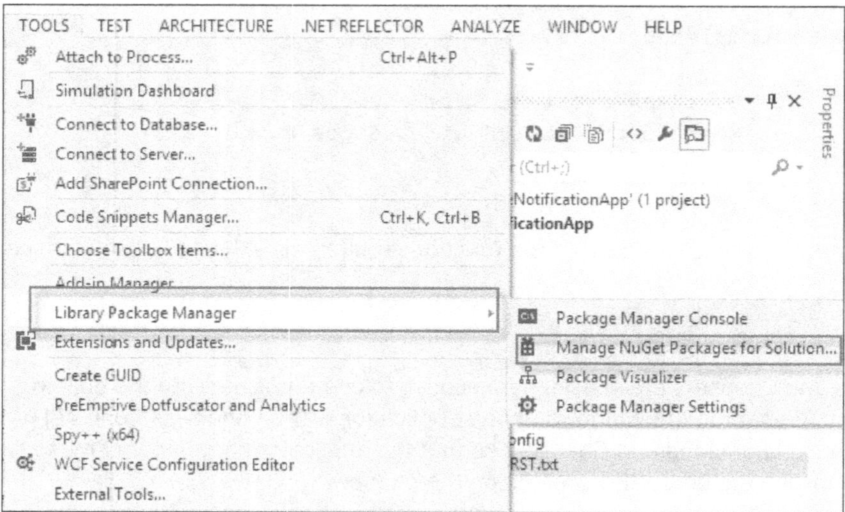

Once you are in **NuGet Package Manager**, select **Online** from the left-hand side of the window and search for **Windows Phone Toolkit**. Add it to the solution.

Finally after the package is installed, add the following namespace to `PhoneApplicationPage`:

```
xmlns:toolkit="clr-
namespace:Microsoft.Phone.Controls;assembly=Microsoft.Phone.
Controls.Toolkit"
```

Creating alarms and reminders

Notifications are one of the most important and primary requirements of any phone. People schedule reminders and alarms on their phone, which lets the phone respond automatically when the certain specified time is reached. As an application developer, you can also schedule a notification to the user so that even though the application is closed, you can still provide the message to the user. When the user gets notified by the environment, a small music file is played and a pop-up message is shown.

There are two types of notifications available:

- **Alarm**: This is a notification to the user at a scheduled time
- **Reminder**: This is a notification that also allows you to specify a URI of a page, which could be opened by clicking on the reminder UI

There is a limit of defining 50 alarms/reminders within a single application. To demonstrate, let's create a page:

```xml
<Grid x:Name="ContentPanel" Grid.Row="1" Margin="12,0,12,0">
        <Grid.ColumnDefinitions>
            <ColumnDefinition />
            <ColumnDefinition/>
        </Grid.ColumnDefinitions>

        <Grid.RowDefinitions>
            <RowDefinition />
            <RowDefinition />
            <RowDefinition />
            <RowDefinition />
            <RowDefinition />
            <RowDefinition />
        </Grid.RowDefinitions>

        <RadioButton x:Name="rbAlarm" GroupName="type"
Content="Alarm" Grid.Column="0" Checked="RadioButton_Checked" />
        <RadioButton x:Name="rbReminder" GroupName="type"
Content="Reminder" Grid.Column="1" Checked="RadioButton_Checked"
/>

        <TextBlock Text="Name" Grid.Row="1"  Grid.Column="0"
/>
        <TextBox  x:Name="txtName" Grid.Row="1"
Grid.Column="1" />
        <TextBlock Text="Title" Grid.Row="2"  Grid.Column="0"
/>
        <TextBox  x:Name="txtTitle" Grid.Row="2"
Grid.Column="1" />
        <TextBlock Text="Content" Grid.Row="3"
Grid.Column="0" />
        <TextBox  x:Name="txtContent" Grid.Row="3"
Grid.Column="1" AcceptsReturn="True" />
        <TextBlock Text="Begin Time" Grid.Row="4"
Grid.Column="0" />
        <StackPanel Orientation="Horizontal" Grid.Row="4"
Grid.Column="1" >
            <toolkit:DatePicker x:Name="dtBegindate" />
            <toolkit:TimePicker x:Name="dtBegintime"/>
        </StackPanel>
```

```
            <TextBlock Text="Expiration" Grid.Row="5"
Grid.Column="0" />
            <StackPanel Orientation="Horizontal" Grid.Row="5"
Grid.Column="1" >
                <toolkit:DatePicker x:Name="dtExpdate" />
                <toolkit:TimePicker x:Name="dtExptime"/>
            </StackPanel>
        </Grid>
```

In the preceding code, we added three textboxes, which represent `Title`, `Content`, and `Name` of a notification entry. Both the reminder and alarm represents a `ScheduledNotification` entry where the alarm cannot have `Title` and `NavigationUri` to open the application. We also added two `RadioButton` controls that control whether the added notification is of the type alarm or reminder. There are also two date entries that we have added two `DatePicker` controls for and two `TimePicker` respectively, which allows you to take `BeginTime` and `Expiration` of the notification. These controls are not a part of general Windows Phone development environment. We added the Windows Phone toolkit to get them as mentioned in the previous topic.

After the toolkit is added to the `MainPage.xaml` file, we can add `DatePicker` and `TimePicker` to the page.

To perform an action on the controls, we will add two `ApplicationBar` commands—one to add the notification and another to cancel it.

Let's add the code at the bottom of the `MainPage.xaml` file below the grid:

```
<phone:PhoneApplicationPage.ApplicationBar>
    <shell:ApplicationBar>
        <shell:ApplicationBarIconButton
x:Name=""btnAddNotification"" Click=""btnAddNotification_Click""
Text=""Add""
                                        IconUri=""/Assets/edit.
png""/>
        <shell:ApplicationBarIconButton x:Name=""btnCancel""
Click=""btnCancel_Click""  Text=""Cancel""
                                        IconUri=""/Assets/cancel.
png""/>
    </shell:ApplicationBar>
</phone:PhoneApplicationPage.ApplicationBar>
```

As we already mentioned, you can add icons that come with the Windows Phone SDK. The icons `edit.png` and `cancel.png` have been added from the location `DriveName\ Program Files\Microsoft SDKs \Windows Phone\v8.0\Icons`.

Now, let's jump back to the code. We create two functions, one of which adds a reminder and another adds an alarm mentioned in the following code:

```
private void AddReminder()
        {
                Reminder reminder = new Reminder(txtName.Text);
                reminder.Content = this.txtContent.Text;
                reminder.Title = this.txtTitle.Text;

                DateTime bdate = this.dtBegindate.Value.Value;
                DateTime beginDateTime = bdate +
this.dtBegintime.Value.Value.TimeOfDay;
                reminder.BeginTime = beginDateTime;

                DateTime edate = this.dtExpdate.Value.Value;
                DateTime exDateTime = edate + this.dtExptime.Value.Value.
TimeOfDay;
                reminder.ExpirationTime = exDateTime;

                reminder.RecurrenceType = RecurrenceInterval.Daily;
                reminder.NavigationUri = new Uri("/MainPage.xaml",
UriKind.Relative);

                ScheduledActionService.Add(reminder);
        }

        private void AddAlarm()
        {
                Alarm alarm = new Alarm(txtName.Text);
                alarm.Content = this.txtContent.Text;

                DateTime bdate = this.dtBegindate.Value.Value;
                DateTime beginDateTime = bdate + this.dtBegintime.Value.
Value.TimeOfDay;
                alarm.BeginTime = beginDateTime;

                DateTime edate = this.dtExpdate.Value.Value;
                DateTime exDateTime = edate +
this.dtExptime.Value.Value.TimeOfDay;
                alarm.ExpirationTime = exDateTime;

                alarm.RecurrenceType = RecurrenceInterval.Daily;

                ScheduledActionService.Add(alarm);
        }
```

In the preceding code, we can see that both the alarm and reminder are of a similar structure. Both of them are of the type `ScheduledAction`, while the alarm does not allow you to specify `NavigationUri` and `Title`. Now when `btnAddNotification_Click` is called, depending on whether `rbAlarm` is checked or not, we add a reminder or an alarm as follows:

```
private void btnAddNotification_Click(object sender, EventArgs e)
    {
        if (this.rbAlarm.IsChecked.Value)
        {
            this.AddAlarm();
        }
        else if(this.rbReminder.IsChecked.Value)
        {
            this.AddReminder();
        }
    }
```

In the preceding code, the action is performed based on the selection of `RadioButton`.

Working with the calendar in Windows Phone

Appointments are some of the most important things that we need while working on a Windows Phone. Even reminders/alarms are important even though appointments can interact with the calendar present on the Windows Phone. To search or access references of other calendar data, we can use the `Appointment` object and search entries. Let's add the UI to show the appointments:

```
<ListBox x:Name="lstAppointments" ItemsSource="{Binding}" Grid.
Row="1">
                <ListBox.ItemTemplate>
                    <DataTemplate>
                        <Grid>
                            <Grid.ColumnDefinitions>
                                <ColumnDefinition />
                                <ColumnDefinition />
                            </Grid.ColumnDefinitions>
                            <TextBlock Margin="5,0,0,0" Text="{Binding
Subject}" TextWrapping="Wrap" Grid.Column="0" />
                            <TextBlock Margin="5,0,0,0" Text="{Binding
Details}" TextWrapping="Wrap" Grid.Column="1"/>
                        </Grid>
                    </DataTemplate>
                </ListBox.ItemTemplate>
            </ListBox>
```

The `ListBox` class contains two `TextBlock` showing `Subject` and `Details` of an appointment entry. To show you the appointments on the `ListBox` class, we need a command that invokes the appointment search task as follows:

```
<phone:PhoneApplicationPage.ApplicationBar>
        <shell:ApplicationBar>
            <shell:ApplicationBarIconButton Text="Search"
IconUri="/Assets/feature.search.png"
Click="SearchAppointment_Click" />
            <shell:ApplicationBarIconButton Text="Add"
IconUri="/Assets/add.png" Click="AddAppointment_Click" />
        </shell:ApplicationBar>
    </phone:PhoneApplicationPage.ApplicationBar>
```

We add two `Appbar` buttons, where the first one searches the appointments and the second one adds an appointment.

To search an appointment, we need to make use of the appointments API available in Windows Phone. To invoke the search operation, we use the following code:

```
private void RefreshAppointments()
    {
        Appointments appointment = new Appointments();
        appointment.SearchCompleted +=
appointment_SearchCompleted;
        DateTime starttime = DateTime.Now;
        DateTime endtime = starttime.AddDays(10);

        int max = 50;

        appointment.SearchAsync(starttime, endtime, max,
null);
    }

    void appointment_SearchCompleted(object sender,
AppointmentsSearchEventArgs e)
    {
        lstAppointments.DataContext = e.Results;
    }
```

The `SearchAsync` method takes three arguments: `startTime`, `endTime`, and the maximum number of appointments to enumerate all the appointments between times. If we call `RefreshAppointments` when the **Search** button is clicked, we see all the appointments between the time specified.

To test an appointment, if you don't have one, you can add an appointment on the Windows Phone environment using `SaveAppointmentTask`. On the `AddAppointment` button, we place the following code to add a sample appointment to the calendar:

```
var saveAppontmentTask = new SaveAppointmentTask();

saveAppointmentTask.StartTime = DateTime.Now.AddHours(1);
saveAppointmentTask.EndTime = DateTime.Now.AddHours(2);
saveAppointmentTask.Subject = "Sample Appointment Demo entry";
saveAppointmentTask.Location = "www.packtpub.com";
saveAppointmentTask.Details = "Sample save appointment entry for
Windows Phone";
saveAppointmentTask.IsAllDayEvent = false;
saveAppointmentTask.Reminder = Reminder.FifteenMinutes;
saveAppointmentTask.AppointmentStatus = AppointmentStatus.Busy;

saveAppointmentTask.Show();
```

Each appointment has `StartTime`, `EndTime`, `Subject`, and `Location` (which takes `Uri` and `Details`). An appointment can also be `AllDayEvent` and automatically add a reminder before a stipulated time. As you can see, `SaveAppointmentTask` is a launcher; hence, you cannot silently add an appointment for the time being.

An appointment needs the `ID_CAP_APPOINTMENTS` capability.

See also

- Check out more about Launchers at `http://bit.ly/Launchers`
- Check out more about Choosers at `http://bit.ly/Choosers`

Working with relational databases and persistent storage

Persistent storage is one of the most important areas that every application developer needs to know. Even though the architecture of the Windows Phone environment is in general built to have connected applications, many times there could be a case where there is a need to store data in persistent storage areas so that it can be fetched later for use. Windows Phone persistent storage exists in the form of the `IsolatedStorage` classes, where the application can store data on a Sandboxed environment where the other application does not have access to. Windows Phone provides a separate filesystem structure for each application, where the application can store and retrieve files and data from.

To store data in persistent storage, we use the following code:

```
public async void SaveToStore(string fileName, string data)
    {
        IsolatedStorageFile store =
IsolatedStorageFile.GetUserStoreForApplication();
        using (StreamWriter sw = new StreamWriter(new
IsolatedStorageFileStream(fileName, FileMode.Append, store)))
        {
            await sw.WriteAsync(data);
            sw.Close();
        }
    }
```

Here, we first get the reference of the user store using `IsolatedStorageFile.GetUserStoreForApplication`. The store is specific to the application that calls the store. Later on, we use a normal `StreamWriter` to write data to the file opened using `IsolatedStorageFileStream`.

We can also use `StreamReader` in a similar way to read from `IsolatedStorageFileStream`, as shown in the following code:

```
Public async Task<string> ReadFromStore(string fileName)
{
    IsolatedStorageFile store = IsolatedStorageFile.
GetUserStoreForApplication();
    if (!store.FileExists(fileName))
    {
        IsolatedStorageFileStream dataFile =
store.CreateFile(fileName);
        dataFile.Close();
    }

    using (StreamReader reader = new StreamReader(new
IsolatedStorageFileStream(fileName, FileMode.Open, store)))
    {
        string rawData = await reader.ReadToEndAsync();
        reader.Close();

        return rawData;
    }
}
```

Here, we first check whether the file exists before opening the `FileStream` class again and then read from it. We can also use miscellaneous functions like the following ones:

```
store.DeleteFile(fileName);
store.MoveFile(sourcefile, destinationfile)
store.CopyFile(sourcefile, destinationfile)
store.CreateDirectory(dirName)
```

We can also use many functions to perform normal file operations on the allotted filesystem for the application. We can also use `store.Remove()` to remove the whole filesystem for the application.

In addition to the file store for the application, there is also a separate concept of storage where the data is stored in relational databases. Windows Phone supports **Entity Framework** (**EF**), which can be used to store data in a relational database structure.

The LINQ to SQL object model is primarily made up of the `System.Data.Linq.DataContext` object, which acts as a proxy for the local database stored in `IsolatedStorage` for the application. It is a bridge between the object data and the relational data, as shown in the following figure:

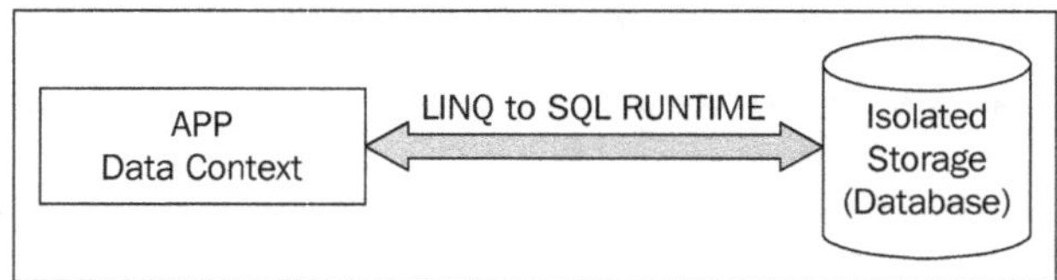

As shown in the preceding figure, the app stores **Data Context**, which bridges the data from relational database stored in **Isolated Storage** for the application using **LINQ to SQL RUNTIME**.

When considering local databases in Windows Phone, here are some points that we need to consider:

- Database files will be stored in an isolated storage container
- Databases are application specific and cannot be shared across applications
- LINQ is used to query database as TSQL is not supported
- A connection string must be used in the format `"Data Source='isostore:/ DirectoryName/databaseName.sdf;Password='securepassword'"`
- A database is encrypted using AES – 128 and password is hashed using SHA-256
- Encrypting the whole database can have performance penalty and a lot of automatic optimizaticns are not being performed

Getting ready

In this recipe, we are going to perform the CRUD operation on a database. We will cover the following topics:

- Creating a local database
- Creating table, indexes, associations, and so on
- Adding data to tables
- Fetching data from tables
- Deleting data from tables
- Deleting a local database

As I have already told you, the application fetches data from databases using LINQ to SQL; there are a few concepts that are worth notifying before continuing further. In LINQ to SQL data models, classes represent tables and properties represent fields. Hence, you can think of indexes that can be applied on tables, that is, classes and association or foreign-key relationship that can be applied on a field, that is, property. The object model is annotated with a number of properties that define the schema of the database structure. Let's take a quick pick on these attributes:

- `TableAttribute`: This designates a class to be an entity with an associated database table
- `ColumnAttribute`: This associates a class with a column of a table
- `IndexAttribute`: This adds an index on a table. Each index covers one or more columns
- `AssociationAttribute`: This designates a property to represent an association

In addition to these attributes, there is `DataContext` that acts as a proxy for the whole database. The `DataContext` class opens a connection to the database using `ConnectionString`, which is main object to save/submit data modifications on entities.

How to do it...

Now let's build the database in object models:

1. Create a Windows Phone project and add a folder called `Model`. We will use this folder to create our model classes.

2. Create a class `Department` with the following definition:

```
[Table]
    public class Department
    {
        public Department()
```

```
        {
        }

        [Column(DbType = "INT NOT NULL IDENTITY", IsDbGenerated =
true, IsPrimaryKey = true)]
        public int Id { get; set; }

        [Column]
        public string Name { get; set; }

        [Column(IsVersion = true)]
        private Binary _version;
}
```

You might have already noticed that the `Department` class is annotated with a `Table` attribute. This attribute indicates that the class is a part of the database table. We define two properties: `Id` and `Name`. The `Id` property is an autogenerated column of INT type, while `Name` is a string. There is also a `version` field of binary type. The `version` field is useful while updating entries.

3. Next, let's define an `Employee` class that has an individual department as the foreign key:

```
[Table]
[Index(Columns="EName", IsUnique=true,
Name="employee_EName")]
public class Employee
{
    [Column(IsPrimaryKey = true, IsDbGenerated = true,
CanBeNull = false, DbType = "INT NOT NULL Identity",
AutoSync = AutoSync.OnInsert)]
    public int EmpId { get; set; }

    [Column(CanBeNull=false, DbType="NVarchar(100) NOT
NULL")]
    public string EName { get; set; }

    [Column(CanBeNull= false)]
    public int Age { get; set; }

    [Column(IsVersion=true)]
    public Binary Version { get; set; }

    // Internal column for the associated department ID
value
    [Column]
    internal int _departmentId;
```

```
    private EntityRef<Department> _department;
    [Association(Storage = "_department", ThisKey =
"_departmentId", OtherKey = "Id", IsForeignKey = true)]
    public Department Department
    {
        get { return _department.Entity; }
        set
        {
            _department.Entity = value;
            if (value != null)
                _departmentId = value.Id;
        }
    }
}
```

In the preceding entity definition, we kept `EmpId` as a primary key. The `EName` and `Age` columns are the two specified columns, each of which are not null. We have also defined an internal column to store `departmentId`.

The `EntityRef` class is used to fetch actual object from the column using the association specified for a particular entity. We defined `departmentId` as a foreign key, which maps the entity reference of the department table.

In the preceding class, we have also added an extra index for the `Employee` entity so that when the `Employee` table is searched using the `EName` column, the query will use the index to improve search performance.

In the case of using the `Where` clause, the order by, or join the appropriate index on the columns can improve performance tremendously. The `index` attribute is used internally by the database engine, where it optimizes it by reindexing at an interval. If you are using an encrypted database with a password, these optimizations will not perform correctly.

4. As we have shown how to use `EntityRef` to refer to the actual object from a foreign key reference, it is also a good idea to define a property that enumerates all the employees present in a particular department, as shown in the following code:

```
public Department()
{
    _employees = new EntitySet<Employee>(
        new Action<Employee>(this.attach_Employee),
        new Action<Employee>(this.detach_Employee)
        );
}
```

```
private EntitySet<Employee> _employees;
[Association(Storage = "_employees", OtherKey =
"_departmentId", ThisKey = "Id")]
public EntitySet<Employee> Employees
{
    get { return this._employees; }
    set { this._employees.Assign(value); }
}


private void attach_Employee(Employee emp)
{
    emp.Department = this;
}


private void detach_Employee(Employee emp)
{
    emp.Department = null;
}
```

The `EntitySet` class enumerates all the foreign key reference objects into the key table. In the preceding context, we create an object of `EntitySet<Employee>`, which automatically fetches all the objects associated with that particular department. The `EntitySet` class also takes two callbacks to attach or detach an employee from a particular department.

5. Once the entities are created, we need to create the `DataContext` object to proxy the actual database to the entities, as shown in the following code:

```
public class EmployeeDataContext : DataContext
{
    public EmployeeDataContext(string connectionString)
        : base(connectionString) { }

    public Table<Employee> Employees;

    public Table<Department> Departments;
}
```

Here, `EmployeeDataContext` inherits from `DataContext` and passes `ConnectionString` to it. As we have defined two tables, we can specify the references of them on `EmployeeDataContext` to access them individually.

6. After the `Object` model is ready, let's use it to create a database for the application. Open the `App.xaml.cs` file and add the following line at the beginning of the `App` class:

```
public const string ConnectionString = "Data
Source=isostore:/Employeedb.sdf";
```

The `ConnectionString` property must have a location reference of the `IsolatedStore` location. We could also add a password to encrypt the whole database.

7. Now, go to the bottom of its constructor and add the following lines of code:

```
string DbConnectionString = ConnectionString;
using (EmployeeDataContext db = new EmployeeDataContext(DbConnecti
onString))
{
    if (!db.DatabaseExists())
    {
        db.CreateDatabase();
        db.Departments.InsertOnSubmit(new Department { Name
= "Accounts" });
        db.Departments.InsertOnSubmit(new Department { Name
= "Sales" });
        db.Departments.InsertOnSubmit(new Department { Name
= "Transfer" });

        db.SubmitChanges();
    }
}
```

Here, we defined the filename of the database using the `ConnectionString` property and created the `Employee` database if it doesn't exist. While creating a database, sometimes we need to pre-populate some data so we added some departments during its creating. The `SubmitChanges` method commits the changes made to the database.

8. Now, let's define an UI for the **Employees** database, as shown in the following screenshot:

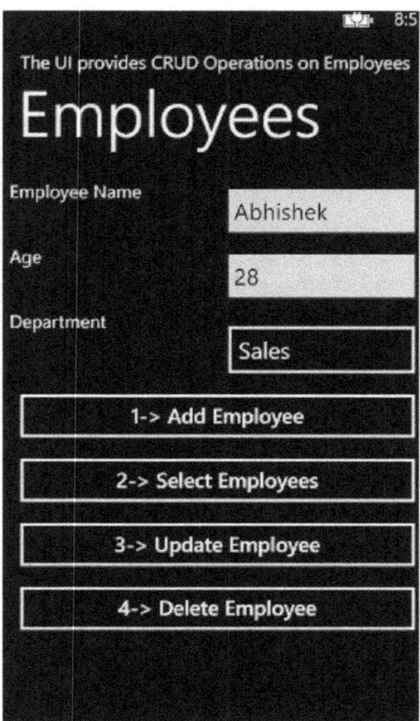

There are a few buttons with `TextBoxes` and `ListPicker` on the UI to create an employee type. We are going to create this UI for our application.

9. Before we do so, we added the Windows Phone toolkit from the NuGet Package Manager and added the namespace for the toolkit to `MainPage.xaml`:

```
xmlns:toolkit="clr-
namespace:Microsoft.Phone.Controls;assembly=Microsoft.Phone
.Controls.Toolkit"
```

10. Once the toolkit is added, we add two `TextBox` methods and a `ListPicker` method to create an `Employee` type as follows:

```
<TextBlock Text="Employee Name" Grid.Row="0"
Grid.Column="0" />
<TextBox x:Name="txtName" Grid.Row="0" Grid.Column="1" />
<TextBlock Text="Age" Grid.Row="1" Grid.Column="0" />
<TextBox x:Name="txtAge" InputScope="Digits" Grid.Row="1"
Grid.Column="1" />
<TextBlock Text="Department" Grid.Row="2" Grid.Column="0"
/>
```

```
<toolkit:ListPicker x:Name="lstDepartment" Grid.Row="2"
Grid.Column="1">
    <toolkit:ListPicker.ItemTemplate>
        <DataTemplate>
            <TextBlock Text="{Binding Name}" />
        </DataTemplate>
    </toolkit:ListPicker.ItemTemplate>
</toolkit:ListPicker>
<StackPanel Orientation="Vertical" Grid.Row="3"
Grid.ColumnSpan="2">
    <Button Content="1-> Add Employee" x:Name="btnAddEmployee"
Click="btnAddEmployee_Click" />
    <Button Content="2-> Select Employees"
x:Name="btnSelectEmployees"
Click="btnSelectEmployees_Click"/>
    <Button Content="3-> Update Employee"
x:Name="btnUpdateEmployee" Click="btnUpdateEmployee_Click"/>
    <Button Content="4-> Delete Employee"
x:Name="btnDeleteEmployee" Click="btnDeleteEmployee_Click"
/>
</StackPanel>
```

In the preceding XAML, we added four buttons each for `Add`, `Select`, `Update`, and `Delete`; hence, the UI is capable of utilizing all the CRUD operations.

11. Now, we add some code for the buttons:

```
private void AddEmployee()
{
    using (EmployeeDataContext context = new
EmployeeDataContext(App.ConnectionString))
    {
        var department = this.lstDepartment.SelectedItem as
Department;
        var contextualDepartment =
context.Departments.FirstOrDefault(e => e.Id ==
department.Id);
        Employee emp = new Employee
        {
            EName = this.txtName.Text,
            Age = Convert.ToInt32(this.txtAge.Text),
            Department = contextualDepartment
        };

        context.Employees.InsertOnSubmit(emp);
```

```
            context.SubmitChanges();
        }
    }
```

 Database activity holds the UI thread when `SubmitChanges` is called. Be sure to use `Async/await` when using it in an actual application to avoid sudden crash of your application.

The preceding code creates a new employee and adds it to the database. It is worth noting that as we are not holding the `DataContext` class, the department created on another `DataContext` cannot be as a type of the current context. For this reason, we need to fetch the department again for each operation.

12. Similarly, you can select all the existing employees using the following code:

```
private IList<Employee> GetEmployees()
{
    using (EmployeeDataContext context = new
EmployeeDataContext(App.ConnectionString))
    {
        var query = from e in context.Employees select e;
        return query.ToList();
    }
}
```

The LINQ query is used to fetch data from the `DataContext` class. You should always remember, that the query is of the `IQueryable` type; hence, until we actually fetch either using `ToList` or looping through the `IEnumerator` interface, the actual data isn't been retrieved.

13. We can also delete an employee using the `Delete` method:

```
private void DeleteEmployee()
{
    using (EmployeeDataContext context = new
EmployeeDataContext(App.ConnectionString))
    {
        IQueryable<Employee> empQuery = from e in
context.Employees where e.EName == this.txtName.Text select e;
        Employee empToDelete = empQuery.FirstOrDefault();
        if (empToDelete != null)
        {
```

```
            context.Employees.DeleteOnSubmit(empToDelete);
        }

        context.SubmitChanges();
    }
}
```

The `DeleteOnSubmit` method requires a call `SubmitChanges` to update the changes to persistent storage. If we are doing a batch operation, it is recommended to do all the batch statements and finally call `SubmitChanges` to improve performance.

14. Similar to these, you can also implement the `Update` operation yourself by changing the object in memory and apply `SubmitChanges` again.

15. Finally, if you need to delete the entire database, you can call `DeleteDatabase` on `DataContext` and the entire database with all existing data would be deleted.

How it works...

The Windows Phone does not inherently support SQL databases, even then you can use SQLite (`http://bit.ly/WPSqlLite`) if you want, but it has an in-built API to make use of relational databases using LINQ to SQL. The LINQ to SQL classes automatically convert the calls to the databases to generic data calls and fetches the data from the database. The LINQ to SQL classes need models to be created on the application end and the data to be retrieved and added only by the application. In the case of Windows Phone databases, the database is virtually a file stored in the `IsolatedStorage` namespace for that particular application, and hence the sharing of database is not possible.

There's more...

In addition to the exciting way of creating and altering data to and from persistent storage, there are also some additional features that we can use to make full use of the storage capabilities.

Encrypting data before storing it in the filesystem

Encryption is an important concern for data security. When dealing with sensitive information and storing data to the application storage, it is sometimes required to encrypt the data to enhance the security of the data used by the application. However, encrypting the data will not increase the security if the decryption key resides within the phone itself. No matter how you hide the key, it is always exposed. **Data Protection API** (**DPAPI**) solves the problem by providing an explicit key using the device credentials and the user to encrypt and decrypt data. This method improves security as the data protection key is different for every device and it becomes virtually impossible to get encrypted data for an external hacker.

Windows Phone API provides a class called `ProtectData` that provides you with access to DPAPI through the `Protect` and `Unprotect` methods. You can use the `Protect` method to encrypt data while `Unprotect` will decrypt data, as shown in the following code:

```
public string EncryptData(string data)
        {
                byte[] databytes = Encoding.UTF8.GetBytes(data);
                byte[] protecteddatabytes = ProtectedData.
Protect(databytes, null);

                string protectedData = Encoding.UTF8.
GetString(protecteddatabytes, 0,
protecteddatabytes.Length);

                return protectedData;
        }

        public string DecryptData(string protectedData)
        {
                byte[] protecteddatabytes =
Encoding.UTF8.GetBytes(protectedData);
                byte[] databytes = ProtectedData.
Unprotect(protecteddatabytes, null);

                string data = Encoding.UTF8.GetString(databytes, 0,
databytes.Length);

                return data;
        }
```

It is very easy to use DPAPI to protect and unprotect data. The only thing you need to do is to convert the data to a byte array and pass it to the `ProtectedData` class to perform the encryption. The preceding methods encrypt or decrypt a string passed to it.

When dealing with complex objects, you can use serializer to get the data in a format supported to protect and unprotect. For instance, if you need to protect `DataModel`, you can use `DataContractJsonSerializer` to serialize the `Model` class and get the string:

```
public string EncryptSerializeData(object target)
{
    var serializer = new DataContractJsonSerializer(target.GetType());
    MemoryStream memStream = new MemoryStream();
    serializer.WriteObject(memStream, target);
    string jsondata = Encoding.UTF8.GetString(memStream.GetBuffer(),
0,
(int)memStream.Length);

    return this.EncryptData(jsondata);
}
```

Here, the `DataContractJsonSerializer` class is used to serialize the target object to the JSON notation and then `EncryptData` is used to protect the object data completely.

Working with the settings file in Windows Phone applications

To store the general settings of the application, it is often not required to use relational databases or even `IsolatedFiles`. The `IsolatedStorageSetting` class provides an easy way to store settings of the application key/value pair for easy storage and retrieval of data. Let's take a look at how to store data in `IsolatedStorageSettings`:

```
public class PersistantStorageSettings
{
    IsolatedStorageSettings settings;

    public PersistantStorageSettings()
    {
        settings = IsolatedStorageSettings.ApplicationSettings;
    }

    public bool AddOrUpdateValue(string key, object value)
    {
        bool valueChanged = false;
        if (settings.Contains(key))
        {
            if (settings[key] != value)
            {
                settings[key] = value;
                valueChanged = true;
            }
        }
        else
        {
            settings.Add(key, value);
            valueChanged = true;
        }
        return valueChanged;
    }
    public T GetValueOrDefault<T>(string key)
    {
        T value;
        if (settings.Contains(key))
            value = (T)settings[key];
        else
            value = default(T);
```

```
        return value;
    }
    public void Save()
    {
        settings.Save();
    }


}
```

The `IsolatedStorageSettings` class provides an API to store and retrieve a key/value data for an easy access to settings. Here, `AddOrUpdateValue` is used to store a value for a particular key and `GetValueOrDefault` is used to get a value or the default value of the type. The `Save` method is used to save data to the settings.

To define settings, you can inherit a class from the type and define properties like this:

```
public string Settings1
{
    get
    {
        return base.GetValueOrDefault<string>("settings1");
    }
    set
    {
        if (base.AddOrUpdateValue("settings1", value))
            base.Save();
    }
}
```

Now by setting a value for the `settings1` property, we virtually store the data in the `IsolatedStorageSettings` key and vice versa. Also, you should always remember that the settings key is unique to the application.

Reading a file from an SD card in the Windows Phone application

Windows Phone devices, being smart devices, support additional SD cards to be added to it. You can add them as a `RemovableStorage` media to the device, and later use the files present on the SD card and open it using an application in the device that is capable of opening it.

To add a file type extension, we first add the `ID_CAP_REMOVABLE_STORAGE` capability to the `WMAppManifest.xml` file and save it. Once it is saved, you can open it in the XML editor and specify `FileTypeAssociation`:

```
<FileTypeAssociation TaskID="_default" Name="GPX"
NavUriFragment="fileToken=%s">
  <Logos>
```

```xml
    <Logo Size="small" IsRelative="true">Assets/Route_Mapper_
Logo33x33.png</Logo>
    <Logo Size="medium" IsRelative="true">Assets/Route_Mapper_
Logo69x69.png</Logo>
    <Logo Size="large" IsRelative="true">Assets/Route_Mapper_
Logo176x176.png</Logo>
  </Logos>
  <SupportedFileTypes>
    <FileType ContentType="application/gpx">.gpx</FileType>
  </SupportedFileTypes>
</FileTypeAssociation>
```

As a file association is required to read a specific file type from an SD card, your app automatically gets registered by the type of files that are not present in the SD card. To handle this situation, we can add a custom `Uri` mapper to pass the file association's token to the correct page, as shown in the following code:

```csharp
class CustomURIMapper : UriMapperBase
  {
        private string tempUri;
        public override Uri MapUri(Uri uri)
        {
            tempUri = uri.ToString();

            if (tempUri.Contains("/FileTypeAssociation"))
            {
                // Get the file ID (after "fileToken=").
                int fileIDIndex = tempUri.IndexOf("fileToken=") +
10;
                string fileID = tempUri.Substring(fileIDIndex);
                // Map the file association launch to route page.
                return new Uri("/RoutePage.xaml?fileToken=" + fileID,
UriKind.Relative);
            }
            // Otherwise perform normal launch.
            return uri;
        }
    }
```

In this example, when a file association launches the app, the `Uri` mapper automatically routes the token to the `RoutePage.xaml` file of the application. To add `customURiMapper` to the application, let's add the line to the `InitializePhoneApplication` of `App.xaml`:

```csharp
RootFrame.UriMapper = new CustomURIMapper();
```

When the application is invoked, the parameters of the URI can be accessed by `QueryString` of `NavigationContext` as follows:

```csharp
protected override async void OnNavigatedTo(System.Windows.Navigation.
NavigationEventArgs e)
{
    // Route is from a file association.
    if(NavigationContext.QueryString.ContainsKey("fileToken"))
    {
        _fileToken = NavigationContext.QueryString["fileToken"];
        await ProcessExternalGPXFile(_fileToken);
    }
    // Route is from the SD card.
    else if (NavigationContext.QueryString.ContainsKey("sdFilePath"))
    {
        _sdFilePath = NavigationContext.QueryString["sdFilePath"];
        await ProcessSDGPXFile(_sdFilePath);
    }
}
```

In the preceding code, `sdFilePath` determines the path of the file present on the SD card. Finally, we use the following code to process the file:

```csharp
private async Task ProcessSDGPXFile(string _sdFilePath)
{
    // Connect to the current SD card.
    ExternalStorageDevice sdCard = (await ExternalStorage.
GetExternalStorageDevicesAsync()).FirstOrDefault();

    // If the SD card is present, get the route from the SD card.
    if (sdCard != null)
    {
        try
        {
            // Get the route (.GPX file) from the SD card.
            ExternalStorageFile file = await
sdCard.GetFileAsync(_sdFilePath);

            // Create a stream for the route.
            Stream s = await file.OpenForReadAsync();

            // Read the route data.
            ReadGPXFile(s);
        }
        catch (FileNotFoundException)
```

```
        {
            // The route is not present on the SD card.
            MessageBox.Show("That route is missing on your SD card.");
        }
    }
    else
    {
        // No SD card is present.
        MessageBox.Show("The SD card is mssing. Insert an SD card
that has a Routes folder containing at least one .GPX file and try
again.");
    }
}
```

Here the `ExternalStorageDevice` API is used to get the file stored on the SD card. The `OpenForReadAsync` method opens the file if present and returns a `FileStream` class. The stream can be used to read the data present on the file.

See also

 ▶ Information on creating a local database app can be found
   at `http://bit.ly/MVVMWphone`

Working with notifications in Windows Phone

The push notification is in-built on most of the modern smart phones. A Windows Phone, being no exception, also implements a number of notification techniques that can be used to bring notifications to the client app from an external source. The server can push notifications to the device and when the device receives the notification, an event occurs.

Push notifications are of three types:

 ▶ **Toast notification**: This notification is launched at the top of the screen with a custom message such as an e-mail alert. The notification will be displayed for 10 seconds unless the user dismisses the alert. If user clicks on the alert, then the application that sends the notification will be launched.

 ▶ **Tile notification**: This notification is used to display dynamic representation of an application state. We can control the image, text, and badge count of the notification.

 ▶ **Raw notification**: This notification can be used only when the application is running in the foreground. The notification is not delivered or even gets discarded when the application is not running.

These are the mediums by which the web server can send push notifications to the applications running on the Windows Phone platform:

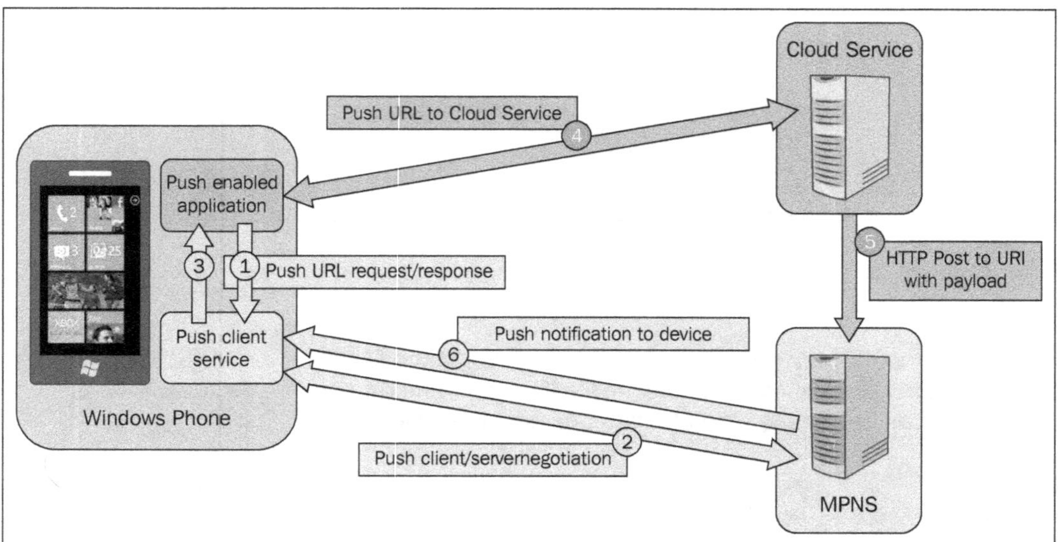

There are a number of steps to set up push notifications and a number of external hosts are involved to enable the push notifications to the clients. For a push notification, there should be a server that a developer can handle. In the preceding figure, we depict how a push notification is received by a Windows Phone. The steps are as follows:

1. The application invokes `PushURIRequest` on the `PushClient` service.

2. The `PushClient` service goes to **Microsoft Push Notification Service** (**MPNS**), which is hosted on live servers to negotiate the device so that it receives push notifications.

3. When the response is received from `Pushclient`, the application receives a signal that it has enabled push notifications and an URI through which the push notification needs to be sent from the server.

4. The application sends `PushUri` to the external server managed by the developer in the cloud.

5. When server needs to push a message, it uses the URI to post the message to the MPNS server.

6. Finally, when the MPNS receives the push notification, it sends the message directly to the phone.

Getting ready

As per the preceding architecture, to implement a full-fledged push notification, we need to create the following applications:

- A Windows Phone application that initiates the push notification channel
- An ASP.NET application that communicates with the live server

How to do it...

Let's create a new application that can enable the web server to use the push notifications:

1. Create a new application and name it `PushClientSample`.

2. Add a button to the `MainPage.xaml` file to create a push notification channel:

```
<Button Content="Bind Channel" x:Name="btnBind" Click="btnBind_
Click" />
```

We name it `BindChannel`.

3. In the preceding code, we create `pushChannel` using `HttpNotificationChannel` and open it:

```
private void btnBind_Click(object sender, RoutedEventArgs e)
{
    string channelName = "PushClientSampleChannel";

    HttpNotificationChannel pushChannel =
HttpNotificationChannel.Find(channelName);
    if (pushChannel == null)
    {
        pushChannel = new HttpNotificationChannel(channelName);
        pushChannel.ChannelUriUpdated += new EventHandler<Notifica
tionChannelUriEventArgs>(PushChannel_
ChannelUriUpdated);
        pushChannel.ErrorOccurred += new EventHandler<Notification
ChannelErrorEventArgs>(PushChannel
_ErrorOccurred);
        pushChannel.ShellToastNotificationReceived += new
EventHandler<NotificationEventArgs>(PushChannel_ShellToast
NotificationReceived);
        pushChannel.Open();
        pushChannel.BindToShellToast();
    }
    else
    {
```

```
        pushChannel.ChannelUriUpdated += new EventHandler<Notifica
tionChannelUriEventArgs>(PushChannel_
ChannelUriUpdated);
        pushChannel.ErrorOccurred += new EventHandler<Notification
ChannelErrorEventArgs>(PushChannel
_ErrorOccurred);
        pushChannel.ShellToastNotificationReceived += new
EventHandler<NotificationEventArgs>(PushChannel_ShellToast
NotificationReceived);
        System.Diagnostics.Debug.WriteLine(pushChannel.ChannelUri.
ToString());
        MessageBox.Show(String.Format("Channel Uri is {0}",
pushChannel.ChannelUri.ToString()));
    }
}
```

We named our push notification channel `PushClientSampleChannel`. We first try to find out whether the notification is already registered. Then, we call `Find` to invoke a web request to the MPNS service to see whether the application is registered for the push notification or not. If it is found, it is used up; otherwise, it is registered using the `Open` command of the `Channel` object.

The `ChannelUriUpdated` event is called when the server updates the URI. This method is used to get the actual URI to which the push messages need to be sent out.

4. When the `ChannelUriUpdated` event is raised, we need to send the URI to the application server using the Internet. For simplicity, we enter the URI in the debugger output window, as shown in the following screenshot:

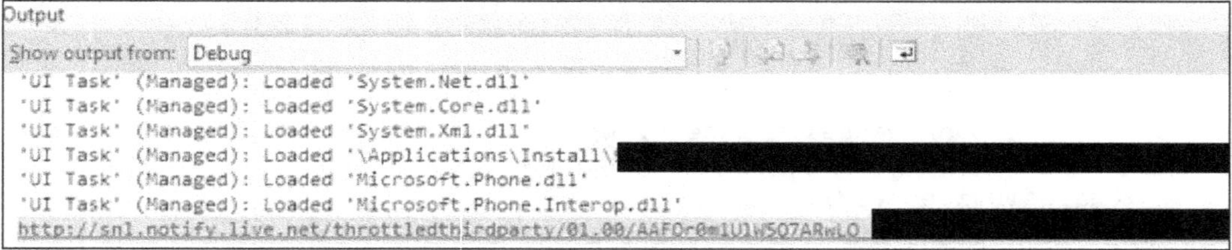

Copy the URI to a safe location, as it is required for the server application to send notifications.

5. Now, create an ASP.NET application and name it `PushServerSample`. In `ToastRequest.aspx`, we add one label, two `TextBox`es, and one button:

```
Server URI :
http://sn1.notify.live.net/throttledthirdparty/01.00/AAE
Title :
SendToast
Message :
Test Message            ×
Send Toast Notification
```

The following code shows how to create an ASP.NET application:

```
<div>
        Server URI :<br />
        <asp:Label runat="server" ID="lblSubscription" />
<br />
         Title : <br />
        <asp:TextBox runat="server" ID="txtTitle" /> <br />
         Message : <br />
        <asp:TextBox runat="server" ID="txtMessage" /> <br
/>
        <asp:Button runat="server" Text="Send Toast
Notification" OnClick="ButtonSendToast_Click" />
    </div>
```

6. To deal with the push notification, we create a class called `PushNotifier` and add a static method `SendPushNotification`:

```
public static void SendPushNotification(string
subscriptionUri, string requestMsg, string type)
        {
            HttpWebRequest sendNotificationRequest =
(HttpWebRequest)WebRequest.Create(subscriptionUri);
            sendNotificationRequest.Method = "POST";

            byte[] notificationMessage =
Encoding.Default.GetBytes(requestMsg);

            sendNotificationRequest.ContentLength =
notificationMessage.Length;
            sendNotificationRequest.ContentType =
"text/xml";
            sendNotificationRequest.Headers.Add("X-
WindowsPhone-Target", type);
```

```
            sendNotificationRequest.Headers.Add("X-
    NotificationClass", "2");


            using (Stream requestStream =
    sendNotificationRequest.GetRequestStream())
                {
                    requestStream.Write(notificationMessage, 0,
    notificationMessage.Length);
                }

                // Send the notification and get the response.
                HttpWebResponse response = (HttpWebResponse)
    sendNotificationRequest.GetResponse();
                string notificationStatus =
    response.Headers["X-NotificationStatus"];
                string notificationChannelStatus =
    response.Headers["X-SubscriptionStatus"];
                string deviceConnectionStatus =
    response.Headers["X-DeviceConnectionStatus"];
            }
```

Here in the preceding code, we send the message to the Microsoft Live server using the URL where the application got registered.

7. Hence, using `ButtonSendToast_Click`, we call the `toastMessage` method with URI for the application:

```
protected void ButtonSendToast_Click(object sender, EventArgs e)
{
    try
    {
        string subscriptionUri =
    this.lblSubscription.Text.ToString();
        string toastMessage = "<?xml version=\"1.0\"
    encoding=\"utf-8\"?>" +
                                "<wp:Notification
    xmlns:wp=\"WPNotification\">" +
                                    "<wp:Toast>" +
                                        "<wp:Text1>" +
    this.txtTitle.Text.ToString() + "</wp:Text1>" +
                                        "<wp:Text2>" +
    this.txtMessage.Text.ToString() + "</wp:Text2>" +
                                        "<wp:Param>/Page2.
    xaml?NavigatedFrom=Toast
    Notification</wp:Param>" +
                                    "</wp:Toast> " +
                                "</wp:Notification>";
```

```
        PushNotifier.SendPushNotification(subscriptionUri,
toastMessage, "toast");
    }
    catch
    {
    }


}
```

In the preceding code, a new `HttpWebRequest` class is invoked with a specific formatted toast message. Once the message is received by the MPNS, it forwards the message to the actual device and a response is returned back.

8. Finally, if you click on the **Send Toast Notification** button, the phone will receive the toast notification. It is to be noted that if the application is running on the phone, it will receive a `ShellToastNotificationReceived` event. If you handle the event handler, it will show the collection that it receives in a message box, as shown in the following screenshot:

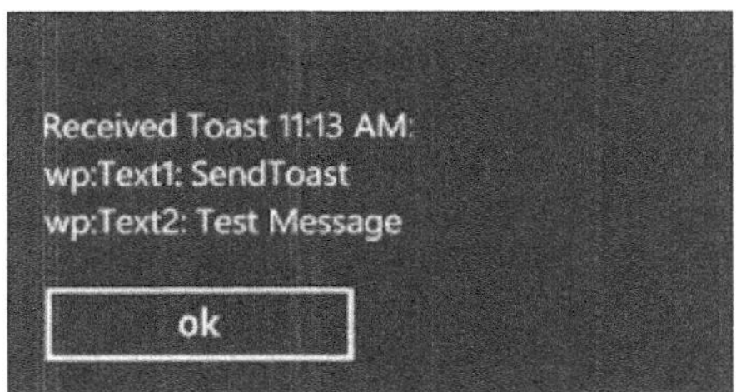

It is to be noted that the `ShellToastNotification` event gets raised automatically by the channel, and a collection of all messages are received as parameter. In the following code, we filter out the message from the `Toast` event:

```
private void PushChannel_ShellToastNotificationReceived(object
sender,
NotificationEventArgs e)
{
    StringBuilder message = new StringBuilder();
    string relativeUri = string.Empty;

    message.AppendFormat("Received Toast {0}:\n",
DateTime.Now.ToShortTimeString());

    // Parse out the information that was part of the
message.
    foreach (string key in e.Collection.Keys)
    {
```

```
        message.AppendFormat("{0}: {1}\n", key,
    e.Collection[key]);

            if (string.Compare(
                key,
                "wp:Param",
                System.Globalization.CultureInfo.InvariantCulture,
                System.Globalization.CompareOptions.IgnoreCase) == 0)
            {

                relativeUri = e.Collection[key];

            }
        }


        // Display a dialog of all the fields in the toast.
        Dispatcher.BeginInvoke(() =>
    MessageBox.Show(message.ToString()));
    }
```

9. If the application isn't running, the environment will show the `Toast` message using a red strip on the top of the phone screen. The message will have the icon of the application on which it is associated as shown in the following screenshot), and it will remain for 10 seconds if user doesn't click on it. You can click on the message to open up the application.

10. Similar to the `Toast` notification, the Windows Phone environment also allows you to send tile notifications so that when that notification is received, the tile that is used to show the application is modified. For the tile notification, let's add a new page to the web project and call it `TileRequest.aspx`. Each tile can have a number of settings, as shown in the following screenshot:

Server URI :
http://sn1.notify.live.net/throttledthirdparty/01.00/AAEehP3nirB1RI8a1
Front Title :
SendTile
Front Background Image :
red jpg
Front Badge Counter :
1
Back Title :
Back of Tile
Back Background Image :
blue jpg
Back Content :
Welcome back!
Send Tile Notification

The preceding screenshot is taken from the web form created using ASP.NET. Here is the sample ASP.NET design that creates the preceding UI:

```
<div>
        Server URI :<br />
        <asp:Label runat="server" ID="lblSubscription" />
<br />
         Front Title : <br />
        <asp:TextBox runat="server" ID="txtTitle" /> <br />
          Front Background Image : <br />
        <asp:TextBox runat="server" ID="txtBackgroundImage"
/> <br />
          Front Badge Counter : <br />
        <asp:TextBox runat="server" ID="txtBadgeCounter" />
<br />
          Back Title : <br />
        <asp:TextBox runat="server" ID="txtBackTitle" />
<br />
        Back Background Image : <br />
        <asp:TextBox runat="server" ID="txtBackgroundBackImage" />
<br />
        Back Content : <br />
        <asp:TextBox runat="server" ID="txtBackContent" />
<br />
         <asp:Button ID="btnTile" runat="server" Text="Send
Tile Notification" OnClick="ButtonSendTile_Click" />
    </div>
```

In this case, we have front- and back-side configuration for the tiles as the tiles flip to show more content.

11. To create the actual tile in the phone, you need to create two images of 176 x 175 pixels—one with a red background, named `red.jpg`, and another with a blue background, named `blue.jpg`—and place the images on the `Content` application. The notification will only be shown when the application is pinned to home screen.

12. Finally, after the application is deployed and the **Send Tile Notification** button is clicked, the web application sends a tile request using the push notification, as shown in the following code:

```
try
            {
                string subscriptionUri =
this.lblSubscription.Text.ToString();
                string tileMessage = "<?xml version=\"1.0\"
encoding=\"utf-8\"?>" +
                    "<wp:Notification
xmlns:wp=\"WPNotification\">" +
                        "<wp:Tile>" +
                          "<wp:BackgroundImage>" +
txtBackgroundBackImage.Text + "</wp:BackgroundImage>" +
                          "<wp:Count>" + txtBadgeCounter.Text + "</
wp:Count>" +
                          "<wp:Title>" + txtTitle.Text +
"</wp:Title>" +
                          "<wp:BackBackgroundImage>" +
txtBackgroundBackImage.Text + "</wp:BackBackgroundImage>" +
                          "<wp:BackTitle>" +
txtBackTitle.Text + "</wp:BackTitle>" +
                          "<wp:BackContent>" +
txtBackContent.Text + "</wp:BackContent>" +
                        "</wp:Tile> " +
                    "</wp:Notification>";
                PushNotifier.SendPushNotification(subscriptionUri,
tileMessage,"tile");
            }
            catch
            {
            }
```

The device receives the notification and displays it as a tile, as shown in the following screenshot:

The tile automatically flips to show more content in the blue background.

How it works...

Each Windows Phone device is well equipped to handle push notifications. The MPNS authenticates the device with the live services using live ID authentication, which is needed for every device. Once the device is authenticated, it can receive a push notification by subscribing a channel for the application. Once the channel is established, the MPNS responds to a unique URL that could be used to receive push notifications.

Now if a third-party application is hosted to that particular URL in cloud requests and it sends a predefined formatted XML document, the MPNS forwards the message as a push notification to the device using either `tile` or `toast` notifications.

There's more...

In addition to the normal toast and tile notifications, there are a number of additional options that may be worth noting. Some of them will be discussed next.

Learning about other tile formats

In addition to normal tiles, there are also a number of XML formats supported by Windows Phones. Based on the configuration and the size of the tile set by the user while pinning, the tile notification can differ a lot. The tile formats are as follows:

- **Flip tile template**: This template flips from front to back, as shown in the following screenshot:

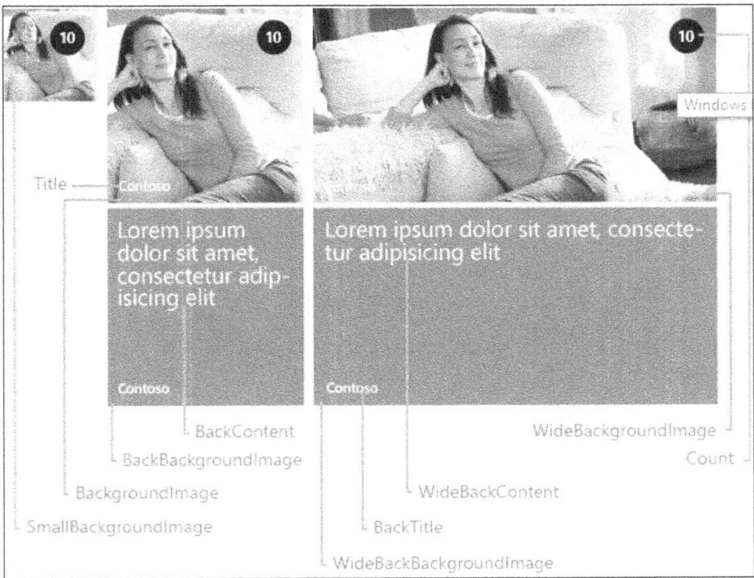

The preceding tile demonstrates the property of the schema that sits on the tile based on the different size of the tile configured. To use this template, you need to send a notification after the following schema:

```
<wp:Notification xmlns:wp="WPNotification" Version="2.0">
  <wp:Tile Id="[Tile ID]" Template="FlipTile">
    <wp:SmallBackgroundImage [Action="Clear"]>[small Tile
size URI]</wp:SmallBackgroundImage>
    <wp:WideBackgroundImage Action="Clear">[front of wide
Tile size URI]</wp:WideBackgroundImage>
    <wp:WideBackBackgroundImage Action="Clear">[back of
wide Tile size URI]</wp:WideBackBackgroundImage>
    <wp:WideBackContent Action="Clear">[back of wide Tile
size content]</wp:WideBackContent>
    <wp:BackgroundImage Action="Clear">[front of medium
Tile size URI]</wp:BackgroundImage>
    <wp:Count Action="Clear">[count]</wp:Count>
    <wp:Title Action="Clear">[title]</wp:Title>
    <wp:BackBackgroundImage Action="Clear">[back of medium
Tile size URI]</wp:BackBackgroundImage>
    <wp:BackTitle Action="Clear">[back of Tile
title]</wp:BackTitle>
    <wp:BackContent Action="Clear">[back of medium Tile
size content]</wp:BackContent>
  </wp:Tile>
</wp:Notification>
```

The template is mostly used for common notification formats.

- **Cycle tile template**: This kind of template is used when it is required to cycle between one to nine images:

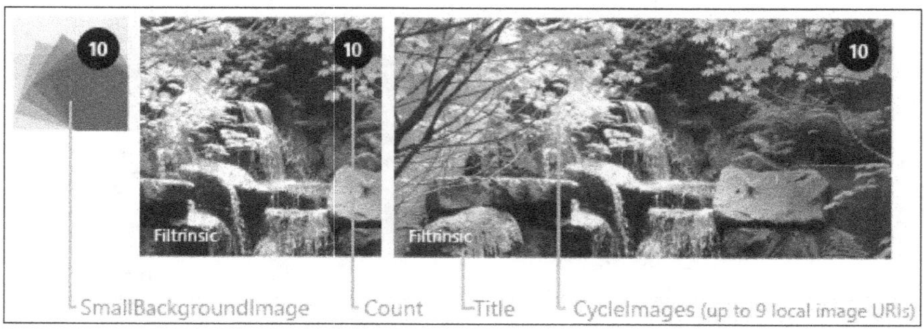

Here, the tile continuously changes after an interval. To send a tile notification, we need to send it using the following format:

```
<wp:Notification xmlns:wp="WPNotification" Version="2.0">
  <wp:Tile Id="[Tile ID]" Template="CycleTile">
```

```
    <wp:SmallBackgroundImage [Action="Clear"]>[small Tile
size URI]</wp:SmallBackgroundImage>
    <wp:CycleImage1 Action="Clear">[photo 1
URI]</wp:CycleImage1>
    <wp:CycleImage2 Action="Clear">[photo 2
URI]</wp:CycleImage2>
    <wp:CycleImage3 Action="Clear">[photo 3
URI]</wp:CycleImage3>
    <wp:CycleImage4 Action="Clear">[photo 4
URI]</wp:CycleImage4>
    <wp:CycleImage5 Action="Clear">[photo 5
URI]</wp:CycleImage5>
    <wp:CycleImage6 Action="Clear">[photo 6
URI]</wp:CycleImage6>
    <wp:CycleImage7 Action="Clear">[photo 7
URI]</wp:CycleImage7>
    <wp:CycleImage8 Action="Clear">[photo 8
URI]</wp:CycleImage8>
    <wp:CycleImage9 Action="Clear">[photo 9
URI]</wp:CycleImage9>
    <wp:Count Action="Clear">[count]</wp:Count>
    <wp:Title Action="Clear">[title]</wp:Title>
  </wp:Tile>
</wp:Notification>
```

- **Iconic tile template**: This template displays a small image in the center of the tile and incorporates Windows Phone Design principles:

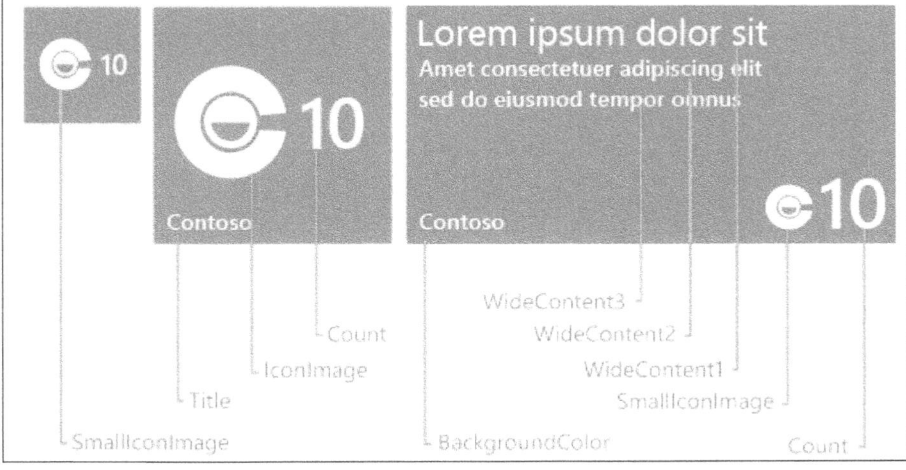

The iconic tile template is sometimes preferred because it has an icon in the middle of the tile and hence promotes branding:

```
<wp:Notification xmlns:wp="WPNotification" Version="2.0">
  <wp:Tile Id="[Tile ID]" Template="IconicTile">
    <wp:SmallIconImage [Action="Clear"]>[small Tile size
URI]</wp:SmallIconImage>
    <wp:IconImage Action="Clear">[medium/wide Tile size
URI]</wp:IconImage>
    <wp:WideContent1 Action="Clear">[1st row of
content]</wp:WideContent1>
    <wp:WideContent2 Action="Clear">[2nd row of
content]</wp:WideContent2>
    <wp:WideContent3 Action="Clear">[3rd row of
content]</wp:WideContent3>
    <wp:Count Action="Clear">[count]</wp:Count>
    <wp:Title Action="Clear">[title]</wp:Title>
    <wp:BackgroundColor Action="Clear">[hex ARGB format
color]</wp:BackgroundColor>
  </wp:Tile>
</wp:Notification>
```

This template can be used to create an Iconic tile notification.

See also

- To learn more about push notifications, visit `http://bit.ly/PushWPhone`

4

Working with Team Foundation Server

In this chapter, we will cover the following recipes:

- Configuring TFS for project hosting and management
- Working with branching and merging in Team Foundation Server
- Creating TFS scheduled jobs

Introduction

Team Foundation Server (**TFS**) is one of the most important components required for any small or big project. Once a project is defined, the optimal utilization of time and management of the team for successful delivery of the project is one of the primary concerns for any development team. This is called **Application Lifecycle management** (**ALM**). To solve issues at different stages of application life cycle, we employ a number of tools and other components, such as product backlogs, source control, and work item management. Visual Studio Team Foundation Server comes with a complete toolset for Microsoft Application Lifecycle Management solution. It provides Agile development practices and can be used either locally or in a cloud to provide tools that can effectively manage the software projects.

Installing TFS

After you have successfully downloaded the latest bits of the TFS installer (you can download TFS at `http://bit.ly/tfsbitdownload`), you can start installing it. You can either install it on a client or a server operating system, but if it is server operating system, you can additionally add a SharePoint portal and SQL Server reporting. We use the basic configuration for standard server installation, but there are options, such as Standard Single Server, which is used for single server installation with all standard features. Also, there is an advanced installation option that allows you to choose components that you need (you can read more about TFS Installation at `http://bit.ly/benjamintfsinstall`). The wizard will install and configure **Install SQL Server (IIS)**, where all the configurations and source codes will be saved. It will create websites for server-side portal and administration, and finally you will see what is shown in the following screenshot:

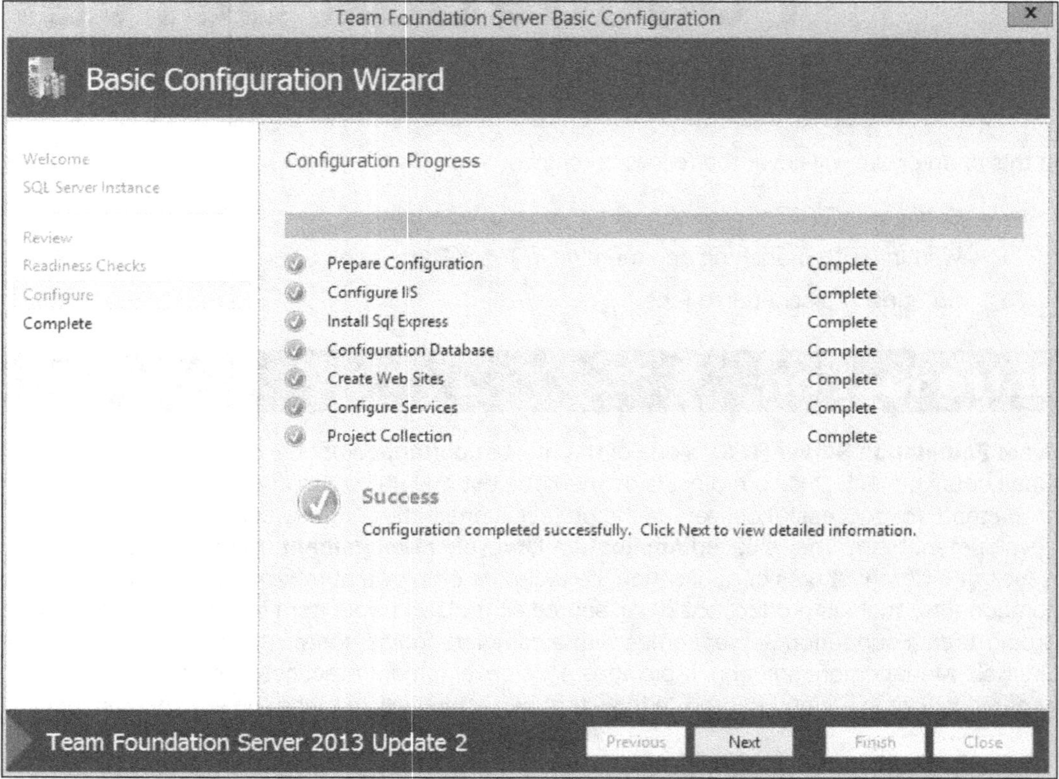

The preceding screenshot shows that everything was successfully installed. After finishing the basic installation of TFS, you can install the build server component on a server. The Build server will automate the builds of your software projects, as shown in the following screenshot:

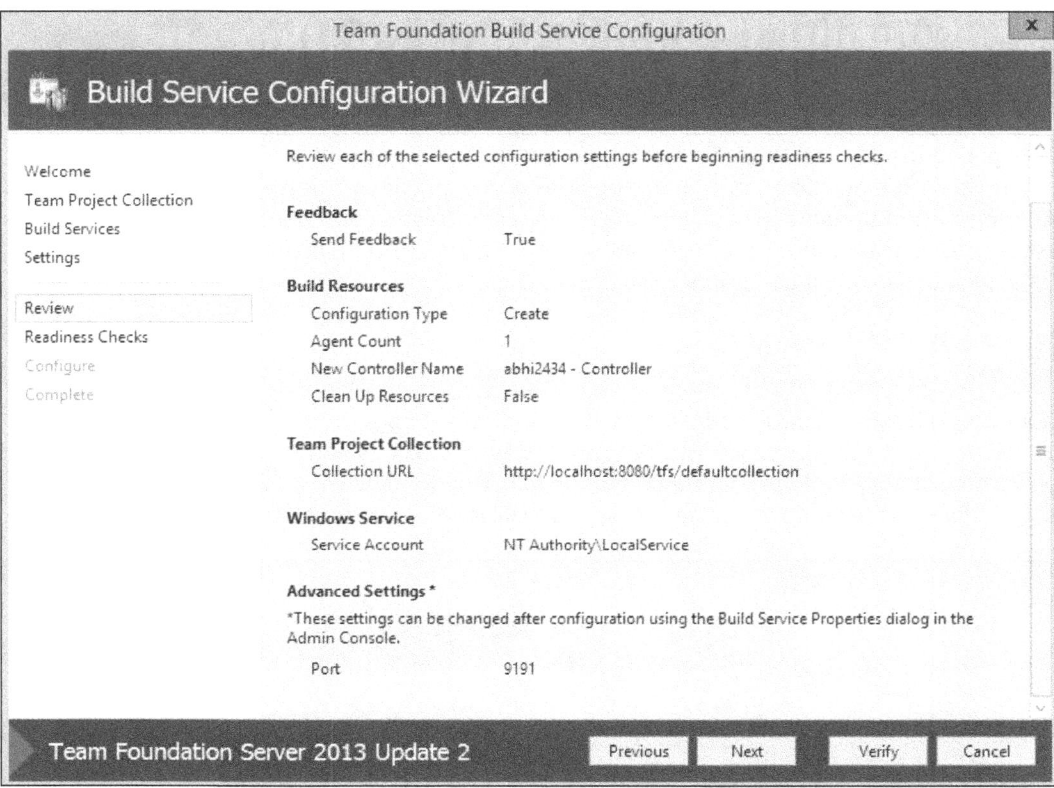

The Build service will automatically create a default collection for which the Build service will work. We can configure the Build service to create a build in the server itself upon updating the source for a project.

TFS has a SharePoint portal as well, which lets the TFS have a website referred to as a team project portal for each team project. This portal will help the team members share the process guidance, project documents, templates, and reports. The SharePoint portal is generally used to share documents and information.

Even though it is not necessary, sometimes to administrate team projects you might also need Team Explorer. Team Explorer provides a unique functionality to create projects for development teams.

To install Team Explorer, go to the `Team Explorer` folder of your setup directory and run `vs_TeamExplorer.exe`.

Configuring TFS for project hosting and management

Configuring the TFS is one of the most important tasks for good utilization of development resources. After installing the TFS in your system, you can open **Team Foundation Server Administration Console** to configure the server so as to add collection, projects, and users. Let's try to configure the most important sections of the TFS administration console and host an application inside it using Team Explorer.

Getting ready

Open the TFS administration console from the path `C:\Program Files\Microsoft Team Foundation Server 12.0\Tools\TfsMgmt.exe` if you have already installed it on your machine. The left-hand section of the following window shows the different types of subsections supported and the right-hand side will load the current section for configuration:

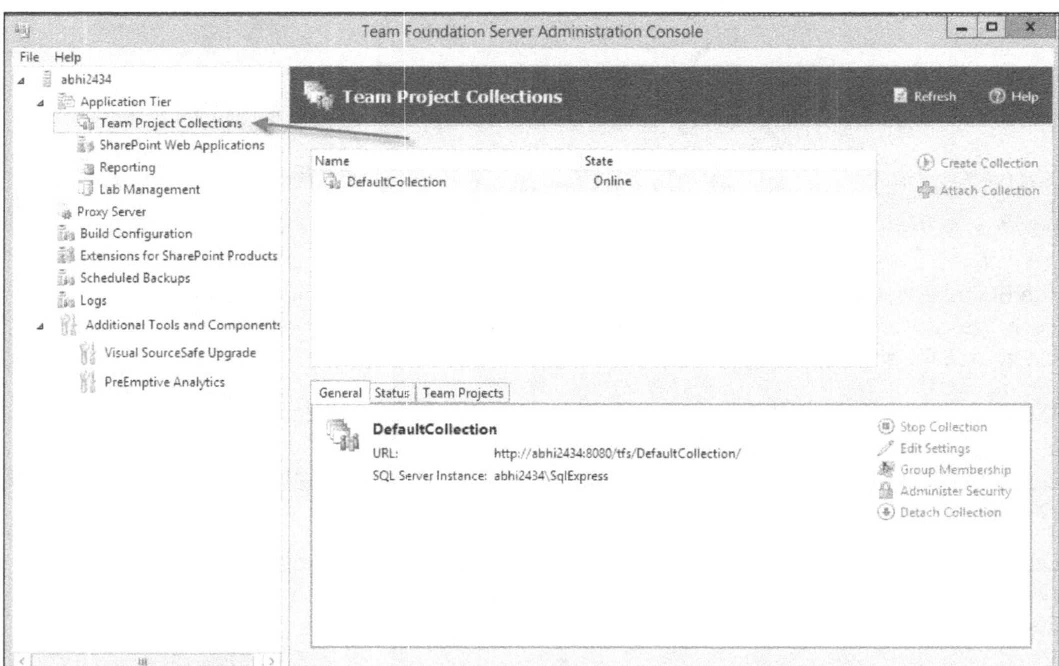

In the preceding screenshot, you can see that the default collection is already created for you. A project collection is a unit of the whole project or application. The users can be assigned to the project collection and each project collection can share a common set of configurations. A project collection holds a number of projects inside it, each of which can have their own solution. It should be worth noting that TFS creates a separate database in the SQL Server physically for each project collection.

Some important keywords you need to understand are as follows:

- **Team project collection**: Each project collection has a separate instance of physical database, which can hold multiple team projects. Generally, we create a team project collection for a big project, which has multiple projects inside it. Each team project collection is totally separate and isolated from one other.

- **Team project**: This is an individual team project that shares a common set of users, even if individual team project permission is given to individual users. A team project is a logical separation of code. A team project can have multiple solutions.

- **Solution**: This is an individual collection of projects that forms an individual solution. Visual Studio opens projects on the basis of the solution.

- **Project**: This is a unit that outputs a `.dll` file or an executable file.

How to do it...

To start configuring, it is important to check the existing configuration settings, such as e-mail alerts, console membership, and reporting server, when you click on the **Application Tier** node. Once things are done, let's follow these steps and create a new project collection:

1. Select **Team Project Collections** from the left-hand navigation section and choose **Create Collection** to create a new project collection.

2. A wizard will open; provide a name and a description for the TFS and then click on **Next**.

3. Supply the **Data Tier** information, choose your SQL database instance where the database needs to be created for the new project collection, and click on **Next**.

4. Finally, click on **Create**. Your project collection should be ready.

5. After the project collection is created, we need to add users to the collection.

6. By selecting the **Project Collection option** created, you can select **Group Membership** to add members to the collection. As TFS uses Windows authentication, you need to have users to be mapped with the domain.

7. There are a number of groups that are already added by default to your Windows user database, as shown in the following screenshot:

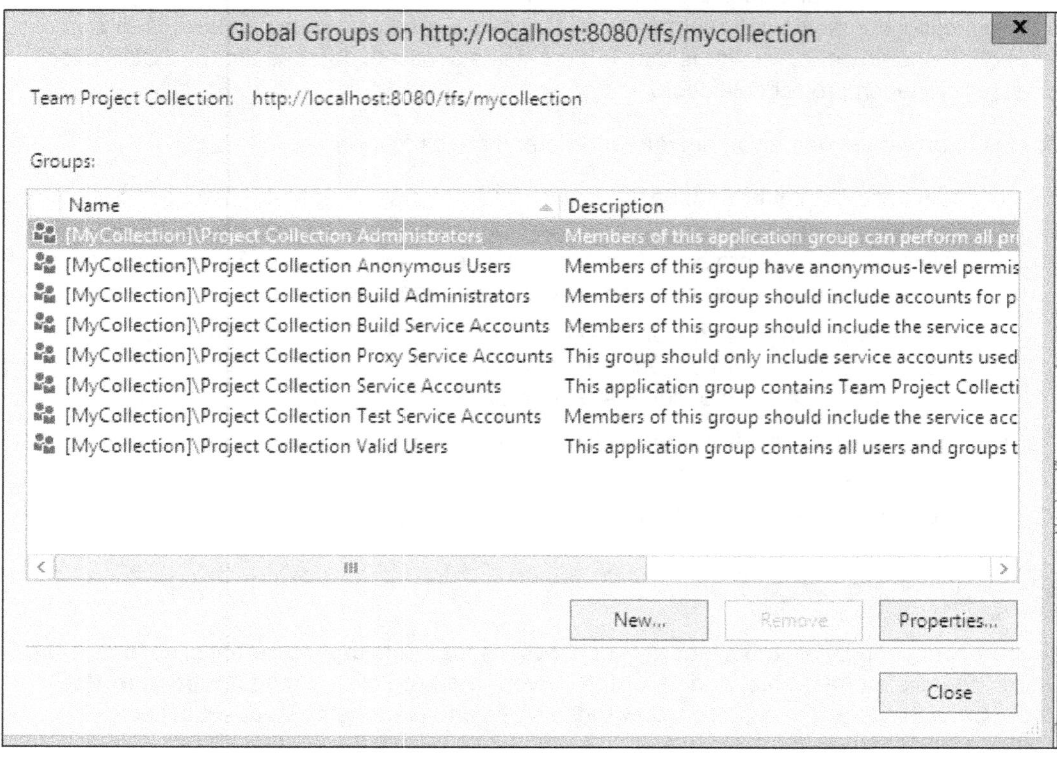

You can either add a user to the specific group to have specific role, or you can create a new one that suits your needs.

You can also use the web portal to do the same task. Enter `http://localhost:8080/tfs/MyCollection/_admin/_security/#_a=members` and you will see the following screenshot, which can be used in the same way:

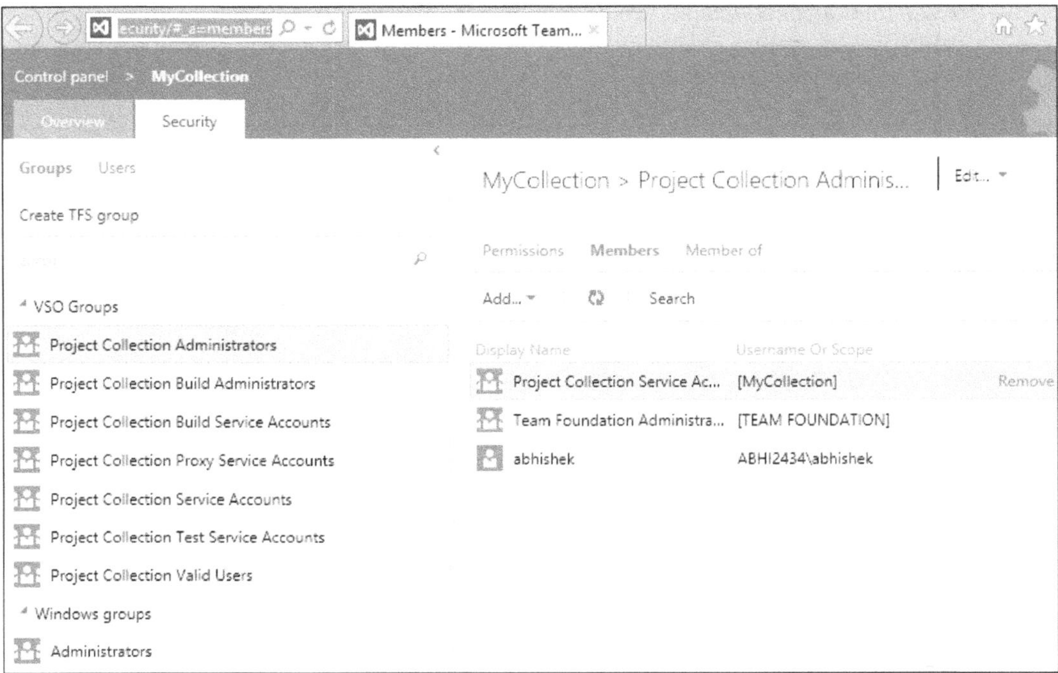

The web portal can also be accessed from outside if it is open to the external world and is backed up with a public IP address.

8. Based on group selection, you can choose **Administer Security** to apply security settings to the groups.

9. Once everything is set up, you can start collecting source in the project using Visual Studio Team Explorer.

10. Open Team Explorer, click on the **Sign up** link, and use `http://localhost:8080/tfs` as your URL (if you didn't choose anything else while installing). Once it is correctly set up, you can connect to the project. You can also protect your TFS behind HTTPS, which requires you to install Microsoft Certificate service and add an additional certificate to the server. You can get more information at `http://bit.ly/tfshttps`.

In the following screenshot, we opened **Source Control Explorer**; you can see the workspace is mapped to the location `D:\TeamProject`. Once it is mapped, you can start adding your source code.

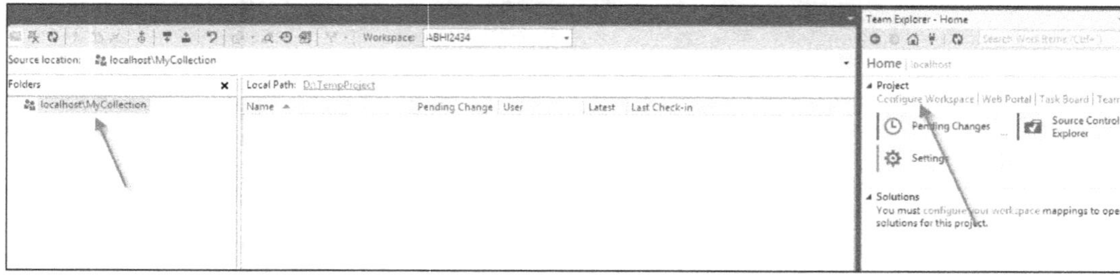

11. Once you're on the **Team Explorer - Home** tab, you will be provided with are a number of different options. You can check the **Pending Changes** button to view all the changes that were not updated on the server. There are **Check In** and **Checkout** buttons that will allow you to hold a file for changes and update it to the server.

12. Now, let's add a new team project. Select the **New Team Project** option in the **File** tab and name it `MyProject`.

13. Select the appropriate template that you want to use for your application development process. For the time being, we implement **Scrum**.

14. Now, select **Team Foundation Server** and then select **Finish**. The project will be created and loaded.

15. You can now add a new file. Select **Add Items to Folder** from the toolbar of the **Source Control Explorer** pane and add the file or folder associated with your project.

16. Once the file is added, it will show a **+** sign corresponding to the file. You can now check **In the file(s)** to upload the file on the server.

17. Right-click on the project and select **Check in pending changes**. You need to add a comment and then select **Check in** in the Team Explorer.

18. The file will be updated on the server.

How it works...

TFS tightly integrates itself with Visual Studio and Visual Studio Team Explorer to deal with projects. The projects can be bound to a TFS project in such a way that any updates that have been made to the server can be easily transferred to the other clients notifying new updates before they start editing the content.

There are a number of components that are used internally to run the TFS. The following diagram shows the partial architecture of the TFS system:

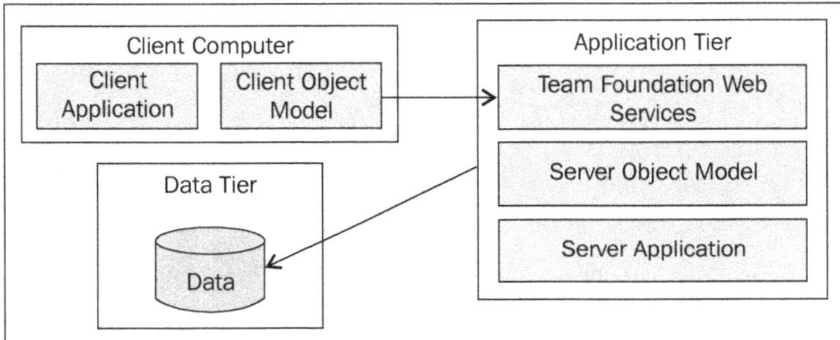

The **Application Tier** is the main section that connects the **Team Foundation Server** and the **Client Computer**. The main engine exposes a number of web services that lets the clients send/receive data. The **Client Computer** holds the **Client Object Model** for communication and the **Client Application** itself. The **Application Tier**, apart from being connected to the client application, is also connected to the **Server Application** that is used for administration. The **Data Tier** represents the actual repository of data. In case of the TFS system, the data is stored in the SQL Server databases.

There's more...

TFS is a vast topic to be considered in a single section. There are lots of other configuration options that we can explore.

How to add a work item to the TFS

TFS can not only be used as a repository of code, but it also allows you with tools for project management. A project is a collection of small individual task items known as work items that can be assigned to a person, and once the item is done, the user can update the item as closed.

In Visual Studio, you can add **Work Items**, which can further be added to the current sprint for the Scrum, as shown in the following screenshot:

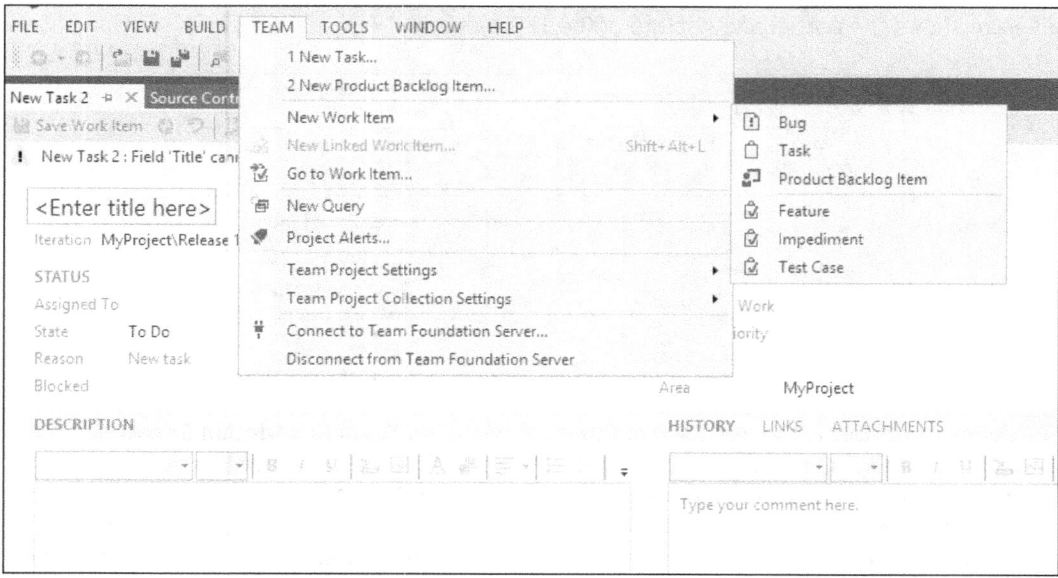

The **Assigned To** option will indicate the user who is responsible for the work. A description can be added and finally when the user clicks on **Save work item**, the user will be notified either using an e-mail notification (if it is configured) or when the user opens Visual Studio and queries its outstanding items.

How to add an e-mail notification to the TFS

A notification is another important thing for any team system. TFS allows you to configure it in such a way that every member is well informed of any changes that are made to the system. There is an option to set rules, which can trigger the appropriate e-mail notification, as shown in the following screenshot:

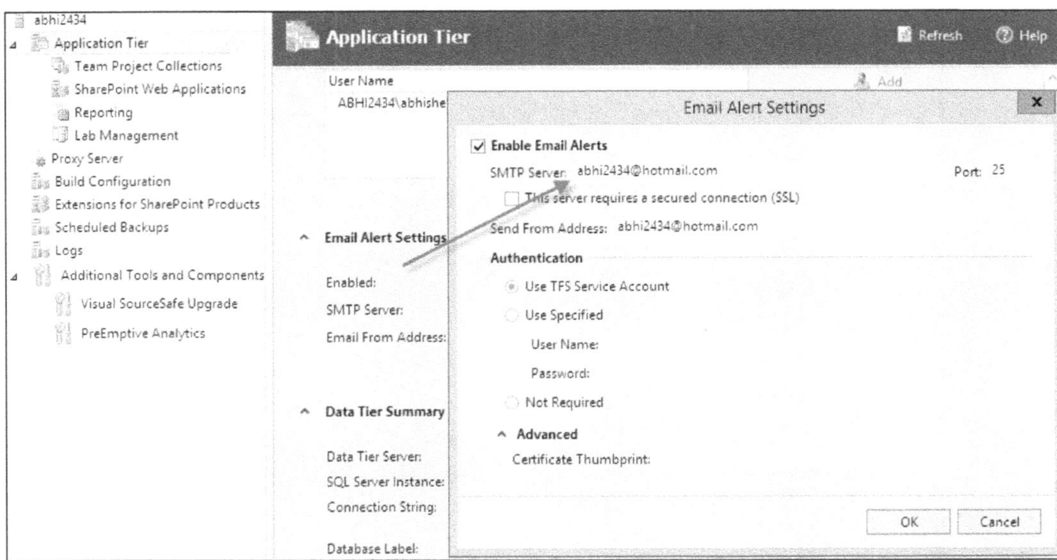

Before we do anything, we need to enable **Email Notification** by providing appropriate SMTP credentials. Open **TFS Administration Console**, select **Application Tier**, and then open the **Email Alerts** section to fill your SMTP details.

Now open the web portal using `http://localhost:8080/tfs` and go to the **Alerts** section. Add an alert to the work item so that when there is any work item change on the current project, the TFS service will notify a particular e-mail address.

The following screenshot shows how the **Alert** filters can be added to/removed from the query for the alert. Once alerts are set up, the TFS service will use the provided SMTP configuration to automatically notify the users.

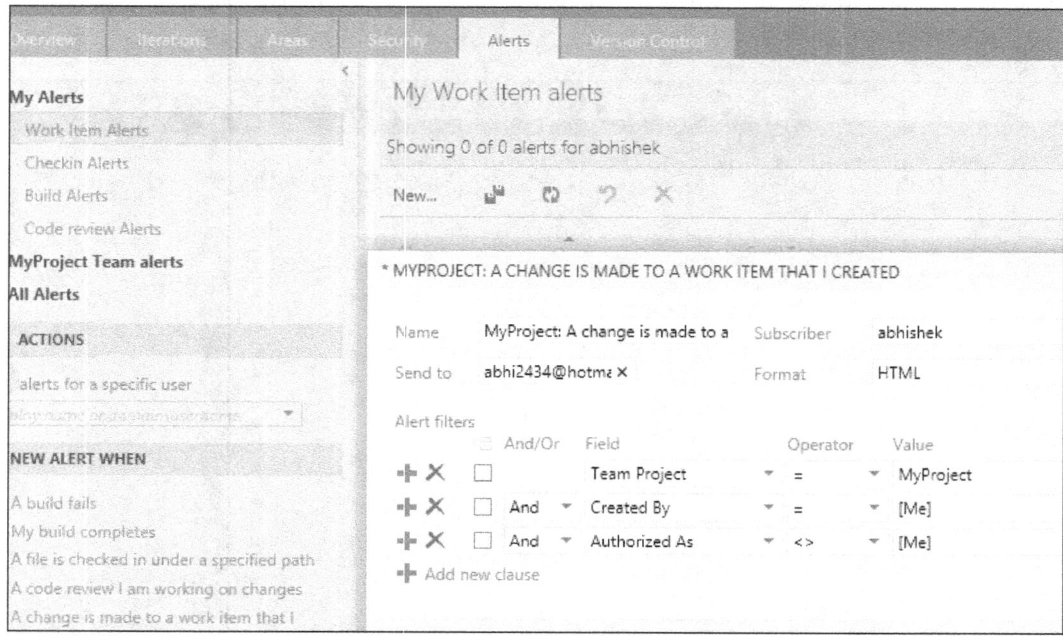

Configuring Agile iterations to a TFS project

TFS can have different project methodologies or processes. By the way, it structures the work items and their relationship (workflow). It already comes with a couple of already defined processes, such as Agile, CMM, and Scrum, which can further be customized as well. Agile is a continuous development process. Every release has a set of iterations. Iterations are divided into weekly sprints where each sprint is individually tracked and backlogs are created. As TFS supports the Scrum methodology of product development, you will see an **Iterations** tab inside the web project when the template is selected for project collection. You can set the dates for the appropriate iterations and apply Scrum.

Go to the web portal using `http://localhost:8080/tfs` and select the project that you want to apply iterations to. Navigate to the **Iterations** tab and set the dates for every release. Remember this option is only available when the Agile project template is chosen while adding a project collection.

In the following screenshot, you can see that **Sprint** is set up on a weekly basis and iterations are named properly. When adding a work item to a particular sprint, choose a particular iteration properly.

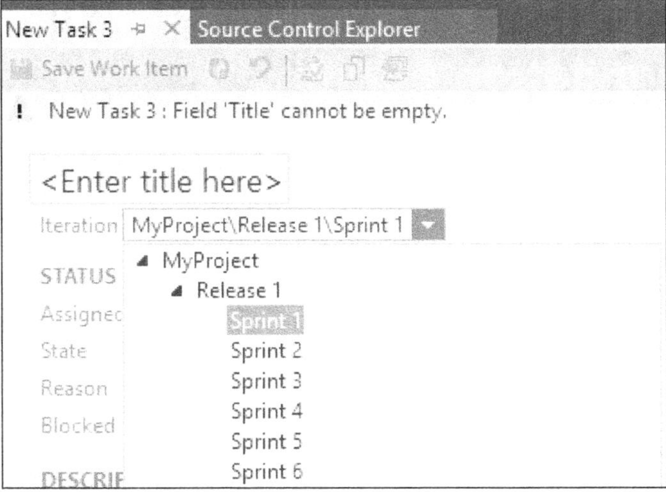

In the following screenshot, you can see the sprints that are listed in a TreeView, and you can choose the appropriate sprint or iteration for a particular work item:

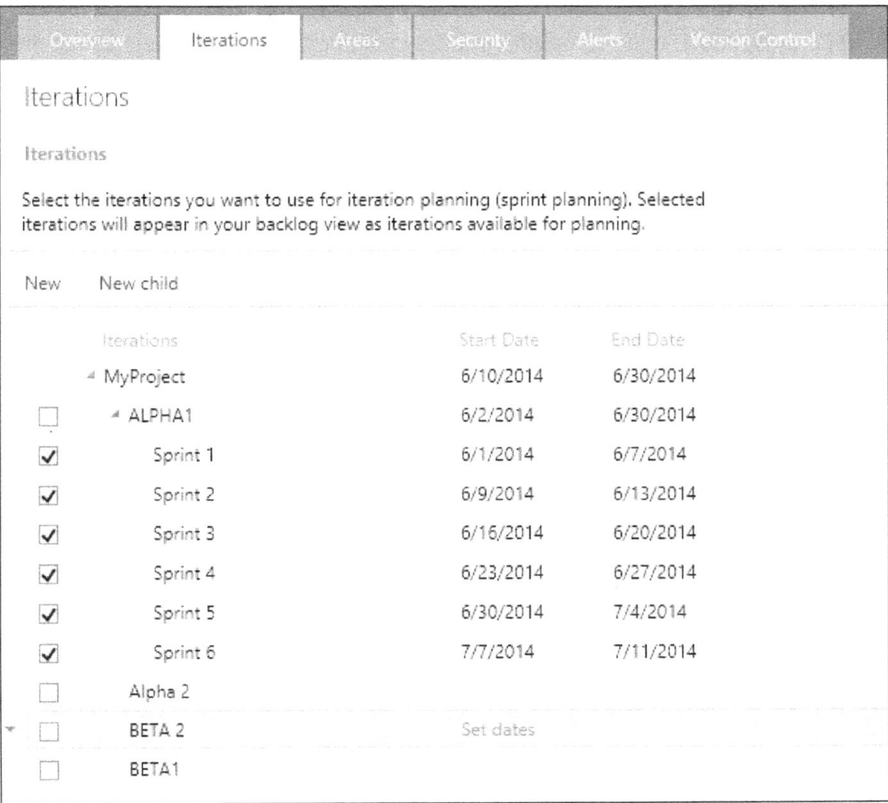

Iterations	Start Date	End Date
MyProject	6/10/2014	6/30/2014
ALPHA1	6/2/2014	6/30/2014
☑ Sprint 1	6/1/2014	6/7/2014
☑ Sprint 2	6/9/2014	6/13/2014
☑ Sprint 3	6/16/2014	6/20/2014
☑ Sprint 4	6/23/2014	6/27/2014
☑ Sprint 5	6/30/2014	7/4/2014
☑ Sprint 6	7/7/2014	7/11/2014
☐ Alpha 2		
☐ BETA 2	Set dates	
☐ BETA1		

Working with branching and merging in Team Foundation Server

Team development is not as simple as we think. If the project is small and has a very small team to work with, it can be configured as a simple deployment. However, in more advanced scenarios where the project is considerably big, there are teams specific to certain aspects of work and are working together on the same code - base.

For instance, the development team works on the core functionalities, the engineering team works on user logical issues and bugs, the quality assurance team works on testing the product, and finally the release team checks the features and releases. Not only this, the environment that these people use is quite different. The codebase that the development team uses is different from the codebase of the engineering team. Also, the development, staging, and production environments work in parallel. For such scenarios and requirements, TFS needs to maintain multiple codebases for the same solution, where the most recent will be with the developer teams while most stable ones will be with the quality assurance and production team. Branching allows you to branch one solution into another such that multiple projects can be maintained, and finally the required branch can be merged again with all the changes.

By branching, we mean creating a separate stream of source code that is capable of maintaining its own source controlling and strongly holding the links to the existing files in such a way that when there is a significant change in branch, it can be merged into the original source without any difficulty.

Before we start with the steps on creating branching and merging, let's discuss some techniques of code sharing. In the previous screenshot, you can see the main stream creates two branches: one for development and another for release, where both of them are merged to the main branch using the merging option. The techniques of code sharing are as follows:

- **File linking**: This is a Visual Studio feature where multiple projects share a single file. This kind of file sharing is best suited to small projects with limited number of shared files. In this mode of file sharing, each file is maintained with multiple links such that changes made to the individual file will automatically reflect to all other files (this resembles file sharing in **Visual Source Safe**.) With file linking, there's only one version of the linked source file to maintain. Changes made to the linked file are immediately received by all projects linking to the file. The disadvantage of file linking is that changes to the linked file should be coordinated with all the dependent project teams. Even carefully coordinated changes might break changes in dependent projects.

- **Binary sharing**: This means when the common source code is shared using the compiled assembly in form of **Dynamic Link Libraries** (`.dll`), teams that own the common code have full ownership and control. In theory, this means that the control, versioning, and quality of the product are probably better. Also, branching and merging complexities are avoided as teams reusing the common code don't have access to the common source code; they're dependent on the owners to add new features and resolve bugs in the common shared code. The assemblies for the common code can be shared by copying them to a well-known file that can be referenced by dependent projects. Signed assemblies may need to be added to **Global Assembly Cache** (**GAC**). Alternatively, the assemblies can be copied from the common code team project to a `bin` folder under the dependent project's main branch.

- **Source code sharing**: With source code sharing, Visual Studio has access to all the source code and can compile all the dependent assemblies together with the application. In Visual studio, the project reference is taken when source code is shared. With very large and complex projects, the compilation time can significantly increase due to source code sharing. Branching allows source code sharing in which a copy of the source code is created for each set of teams. It could be a development team, quality assurance team, implementation team, and so on—each developing on their own source. Finally, the changes made are merged to a main production stream.

How to do it...

To create branching inside a Visual Studio project, perform the following steps:

1. Open Visual Studio and select **Source Control Explorer**.

2. Right-click on the project folder, select the **Branching & Merging** option, and then select **Branch**.

3. A new dialog will pop up. Provide the appropriate location for **Branch** and click on **OK**, as shown in the following screenshot:

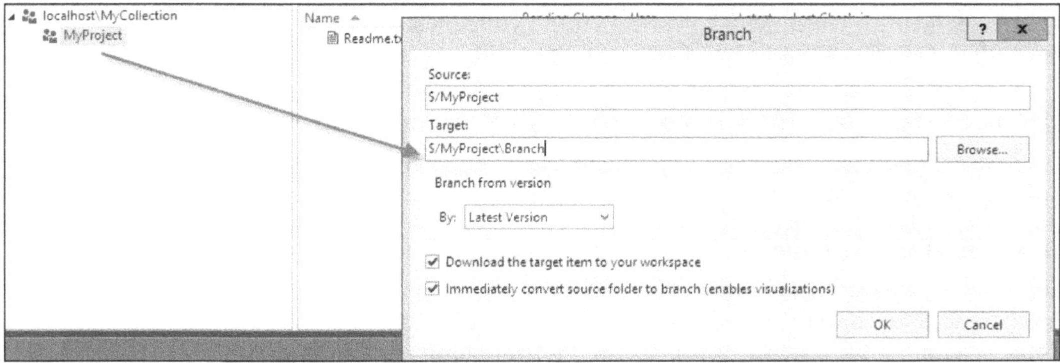

4. The branch will be created, acquiring the latest version of the existing source.

   In the following screenshot, **MyProject** has been branched out as **MyProject-Branch**. Here, both the projects will be under the source control and in both the projects people can work in parallel.

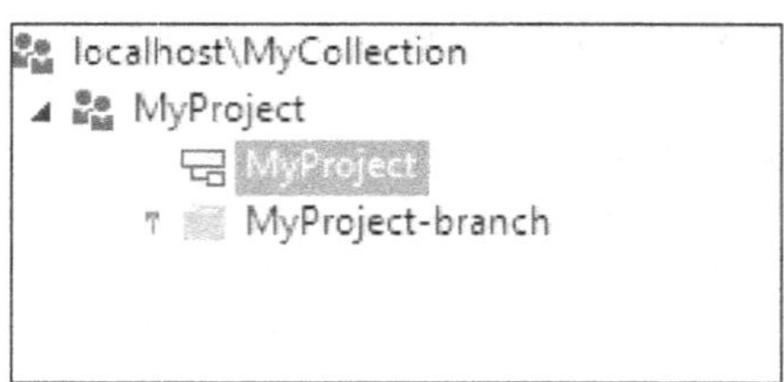

5. These branches can be merged later on when required by right-clicking on the `Branch` folder and selecting the **Merge** option from the **Branching & Merging** tab.

6. For merge, you need to choose the target and source, in such a way that individual files from source are merged to the target. You also need to note that the merging can have conflicts and sometimes TFS can ask to resolve these conflicts before the actual merging takes place.

How it works...

Branching is a process where a separate stream is maintained individually in a separate branch. The TFS System manages a backlink on every file it branches and separately maintains its own source control. The backlink is a unique identifier in the SQL Server tables, which identifies where the actual branch is created from so it can easily merge the source to the actual file later on during the merge operation.

There's more...

Visual Studio provides various tools to show the branching architecture of the TFS system. Here are some of the visualizers that might help.

Inspecting a visualizer to check TFS branching

There are a number of visualizers related to branching and merging that help to clearly inspect the TFS system.

Branch visualization

The branch visualization shows a diagrammatic view of the entire project branch. You can navigate to **Source Control Explorer**, click on the project that has been branched, and right-click on the **View Hierarchy** option in the **Branching** and **Merging** tab.

The following screenshot shows how the main **Agent** project is branched out to **Agent-Dev** and **Agent-Practice**. From this, you can quickly understand the branch hierarchy.

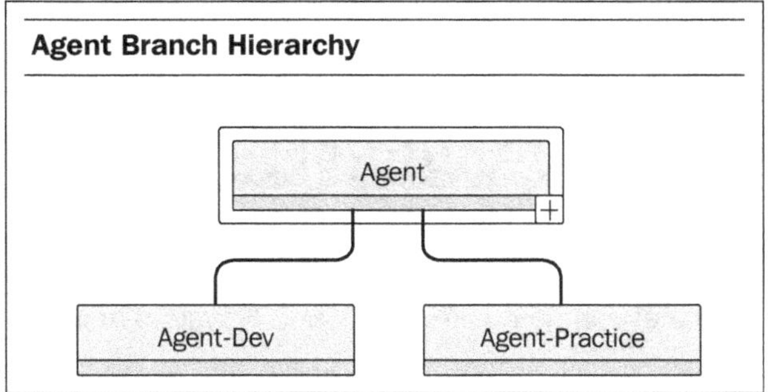

Changeset visualization

In Visual Studio, you can also see the changeset history for each branch to determine the merges to a changeset. Right-click on the project and then select **Track Changeset**. Once the changeset history is open, you can select the branches that you want to view changeset for and click on **Visualize**. This will visualize the changesets in different streams.

The following screenshot shows how a changeset is merged to different versions of streams. For a large project, it will be easier to understand the actual branching and merging using these visualizers.

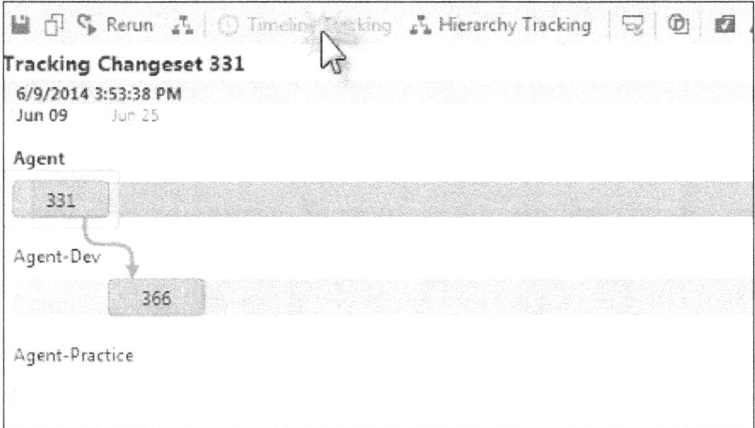

See also

▸ Refer to the ALM Rangers guide at `http://vsarbranchingguide.codeplex.com/`

▸ Learn more about branching and merging at `http://bit.ly/branchmerge`

Creating TFS-scheduled jobs

As TFS runs in the background, there is always a requirement to run scheduled jobs that perform a batch operation silently in the background. The TFS Background Job Agent is used to run certain tasks that can be hooked into the TFS system and that run automatically when scheduled.

Getting ready

Before getting started, create a `library` class and name it `ScheduledJobs`. We need to add a reference to the following files:

▸ `Microsoft.TeamFoundation.Framework.Server.dll` located at `C:\Program Files\Microsoft Team Foundation Server 12.0\Application Tier\ Web Services\Bin`

▸ `Microsoft.TeamFoundation.Common.dll` located at `C:\Program Files (x86)\Microsoft Visual Studio 12.0\Common7\IDE\ ReferenceAssemblies\v2.0`

▸ `Microsoft.VisualStudio.Services.WebApi.dll` located at `C:\Program Files(x86)\Microsoft Visual Studio 12.0\Common7\IDE\Reference Assemblies\v4.5`

Once the setup is ready, let's write the scheduler logic first and later hook it into the TFS system.

We also create a new .NET 4.5 library class called `TFS.ScheduledJobs` and add a reference to the following files:

▸ `Microsoft.TeamFoundation.Framework.Server.dll` located at `C:\Program Files\Microsoft Team Foundation Server 12.0\Application Tier\ Web Services\bin`

▸ `Microsoft. TeamFoundation.Common.dll` located at `C:\Program Files (x86)\Microsoft Visual Studio 12.0\Common7\IDE\ ReferenceAssemblies\v2.0`

▸ `Microsoft.VisualStudio.Services.WebApi.dll` located at `C:\Program Files (x86)\ Microsoft Visual Studio 12.0\Common7\IDE\ ReferenceAssemblies\v4.5`

We will be writing the `ScheduledJob` logic inside the `library` class and will later hook it to the main job project to run it.

How to do it...

Now let's create `ScheduledJob` inside TFS using these simple steps:

1. Create a new class called `IdCheckJob` and make it inherit variables from `ITeamFoundationJobExtension`. Then implement the interface. This should now give you the following code:

```
using System;
using Microsoft.TeamFoundation.Framework.Server;
namespace TFS.ScheduledJobs
{
    public class IdCheckJob : ITeamFoundationJobExtension
    {
        public TeamFoundationJobExecutionResult Run(TeamFounda
tionRequestContext requestContext, TeamFoundationJobDefinition
jobDefinition,  DateTime queueTime, out         string
resultMessage)
    {
        throw new NotImplementedException();
    }
    }
}
```

2. Now let's implement the `Run` method, as shown in the following code. The idea is to check every work item and then check which work items have been updated:

```
try
{
  TfsTeamProjectCollection tfsServer = new TfsTeamProjectCollectio
n(GetTFSUri(requestContext));
  WorkItemStore workItemStore = tfsServer.
GetService<WorkItemStore>();
List<WorkItem> changedWorkItems = new List<WorkItem>();
  foreach (WorkItem workItem in workItemStore.Query("SELECT * FROM
WorkItems"))
    {
      if (!workItem.Title.StartsWith("#" + workItem.Id + " - "))
      {
        workItem.Title = "#" + workItem.Id + " - " + workItem.Title;
        changedWorkItems.Add(workItem);
      }
    }
    if (changedWorkItems.Count > 0)
    {
        workItemStore.BatchSave(changedWorkItems.ToArray());
        resultMessage = changedWorkItems.Count + " work item titles
updated.";
```

```
      }
      else
      {
         resultMessage = "no work item titles to update.";
      }
   return TeamFoundationJobExecutionResult.Succeeded;
}
catch (Exception ex)
{
    resultMessage = "Job Failed: " + ex.ToString();
    EventLog.WriteEntry("TFS Service",
resultMessage,EventLogEntryType.Error);
    return TeamFoundationJobExecutionResult.Failed;
}
```

The code selects the updated work items and updates the database with a message.

You can see that the `resultMessage` variable is also updated so that we can see the job history.

3. Now compile the project and place the `.dll` and `.pdb` files in `C:\Program Files\Microsoft Team Foundation Server 12.0\Application Tier\ TFSJobAgent\Plugins`.

4. Once the file has been successfully placed, we need to register the TFS job. To register the job, we simply write a console application and run the following code:

```
var tfsUri = new Uri("http://localhost:8080/tfs");
var config = TfsConfigurationServerFactory.
GetConfigurationServer(tfsUri);
var jobService =  config.GetService<ITeamFoundationJobService>();
var jobDefinition = new TeamFoundationJobDefinition("Check
WorkItem Job", "TFS.ScheduledJobs.IdCheckJob");
jobDefinition.EnabledState = TeamFoundationJobEnabledState.
Enabled;
jobDefinition.Schedule.Add(new TeamFoundationJobSchedule(DateTime.
Now,300));
jobService.UpdateJob(jobDefinition);
```

The code will retrieve the job that has been added as a plugin to the TFS job agent and we call `UpdateJob` to service the plugin.

5. Once the job is registered, you can verify it using the following SQL statement:

```
select * from Tfs_Configuration.dbo.tbl_JobDefinition where
JobName = 'Check WorkItem Job'
```

   If you see an entry that exists in the database, this means the job is running.

6. You can copy `JobId` from the data and select `JobHistory` to verify how the scheduled job is working, as shown in the following code:

```
select * from Tfs_Configuration.dbo.tbl_JobHistory WITH (NOLOCK)
where JobId = '62FDDA25-4938-4BF7-A7C3- 6A9BF527A20C
```

   For instance, in my case it gives the appropriate results.

7. Finally, when you want to stop the scheduled job, you can easily write a console application again to delete the job. Let's take a look at the following code:

```
var tfsUri = new Uri("http://localhost:8080/tfs");
var config = TfsConfigurationServerFactory.GetConfigurationServer(
tfsUri);
var jobService = config.GetService<ITeamFoundationJobService>();
jobService.DeleteJob(new Guid("62FDDA25-4938-4BF7-A7C3-
6A9BF527A20C"));
```

Here, you can see that I used the `Guid` to identify the job rather than using the name. The `DeleteJob` method will de-register the job from the TFS job agent.

How it works...

TFS is hosted using IIS. There is a specific TFS job agent associated with the TFS, which runs periodically in the background to perform some batch operations. The TFS provides a plugin model to integrate your own scheduled tasks so that when the jobs are being dispatched, it can also run the user code automatically.

Until and unless the job has been deregistered, the TFS automatically picks it up and performs the tasks assigned to it.

See also

▶ To learn more about the TFS Background Job Agent,
   visit http://bit.ly/tfsbackgroundjob

5

Testing Applications Using Visual Studio 2013

In this chapter, we will cover the following recipes:

- Understanding Visual Studio unit test projects
- Working with the Microsoft Fakes framework in Visual Studio
- Understanding how Coded UI testing works in Visual Studio

Introduction

Testing is one of the most important parts of any development process cycle. Starting from the classic **Waterfall Software Development Life Cycle** (**SDLC**) model to the modern Agile-based SDLC, testing forms one of the most important sections of any development process. After the development phase is complete, the application is sent for testing. Every application, irrespective of its volume or size, is thoroughly tested before it is released for production. Testing software is so important that no software can ever be successful without going through this phase. Large enterprises keep separate teams that dedicatedly test applications and frameworks before finalizing the release. The purpose of these testing teams is to find out hidden flaws/bugs in the software, which might have been produced because of some wrong or illegal input that has not been taken care of by the developers during the phase of development. Most of these bugs come from the validation of code blocks or even logical bugs. The main motive of the testing team is to produce test cases and a bug report, which is then sent back to the development team for rectification.

As we already know, **Team Foundation Server** (**TFS**) supports a number of critical and important features, which makes communication between the development and testing teams easy and quicker than ever before using Visual Studio 2013.

When we talk about testing, the most important and common form of testing that comes to mind is unit testing. Unit testing is a method by which the developers test their source code by factoring the smallest portion of the program called units, which can be individually tested, and calling these units from outside using various logical test cases or a range of values. This method finally asserts the expected output with the actual output from the program. In most cases, unit tests are written by the White Box testers during the development process.

White Box testing is done by testing the internal structure and working of an application.

Visual Studio 2013 comes with lot of advanced tools and techniques that can be used from inside the IDE to help developers easily write and run test cases on the code that they have been working on. Some of the interesting tools include:

- **Test Explorer**: This lists all the unit tests that can be run from inside the IDE with logical grouping of tests based on the status of the test case. Test Explorer can also include third-party frameworks that have an adapter for the Test Explorer.

- **Microsoft Unit Test Framework**: This is a general purpose test framework that is installed with the Visual Studio IDE to write unit tests.

- **Code Coverage Tools**: This tool helps to find the amount of code that the unit test covers from a single command in the Test Explorer.

- **Microsoft Fakes Isolation Framework**: This allows you to create classes and methods that can generate fake dependencies between various modules of the code that are in the testing phase.

It is worth noting that unit testing is a part of Visual Studio Test Framework defined inside the `Microsoft.VisualStudio.QualityTools.UnitTestingFramework.dll` assembly, which is not a part of the .NET framework but a part of the Visual Studio IDE. You can work with the unit testing capabilities of Visual Studio using any version of Visual Studio except the Express edition.

In this chapter, we are going to cover some of the interesting and useful ways to define tests for our code.

Understanding Visual Studio unit test projects

Writing a test project inside the Visual Studio IDE has never been easier than that in Visual Studio 2013. A lot of tools inside the IDE makes it very easy to work on unit testing for an existing project and write superior test cases for the application. Microsoft has invested special efforts to make testing inside Visual Studio 2013 seamless for a developer who is already aware of how to write code inside Visual Studio. For instance, rather than running the project in the debugging mode, Visual Studio also provides shortcuts to build a project and run tests on it simultaneously. Now, let's see how to test an application inside Visual Studio in simple terms.

Getting ready

Before writing the actual test projects, let's first define a class that we need to test. For simplicity, let's consider a simple class called `Salary`, which will get the salary of an employee based on certain logic around his age. To implement, let's Open Visual Studio 2013 and create a library class and name it `UnitTestingSample`. Get rid of the default class produced and add a new class file called `Salary`. The implementation will look like what is shown in the following code:

```
public class Salary
{
    public const string ARGUMENTLESSTHAN20 = "Cannot calculate salary
of a person below age 20";
    public const string ARGUMENTGREATERTHAN85 = "You are too old to be
valid for pension";
    string name;
    int age;

    public Salary(string name, int age)
    {
        this.name = name;
        this.age = age;
    }

    // For simplicity we define salary by age.
    public float GetSalary()
    {
        int baseSalary = 20000;
        int ageSeed = this.age - 20;
```

```
            if (ageSeed < 20)
                throw new ArgumentOutOfRangeException(ARGUMENTLESSTHAN20);
            if (this.age > 85)
                throw new ArgumentOutOfRangeException(ARGUMENTGREATERTH
    AN85);
            float pensionFraction = 1.0f;
            if (this.age > 60) //retired
            {
                ageSeed = 40; //(60 - 20)
                pensionFraction = 0.5f;
            }
            float actualSalary = (baseSalary * ageSeed) * pensionFraction;
            return actualSalary;
        }
    }
```

The preceding class takes two arguments in its constructor, which will be stored as the name and age of an employee using a constructor. The `GetSalary` method is a method that will invoke logic to determine the salary of a person based on the following:

- The salary cannot be determined if the age of a person is less than 20 or greater than 85

- Salary equals age multiplied by base salary, which is taken to be 20,000 when the age is less than 60

- Salary equals 50 percent of the final salary at age 60 as pension

How to do it...

Now, let's create a project and see how to test an application:

1. To test the previous method, let's add a new `Unit Test Project` to the solution and call it `UnitTestingSample.Tests`.

2. Remove the default class generated from the template and add a new unit test class to the project. We will call it `SalaryTests`.

3. Add a reference to `UnitTestingSample` using the **Add Reference** dialog box to test the project.

4. Add a new method to test the `GetSalary` method. The test method should always be named according to the `NameofMethod_WhatToTest_ExpectedResult` logic. For the first `TestMethod`, we are going to pass `ValidValues` and expect a valid result:

```
[TestClass]
public class SalaryTests
{
    [TestMethod]
    public void GetSalary_ValidValues()
    {
        //arrange
        int age = 50;
        float expected = (20000 * (age - 20)) * 1;
        Salary osalary = new Salary("John", age);

        //act
        float actual = osalary.GetSalary();

        //assert
        Assert.AreEqual(expected, actual, string.Format("Expected
{0} not equals actual {1}", expected, actual));
    }
}
```

In the preceding `TestMethod`, we use `50` as the age of the employee `John` so that we receive the value based on the logic as expected. Notice that we defined the name of the method based on the nomenclature defined to write test methods.

We divide any `TestMethod` into the following three sections:

▶ **Arrange**: This section defines the prerequisites to call the method

▶ **Act**: Here, the method is actually called and the result is stored

▶ **Assert**: In this section, we write various assert statements on the expected and actual

We also need to annotate the method with `TestMethod`, and the actual class that defines the `Test` class with the `TestClass` attribute.

5. Build the project and open Test Explorer. Test Explorer will identify the `TestMethod` automatically and list them inside Visual Studio.

6. Run the `TestMethod` that states `GetSalary_ValidValues` and you should see the test pass.

7. Now, to check whether the test actually ran before giving the result using `TestExplore`, add a value with the expected result and rerun the test again; the test will eventually fail. When the test fails, the assert failure message is shown to indicate failure, as shown in the following screenshot:

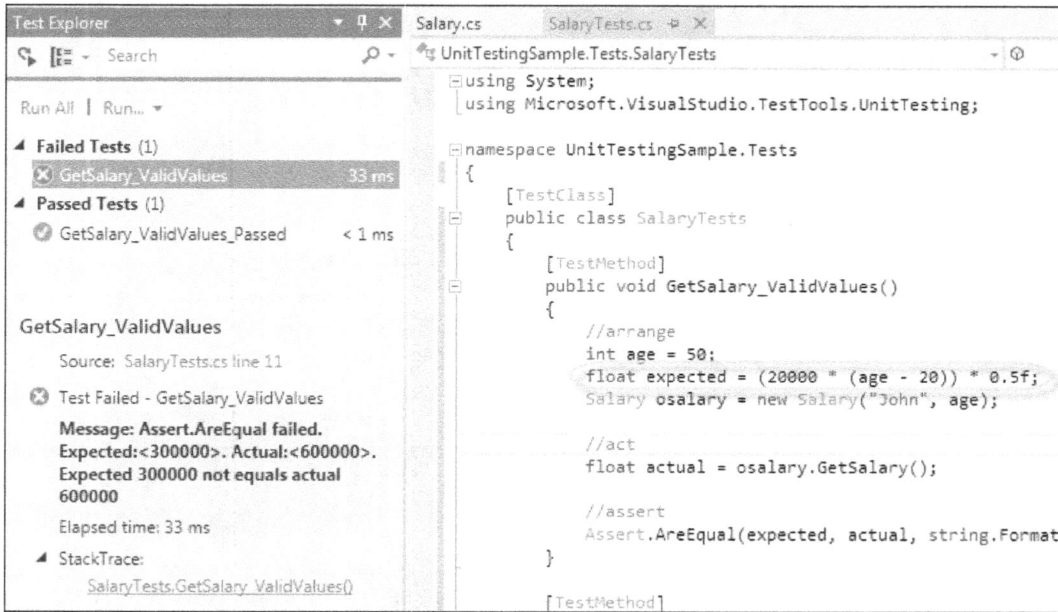

In the preceding screenshot, the **Test Explorer** lists the tests that have intentionally failed by changing the value of expected. When you click on any of the failed tests, the Explorer lists the assert failure message returned with a complete listing of the actual and expected values. You can fix the problem easily by clicking on the test result, which will directly point you to the code, or using `StackTrace` to find the trace results.

8. Let's add another method to test what will happen when we pass an age less than 15:

```
[TestMethod]
[ExpectedException(typeof(ArgumentOutOfRangeException))]
public void GetSalary_WhenAgeLessThanTwenty__
ShouldThrowException()
{
    //arrange
    int age = 15;
    Salary osalary = new Salary("John", age);

    //act
```

```
    float actual = osalary.GetSalary();

    //assert
}
```

When the value for the age is less than 20, we get an exception from the method, which indicates that the salary cannot be returned for a person below age 20. To assert an exception, we have used the `ExpectedException` attribute and annotated it with a method. This attribute indicates that the method should throw an exception when the test runs.

9. Run the test again to ensure that it passes.

10. The method can throw `ArgumentOutOfRangeException` for cases where the age is less than 20 or greater than 85. Let's test the second case where the age is greater than 85:

```
[TestMethod]
public void GetSalary_WhenGreaterThanEightyFive_
ShouldThrowException()
{
    //arrange
    int age = 90;
    Salary osalary = new Salary("John", age);

    //act
    try
    {
        float actual = osalary.GetSalary();
    }
    catch (ArgumentOutOfRangeException e)
    {
        //assert
        StringAssert.Contains(e.Message, Salary.
ARGUMENTGREATERTHAN85);
        return;
    }
    Assert.Fail("No exception was thrown");
}
```

In the preceding code, we have used the `try/catch` blocks to determine the argument. The `StringAssert.Contains` method will compare the message that is received by the argument exception with the expected string to indicate whether the assertion is passed. In the preceding code, we place `Assert.Fail` in the final step to indicate that we don't have an exception. Finally, run the tests again and ensure everything is passed.

How it works...

The Visual Studio IDE has built-in unit testing. Visual Studio is capable of determining `TestClass` and `TestMethod` automatically when tests are run. It automatically browses the entire project hierarchy and finds all the classes that are annotated with the `TestClass` attribute. It also lists the names of all the methods defined inside them and annotated with the `TestMethod` attribute inside the Test Explorer of Visual Studio. The Test Explorer can be used to run the test methods directly within it, which will call the tests, run them, and show the asserted result on the screen.

The IDE determines the failure or success based on the assert statements. An assert statement determines the validity of the statement when Visual Studio runs the method. The method produces an exception when an assert statement fails logically, which is captured by the IDE and the results are shown on the screen. In other words, if you call the `TestMethod` from outside, it will produce `AssertFailedException` if the expected and actual value differs. This exception is handled by Visual Studio to show a failure inside the IDE.

There are a number of APIs available for the `Assert` method, which are useful in various ways:

- `Assert.AreEquals`: This fails when two values differ
- `Assert.AreSame`: This fails when two objects point to different locations
- `Assert.Fail`: This fails irrespective of any logic
- `Assert.IsTrue/Assert.IsFalse`: This determines the failure based on a true or false condition
- `Assert.IsNull/Assert.IsNotNull`: This fails when an object points to `null`

Similar to `Assert`, there are a number of other classes that are used to test values, such as `StringAssert` and `CollectionAssert`, which work specially on a set of types.

There's more...

As you've already got the basic idea of unit testing, let's help you further understand the additional features.

Testing private types and members

Sometimes, it becomes essential to test a private type or a private member of a type. Let's create a new `UnitTest` class on the same project and call it `SalaryPrivateTests`. The unit testing API provides two classes to handle private types and members:

- `PrivateObject`
- `PrivateType`

The `PrivateObject` class is used to invoke private members of a type. To test this feature, let's test the validity of the `Salary` class constructor as follows:

```
[TestMethod]
public void TestPrivateMembers()
{
    //arrange
    string name = "Abhishek";
    int age = 30;
    Salary osalary = new Salary(name, age);

    //act
    PrivateObject pObj = new PrivateObject(osalary);

    //asset
    Assert.AreEqual<int>(age, Convert.ToInt32(pObj.GetField("age")));
    Assert.AreEqual<string>(name, pObj.GetFieldOrProperty("name") as
string);
}
```

In the preceding code, the instance of `PrivateObject` is used to get the private data members defined in the `Salary` class using `GetField` or `GetFieldOrProperty` to determine the validity of the constructor. The `PrivateObject` class provides methods such as `GetField`, `GetProperty`, `SetField`, and `SetProperty` to handle private fields, properties, or methods. You can call a `Private` method using the `Invoke` method from the `PrivateObject` instance.

The `PrivateObject` class is used to test instance members of a private type. When there is a need to test a private static member, we need to use `PrivateType` instead of `PrivateObject`. Let's add a simple static method to the `Salary` class, which takes an object of the salary and returns the name associated with the object:

```
static string GetName(Salary oSalary)
{
    return oSalary.name;
}
```

The preceding code takes an object of the `Salary` class and retrieves the name associated with it. To test this method, we need to create an instance of the `PrivateType` class as follows:

```
[TestMethod]
public void GetName_StaticMethodTest()
{
    //arrange
    string name = "Abhishek";
```

```
    int age = 30;
    Salary osalary = new Salary(name, age);

    //act
    PrivateType pType = new PrivateType(typeof(Salary));
    string returnValue = pType.InvokeStatic("GetName", osalary) as
string;

    //assert
    Assert.AreEqual(name, returnValue);
}
```

In the preceding code, the `PrivateType` class allows you to call the private static member `GetName` and get the result of the method. Similarly, using the object of `PrivateType`, we can call the static field, properties, and so on using `GetField` and `GetProperty`.

Using code coverage results

From Test Explorer, Visual Studio 2013 allows you to analyze a project to ensure that all the lines of the project are tested. The **Code Coverage** window allows you to get an estimate on how much code has already been tested by the test cases defined in the unit testing project.

Let's say we comment out all the tests other than the `GetSalary_ValidValues` method from the project and rerun them. You will see that the tests have been passed to the Test Explorer. Once the tests have been passed, right-click on the test entry in the Test Explorer and select **Analyze Code coverage for Selected Tests**. The project will be analyzed and the result will be displayed inside the IDE.

In the following screenshot, how much code has been covered by the selected test has been shown. The `GetSalary` method listed on the **Code Coverage Results** window shows **50%**. If you choose **Show code coverage coloring** form the **Result** pane, it will annotate all the lines that have been tested.

If you uncomment all the test cases for the project and run the code coverage, you will see that a lot more lines of the `GetSalary` method are colored in blue, which indicates that the lines are covered by test cases.

Dealing with test-driven development in Visual Studio

Test-driven development is a new way of developing code, where the test cases are written before the actual code is written. Visual Studio IDE helps in developing the actual code from the test cases easily. To create a test-driven method, let's create a unit testing project in Visual Studio and name it `TDDSample.Tests`.

Get rid of the default test file and create a new unit test class on the project. Create a test case and name it `BasicDivideTest`:

```
[TestMethod]
public void BasicDivideTest()
{
    //arrange
    Calculator ocalc = new Calculator();
    double expected = 4d;
    //act
    double actual = ocalc.Divide(20d, 5d);

    //assert
    Assert.AreEqual(expected, actual);
}
```

In the preceding code, we created an instance of the `Calculator` class that does not exist and call its `Divide` method with two double arguments. Now, we need to generate the class and the method automatically.

Let's add a new project to the solution and call it `TDDSample`. Right-click on **Calculator** in the code and select the **New Type** option from **Generate**, as shown in the following screenshot:

The new type pops up a new window, where you need to choose the correct project to autogenerate the `Calculator` class. Once the class is generated, you can again right-click on the `Divide` method and generate it inside the `calculator` class in a similar way.

Next, when we run the test from Test Explorer, it fails as the method throws `NotImplementedException` by default. If you select the test entry from Test Explorer, you will be navigated to the actual method. Let's now write the code that will ensure that the test passes:

```
public double Divide(double p1, double p2)
{
    return p1 / p2;
}
```

If we run the test again, it will pass because the result returned by the `Divide` method is valid for the test case.

Now, let's validate our test using a range of values:

```
[TestMethod]
public void RangeDivideTest()
{
    //arrange
    Calculator ocalc = new Calculator();

    //act
    for(double p1 = -100d; p1 < 100d; p1 ++)
        for (double p2 = -100d; p2 < 100d; p2++)
        {
            double expected = p1 / p2;
            AssertRange(ocalc, p1, p2, expected);
        }
```

```
    }

    private void AssertRange(Calculator ocalc, double p1, double p2,
    double expected)
    {
        double actual = ocalc.Divide(p1, p2);

        //Assert
        Assert.AreEqual(expected, actual);
        Assert.IsFalse(Double.IsInfinity(actual));
    }
```

In the preceding code, we try to test a range of values for `p1` and `p2` from `-100` to `+100`. The test will fail because when the value of `p2` is `0`, the result will be returned as infinity. A check of `Double.IsInfinity` will ensure that the assert statement fails.

Let's add a code snippet to fix the problem:

```
    public double Divide(double p1, double p2)
    {
        if (p2 == 0 || p1 == 0)
            return 0;

        return p1 / p2;
    }
```

Here, we validated `p1` and `p2` to return `0`. Hence, the code will run.

See also

- Refer to creating and running unit tests in a managed environment at `http://bit.ly/TestRuntime`

Working with the Microsoft Fakes framework in Visual Studio

Isolation of the dependencies in code by mocking or faking objects is one of the common norms when developing unit tests or creating a Test-driven development. People write mocking objects that can be used to redirect calls to some dependent objects in order to independently test modules. There are also a number of frameworks that generate mocking objects automatically based on the existing dependencies without having to use any handwritten objects. The Visual Studio 2013 Ultimate edition comes with a new Microsoft Fakes framework that takes mocking to a new level.

If you have used Microsoft Moles before, you will find that the Fakes framework has a very similar workflow. Moles was originally designed for Microsoft Pex, which is another great unit testing tool by Microsoft Research. Moles became popular because it could virtually create mocks on anything and was so simple that there was hardly any overhead on using it. Moles provided a type safe detour framework with very clear semantics. For example, any .NET method in Moles is represented by a delegate. Microsoft replaces Moles in Visual Studio 2013 with the Microsoft Fakes framework, with the working principles defined almost the same as it.

Microsoft Fakes uses stubs and shims to replace other parts of the dependencies while testing a unit. These are small pieces of code that are used in tests. Thus, replacing unnecessary dependencies using stubs and shims ensures that you find an appropriate cause of a test failure. Stubs and shims are helpful to test parts of the code that are still to be implemented.

> - **Stubs**: This replaces the call of one class with another class implementing a common interface. To use stubs, the design of the test method should always use an interface to call an object rather than calling the class directly. Typically, we use stubs for the components that are defined inside the same assembly.
>
> - **Shims**: This modifies the compiled code of the application at runtime replacing the original calls to some API with a shim code defined inside the test providers. Shims are slow and require runtime to rewrite the code during compilation.

In this recipe, we are going to create tests for the code that has external dependencies either from the .NET class library or from inside our own code.

Getting ready

Before going ahead, it would be a good idea to create code that can be tested using the Microsoft Fakes framework. The following `static` method checks whether the current date is December 21, 2012, and based on this, it will throw an exception:

```
public static void DoomsDay()
{
    if(DateTime.Now.Equals(new DateTime(2012, 12, 21)))
        throw new Exception("Time's Up !!!! World will end now");

    //Other code
}
```

You can see that it is as a `static` method but it has the `DateTime.Now` static property tied to it, which makes it very hard to test the method and generate an exception. As the `DateTime.Now` property is defined inside the .NET framework and will evaluate `DoomsDay` only when the system date reaches that particular day, it will become mandatory to replace the call with some fake calls:

```
public static void DeleteTemporaryData(string dirLocation)
{
    Directory.Delete(dirLocation, true);
}
```

Similar to the preceding code, `DeleteTemporaryData` will delete the entire directory that has been passed recursively.

We will create an interface `ILogger` to implement the `Logger` utility. To test the stubs, we will call the interface to create an external dependency:

```
public string GetEventName(ILogger logger)
{
    if (logger.IsLoggerEnabled)
        logger.Log("GetEventName method is called");

    return "Sample Event";
}
```

Here, the `ILogger` interface has one Boolean property `IsLoggerEnabled` and a `Log` method to write the log entry from the logger.

How to do it...

Let's take a look at how we can create a Fakes project solution in the following steps:

1. Add a new unit test project to the solution and name it `MSFakesSample.Tests`.
2. Get rid of the default file and create a test unit.

3. Add a reference to the class library that we need to test the test project. To enable Fakes types for an assembly, go to the **Solution Explorer** pane, open **References**, right-click on the assembly that you want to Fake, and select **Add Fakes Assembly**. This will automatically create a Fake assembly with all the additional features to call it just like a normal one. It is necessary to create a Fake assembly for `System.dll`. We can right-click on the normal assembly to create its Fake, as shown in the following screenshot:

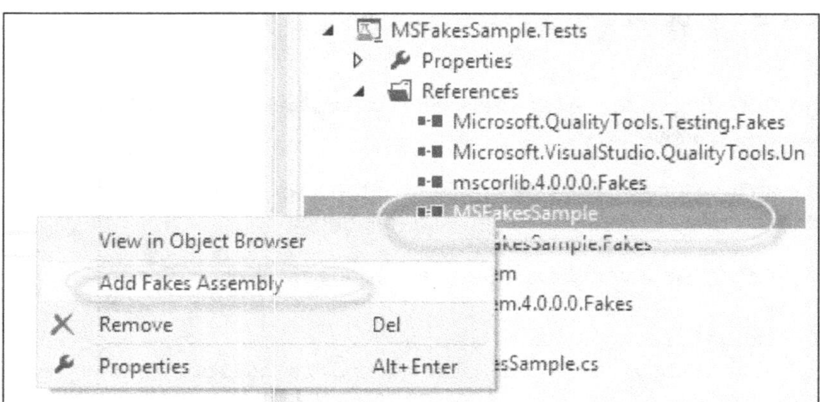

4. Once the Fake assembly is created, let's test the `DoomsDay` method we created earlier. As a test case, we need to generate an exception, which is only intended for December 21, 2012. We use shims to define a Fake implementation of `DateTime.Now` inside `ShimsContext`:

```
[TestMethod]
[ExpectedException(typeof(Exception))]
public void DoomsDay_Test_Shims()
{
    using (ShimsContext.Create())
    {
        ShimDateTime.NowGet = () => new DateTime(2012, 12, 21);
        DiagonizeShims.DoomsDay();
    }
}
```

In the preceding unit test, the Fakes assembly for the project automatically creates intercepts that can redefine the existing APIs. Here, inside `ShimsContext` we redefine the `Get` method of the property. Now using `Delegate`, which returns a valid date, a call to the `DoomsDay` method generates the expected exception.

5. Notice that `DateTime.Now` is defined in `mscorlib.dll`, which has been faked using the Fakes framework. You can also specify `BehaveAsNotImplemented` to ensure that an API throws `NotImplementedException` when it is called:

```
[TestMethod]
[ExpectedException(typeof(ShimNotImplementedException))]
public void DeleteDirectory_BehaveNotImplemented()
{
    using (ShimsContext.Create())
    {
        ShimDirectory.BehaveAsNotImplemented();
        DiagonizeShims.DeleteTemporaryData(Environment.
GetFolderPath(Environment.SpecialFolder.ApplicationData));
    }
}
```

In the preceding code, `DeleteTemporaryData` generates `ShimNotImplementedException` because we defined the Fakes implementation of the `Directory` class to `BehaveAsNotImplemented`. Remember that the shims implementation will only work on the calls inside `ShimsContext`.

6. Unlike shims, stubs on the other hand are used to fake virtual types, such as interfaces, abstract classes, and virtual methods. Stubs cannot be used in a nonvirtual context, such as private, sealed, or static types. To write a unit test for the `GetEventName` method, we use a stub for the `ILogger` interface so that it does not actually log data, rather it calls the custom test logger stubs:

```
[TestMethod]
public void GetEventName_Test()
{
    //Arrange
    var sLogger = new StubILogger
    {
        IsLoggerEnabledGet = () => true
    };
    var sut = new DiagonizeStubs();
    //Act
    var result = sut.GetEventName(sLogger);

    //Assert
    Assert.IsFalse(string.IsNullOrEmpty(result));
}
```

In the preceding code, the test will call `StubILogger`, which is a fake implementation of the `ILogger` interface and is used instead of the actual `Logger` class. The `StubILogger` variable exposes properties that enable the tester to assign a delegate for the `Get` and `Set` methods of the properties and other methods associated with the interface. Here, we have changed the default implementation of the `Get` method of `IsLoggerEnabled` to return the `true` value.

7. Stubs can also be associated with an observer. An observer allows you to record calls on stubs. The Fakes framework ships its own observer, which allows you to record every call and argument made in the stub just like any other standard isolation framework. Thus, we can rewrite the preceding test with an observer like the following one:

```
[TestMethod]
public void GetEventName_Test_Fakes()
{
    //arrange
    var stubLogger = new StubILogger { IsLoggerEnabledGet = () =>
true };
    var diagonizeStub = new DiagonizeStubs();
    var observer = new StubObserver();
    stubLogger.InstanceObserver = observer;

    //act
    diagonizeStub.GetEventName(stubLogger);
    var calls = observer.GetCalls();

    //assert
    Assert.IsNotNull(calls);
    Assert.AreEqual(2, calls.Length);
}
```

Here, we have created an instance of `StubObserver`, which is assigned to `InstanceObserver` for the logger implementation. If you remember the actual definition of `GetEventName`, it first checks the value of `IsLoggerEnabled` before calling `Log`. The preceding code will observe two calls: one to the `IsLoggerEnabledGet` method and another to the `LogString` method.

8. Finally, if we run all the tests, they will pass. This indicates that the stubs and shims actually injected Fake code to isolate dependencies in the application.

How it works...

The Microsoft Fakes framework provides a superior technique to isolate a portion of the code from external sources. Shims and stubs are important picks to implement the level of isolation. Shims are used mainly to test the untestable code that comes with calls from third-party components with a lot of statics and privates. Shims rewrite the code completely during compilation to replace the actual calls during testing, and hence it requires a long time to load. Stubs, on the other hand, are recommended for virtual types, which are much faster with minimum or no code replacement during compile time.

In the following diagram of the component, the test uses the component that has the dependency of some external files (`System.dll`) and some other components defined in the assembly. When an isolation technique is taken, the component replaces the calls to the external components with shim methods and other internal calls, using stubs.

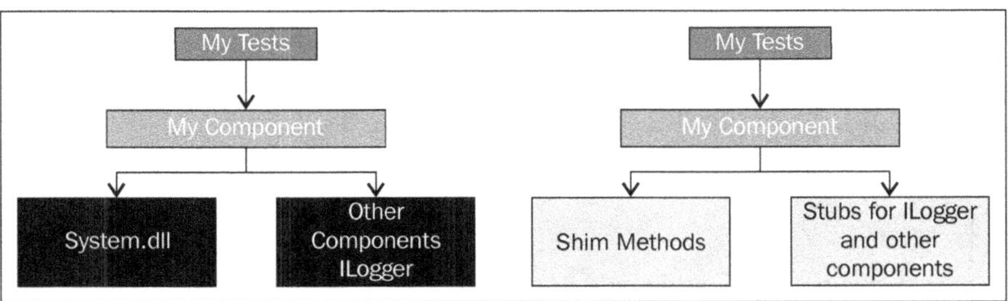

Shim replaces all the calls to a method inside its context with a new implementation, if provided. For instance, if you take a closer look at the implementation of `ShimDateTime.NowGet` in the preceding assembly using .NET Reflector, you will find that `ShimRunTime` replaces `DateTime`. The `NowGet` property with the delegate that we have passed data to the `TestMethod` is shown in the following code:

```
public static FakesDelegates.Func<DateTime> NowGet
{
    [ShimMethod("get_Now", 24)]
    set
    {
        ShimRuntime.SetShimPublicStatic((Delegate) value,
typeof(DateTime),        get_Now", typeof(DateTime), new Type[0]);
    }
}
```

In the preceding implementation of `NowGet`, you can see that the delegate we passed to the property is replaced with the actual `get_Now` method of the `DateTime` object only within the current context. On the other hand, calling the `BehaveAsNotImplemented()` method injects `NotImplementedException` inside the actual definition of the methods that are defined in the `Directory` class present inside the context. Thus, shims ensure that calls to any API are properly replaced to call a Fake assembly rather than the actual API call.

Unlike shims, stubs implement interfaces inside the Fake assembly. It ensures that all the methods (even the `Get` and `Set` methods of property) expose a matching property of the delegate type to enable the test environment to replace the default content when required. Shims also make calls to the observer to ensure that all the calls to the methods and properties are logged on the observer. If we see the implementation of `StubILogger`, we can also see that there are delegates defined for each of the three methods as follows:

```
public FakesDelegates.Func<bool> IsLoggerEnabledGet;
public FakesDelegates.Action<bool> IsLoggerEnabledSetBoolean;
public FakesDelegates.Action<string> LogString;
```

The delegates passed to these methods will be called when the actual methods are called from the test environment.

See also

 ▸ Refer to the isolating code testing using the Microsoft Fakes section at `http://bit.ly/MSFakesTest`

Understanding how Coded UI testing works in Visual Studio

Visual Studio offers a Coded UI Test builder to record interactions with the application so that the tester can generate UI test cases automatically, and rerun the tests later on the projects to ensure everything is working as expected.

Coded UI Test refers to the black box testing that is performed by the application testers after the application development is finished. These tests include the testing functionalities of the controls to ensure that the whole application including the user interface is working correctly. Coded UI Tests are very useful when there are some validations or other logic in the user interface needed to be tested.

In this recipe, we are going to create a small application and try to test its functionalities using Coded UI Tests.

Getting ready

Let's create a small WPF application project. We will call it `CodedUITestSample`. Once the project is created, it will display a blank window with the designer. Drag a `TextBox`, `Button`, and `TextBlock` class onto the designer. We will add logic to reverse the characters present in the `TextBox` class, which means that whatever we write in the `TextBox` class will be reversed and shown in the `TextBlock` class. We will name the `TextBox` class `txtInput`, the `TextBlock` class `tbReverseText`, and the `Button` class `btnReverse`.

Reversing a string is very easy. It will take a few milliseconds to calculate. We will use a simple method to reverse an input string, as shown in the following code:

```
private string ReverseString(string input)
{
    char[] charArray = input.ToCharArray();
    Array.Reverse(charArray);
    return new string(charArray);
}
```

The code looks very simple and it won't take long to get a visual clue of something the code is working on. So, to create a visual illusion or rather to make the application do something, let's go to the designer again and drag `progressbar` and `Button`. We will call the `progressbar` class `pbProgress` and the `Button` class `btnAgain`.

Now, let's double-click on the **Reverse** button to create its handler method. We will add the following code to reverse a string:

```
private void btnReverse_click(object sender, RoutedEventArgs e)
{
    string reverse = this.ReverseString(this.txtInput.Text);

    string isPalindromeString = string.Empty;
    if (this.txtInput.Text.Equals(reverse))
        isPalindromeString += ", and it is a palindrome";
    var msg = string.Format("The reverse is : {0}{1}", reverse,
isPalindromeString);
    this.Progress();
    this.tbReversedText.Text = msg;
    this.btnAgain.Visibility = System.Windows.Visibility.Visible;
}
```

The `ReverseString` method is called to get the reverse of a string and produces a message. In addition to reversing a string, the `btnReverse_click` method will also check whether the string input is a palindrome (which means the reverse of the input is the same), and adds a message to it.

We also added a `progressbar` class to indicate the progress of the reverse. But `Array.Reverse` works instantaneously and it wouldn't take much time to show the progress of the method. Let's add some code to simulate the progress of the progress bar. To do this, we will add the following delegate:

```
private delegate void ProgressBarDelegate(DependencyProperty dp,
Object value);
```

The delegate will be used to point to `SetValue` of the `progressbar` class. Let's add a code snippet to show the progress of the `ProgressBar` class:

```
private void Progress()
{
    this.pbProgress.Visibility = System.Windows.Visibility.Visible;
    double progress = 0;

    ProgressBarDelegate updatePbDelegate = new
ProgressBarDelegate(pbProgress.SetValue);

    do
    {
        progress++;
        Dispatcher.Invoke(updatePbDelegate, DispatcherPriority.
Background,
            new object[] { ProgressBar.ValueProperty, progress });
        pbProgress.Value = progress;
        Task.Delay(100);
    }
    while (pbProgress.Value != pbProgress.Maximum);
    this.pbProgress.Visibility = System.Windows.Visibility.Collapsed;
}
```

In the preceding code, the `updatePbDelegate` delegate points to the `SetValue` method of the `progressbar` class and the value gets updated in the background using `Dispatcher.Invoke`. In the preceding code, the `progressbar` class iterates by one and halts it by 100 milliseconds with each iteration until finally it reaches the maximum value. Once it is reached, `progressbar` is set to `invisible` again. Hence, we call this method before showing the message on `btnReverse` to ensure that the progress is shown on the screen when the **Reverse** button is clicked.

We again return to the designer and double-click on `btnAgain` to write code for it. In this method, we turn off the visibility of `pbProgress` and `btnAgain` and clear `txtInput` and `tbReverse.Text`.

We finally run the application to ensure everything is working.

How to do it...

Now, as our sample application is ready, it is a good time to start testing the program using Coded UI Tests:

1. Add a new project to the solution, select **Coded UI Test**, and name the project `CodedUITestSample.Tests`.

2. Once the project is added to the solution, you will be prompted with the following pop-up window:

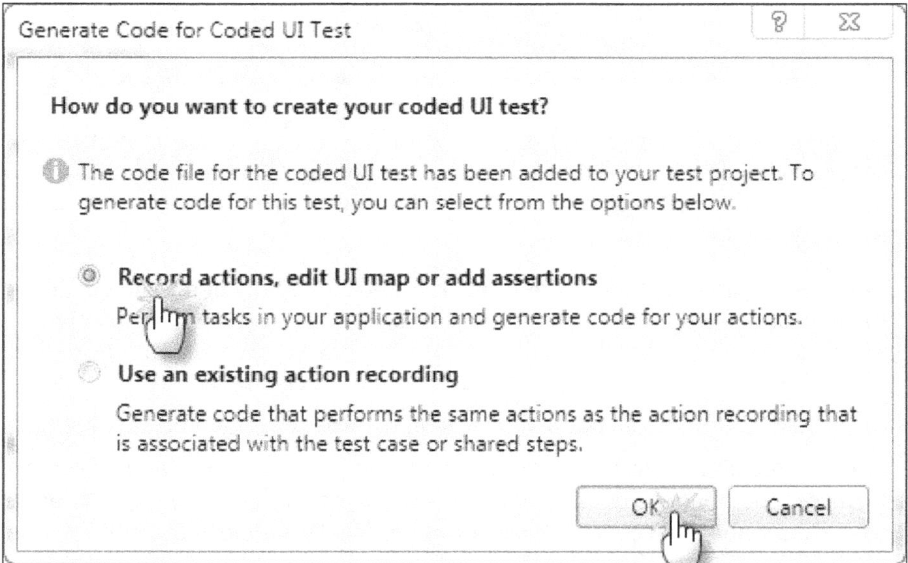

In the pop-up window, the program asks to either click on **Record actions, edit UI map or add assertions** or **Use an existing recording**. An existing action recording is used to load a recording from a file already created. As our application is brand new, we choose the first option to start creating the recording from scratch.

3. After the application gets ready, it will automatically be minimized and you will see a small tool window on the right-hand side of the screen to start the recording.

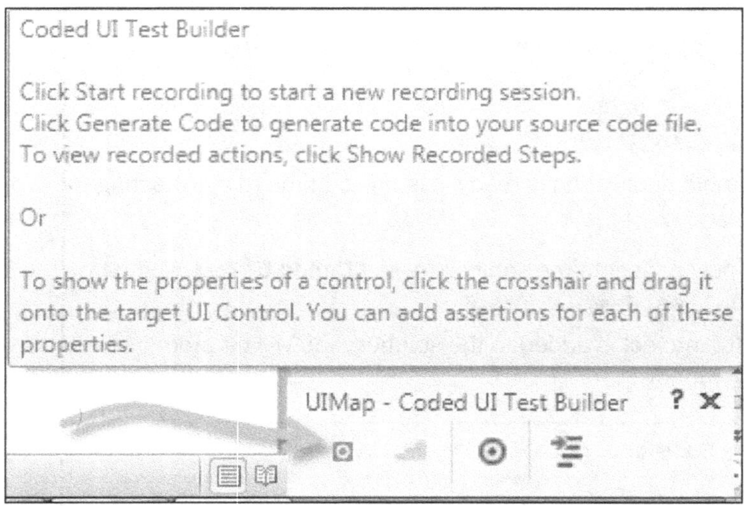

The preceding screenshot shows the tool window, which is shown when Coded UI Test is added. Visual Studio does a good job showing a tooltip that indicates the functionalities of the toolbar buttons. The **Record** button in red is used to start recording the UI test.

4. Before you start the recording, let's go to the `bin` directory of the project and open the application (you can find the project by default at `My Documents\Visual Studio 2013\Projects\CodedUITestSample\CodedUITestSample\bin\debug`), and create a desktop shortcut before you begin recording.

5. Open the file from the desktop and click on the **Record** button of Visual Studio.

6. After the recording has been started, we type `Abhishek` in the window and click on **Reverse**. The progress bar appears to show the message. We click on **Try again** and type `madam` and then click on **Reverse again**. Finally, we close the application.

7. After the recording is finished, we click on **Generate Code** to save the recording as code in a Visual Studio test project.

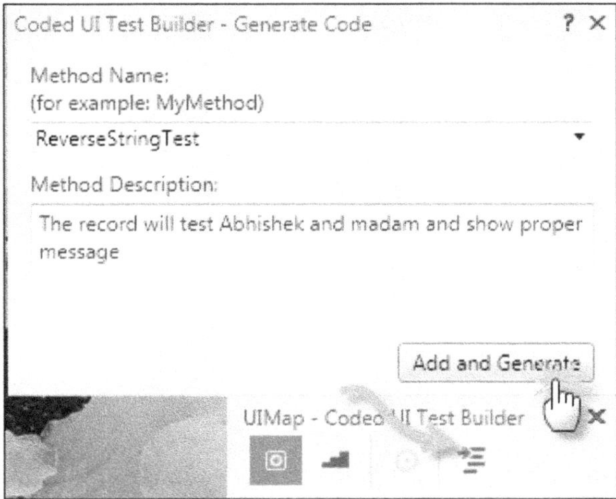

The **Generate Code** option takes a little while and finally asks the method name for the code as shown in the preceding code. We name it `ReverseStringTest` and click on the **Add and Generate** button to generate the code for the test.

8. Once Visual Studio is open, you will see two files. One that represents the `CodedUITest1` and calls recording, and the other one is `UIMap.uitest`. The `UIMap` file holds information about the recording, and the `CodedUITest1` file represents the `Test` method, which calls the recording.

9. Double-click on the `UIMap` file to see the UI actions. On the right-hand side of the screen, the explorer shows all the controls that have been identified by the recording. If you open the application from the desktop again, right-click on any of the node on the right-hand side, and select **Locate the UI control**. The application will mark the control on the application window in a blue border.

10. On the left-hand side, the actions are listed. The header shows a few contextual toolbar buttons, as shown in the following screenshot:

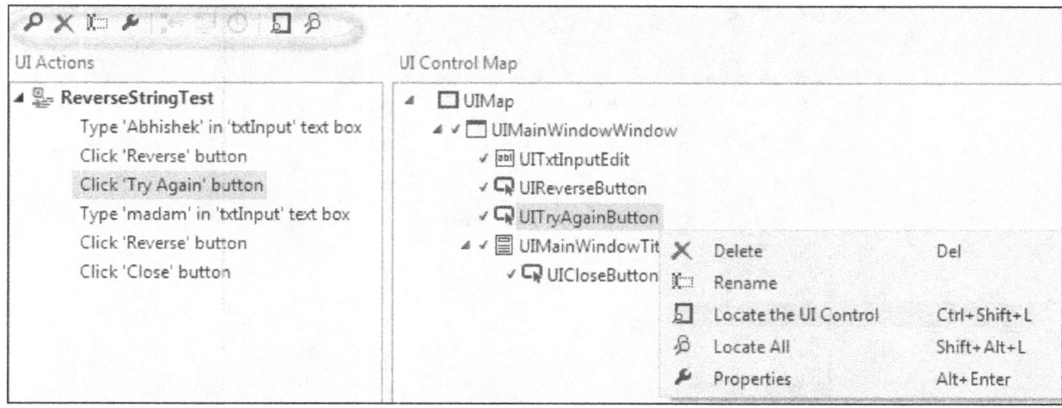

The buttons will help you to modify the UI test actions or perform actions on **UI Control Map**.

11. As we would like to edit the code inside `ReverseStringTest`, it is important to move the actions from the designer file inside `UITests` to the `UIMap.cs` file. We can right-click on the method and select **Move code to UIMap.cs**.

12. If you run the test now from Test Explorer, the test will fail (remember to start the application before calling the test). This is because the test will not pause until `Try Again` becomes visible.

13. Let's open the `UIMap.cs` file and navigate to the `ReverseStringTest` method. You will see all the actions that the method will perform once the test runs. We will add a few lines to it to indicate that our test will always pass when it should:

```
public void ReverseStringTest()
{
    #region Variable Declarations
    WpfEdit uITxtInputEdit = this.UIMainWindowWindow.
UITxtInputEdit;
    WpfButton uIReverseButton = this.UIMainWindowWindow.
UIReverseButton;
    WpfButton uITryAgainButton = this.UIMainWindowWindow.
UITryAgainButton;
    WpfButton uICloseButton = this.UIMainWindowWindow.
UIMainWindowTitleBar.UICloseButton;
```

```
    #endregion

    // Type 'Abhishek' in 'txtInput' text box
    uITxtInputEdit.Text = this.ReverseStringTestParams.
UITxtInputEditText;

    // Click 'Reverse' button
    Mouse.Click(uIReverseButton, new Point(30, 13));

    uITryAgainButton.WaitForControlExist(5000);

    // Click 'Try Again' button
    Mouse.Click(uITryAgainButton, new Point(184, 10));

    uITxtInputEdit.WaitForControlPropertyEqual("Text", "");

    // Type 'madam' in 'txtInput' text box
    uITxtInputEdit.Text = this.ReverseStringTestParams.
UITxtInputEditText1;

    uIReverseButton.WaitForControlEnabled();

    // Click 'Reverse' button
    Mouse.Click(uIReverseButton, new Point(37, 10));

    // Click 'Close' button
    Mouse.Click(uICloseButton, new Point(29, 9));
}
```

Here, we have added the highlighted lines. The first line will wait for the **Try again** button to appear before it is clicked. We have specified a time-out value of 5 seconds, hence if the **Try Again** button does not appear for 5 seconds, the test will fail.

Secondly, the test will wait to ensure that the `Text` property of `txtInput` is empty before writing the next string.

Finally, the **Reverse** button will be checked to be enabled before it is clicked.

14. Now, if you go to the `CodedUITest.cs` file, navigate to the `TestMethod`, and run the test, the test will pass.

15. To add an assertion to the test, we right-click on `UIMap` and select **Edit with Coded UI Test Builder**. A small **Test builder** window will appear.

16. Drag the round crosshair to the control to add an assertion. For instance, let's type `madam` in the application window and drag the crosshair to the label, and add an assertion to detect the reverse. We will choose **Add Assertion** on `DisplayText` of the UI element, and add a comparator **Contains** to it, as shown in the following screenshot:

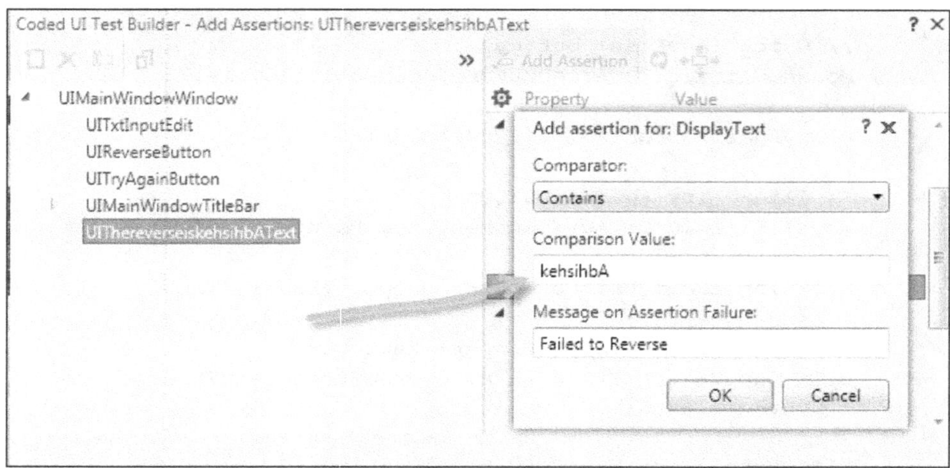

In the preceding screenshot, we have added an assertion using the **Add Assertion** button and checked a string.

17. We will click on the `Generate` method and call it `AssertReverse`. We add similar assertion methods to check other assertions.

18. Finally, we will add the assertion inside the `ReverseStringTest` method to test the reverse of the code appropriately. For instance, we include a reverse assertion to the test by adding the following lines:

```
//Checks whether the label contains reverse string
string reverseString = this.ReverseString(this.
ReverseStringTestParams.UITxtInputEditText);
StringAssert.Contains(uIThereverseiskehsihbAText.DisplayText,
reverseString);
```

We add these lines just before the `Click` operation.

19. We will also place a palindrome check for the next observation:

```
reverseString = this.ReverseString(this.ReverseStringTestParams.
UITxtInputEditText1);
            bool isPalindrome = this.ReverseStringTestParams.
UITxtInputEditText1.Equals(reverseString);

            if (isPalindrome)
```

```
              Assert.IsTrue(uITxtInputEdit.Text.
Equals(reverseString));


               StringAssert.Contains(uIThereverseiskehsihbAText.
DisplayText, "palindrome");
```

The preceding code checks the content of the label that contains a palindrome, and also the input of the reverse of the string passed is a palindrome.

20. Finally, if you run the `TestMethod`, all validations will be observed and the test will pass.

How it works...

To test a user interface, Coded UI Tests plays a vital role. Coded UI Test projects can record user input, which is converted to `TestMethod` to run the tests whenever it is required. The application automatically runs the tests using an operating system and the `SendKeys` or `MouseClick` operation. It hooks the position of the pointer using the pointer location and clicks on the exact same location of the window.

The window is identified by the HWND handle to run the test appropriately. Each Coded UI Test has a few files associated with it, which are as follows:

- `UIMap.uitest`: This is an XML file that represents the structure of the recording. Visual Studio provides a good designer to work with the XML, which is created during recording. The `uitest` file contains all the information about the controls and properties. This file shouldn't be edited manually.
- `UIMap.designer.cs`: This contains autogenerated code for the recording. This file is recreated every time the test changes.
- `UIMap.cs`: This is a partial class that contains customized code to extend the functionalities of the `UIMap` class.
- `CodedUITest.cs`: This is the main file that comprises the `TestMethod`. It calls the `Recorded` method created on `UIMap` and runs when the test runs. It is the starting point of the test and should contain at least one `TestMethod`.

There's more...

As we move forward on Coded UI Tests, we may require more options to fetch our needs. Let's discuss some of the additional options that we have.

How to drive a test using predefined data

It is sometimes required to test an application with different kinds of data. The test can be configured in such a way that it gets data from a certain data source and runs the tests continuously using data one after another.

Let's create a CSV file to store data for our test inputs. In the application we built, the first input is reversed, and the second input is reversed and checked whether it is a palindrome or not. Let's say we create a data source with the following data and save it as a CSV file:

```
Input1,Input2
Hello,madam
Father,dad
Mother,mom
Store,refer
God,devoted
```

There are two columns for the CSV file and we will place a string in the first column and a palindrome in the second column. Notice that the last row contains a word that is not a palindrome, so any test using this data source will fail.

Now open `CodedUITest` and create another method. We will call it `CodedUITestMethod2_DataDriven`. This method is not marked only as `TestMethod`, rather we will be using the `DataSource` attribute in addition to the `TestMethod`:

```
[DataSource("Microsoft.VisualStudio.TestTools.DataSource.CSV",
    "|DataDirectory|\\DataDrivenTest.csv", "DataDrivenTest#csv",
    DataAccessMethod.Sequential),
DeploymentItem("DataDrivenTest.csv"), TestMethod]
public void CodedUITestMethod2_DataDriven()
{

    this.UIMap.ReverseStringTestParams.UITxtInputEditText =
TestContext.DataRow["Input1"].ToString();
    this.UIMap.ReverseStringTestParams.UITxtInputEditText1 =
TestContext.DataRow["Input2"].ToString();
    this.UIMap.ReverseStringTest();
}
```

> The `DataSource` attribute takes a CSV file called `DataDrivenTest.csv` with Sequential access. The `DeploymentItem` attribute specifies the files and directories that are to be used by the method. We specify the filename. We can also use the whole path here to define the custom URL of the file. By default the file is searched in the `bin` folder.

The `REverseStringTestParams` function contains the two inputs that are used by the `TestMethod`. So before calling the `ReverseStringTest` method, we will change the value of `Params` using the contextual parameter `Textcontext`. The `DataRow` method will contain values from `DataSource`.

When you run the test from Test Explorer and then run the application, you will see that the application automatically gets values from the CSV file and the test runs.

You can also use Excel, Test Case in Team, Foundation Server XML, or SQL Server to get the data source.

For more information, you can refer to `http://bit.ly/XRirt7`.

How to analyze UI tests

When running Coded UI Tests, the application logs a screenshot with some additional items in the `TestResults` folder of the test. If you check the contents of the folder, you will see that there are a few folders that take screenshots of all the times the application is executed. These screenshots are available from Test Explorer when running the test.

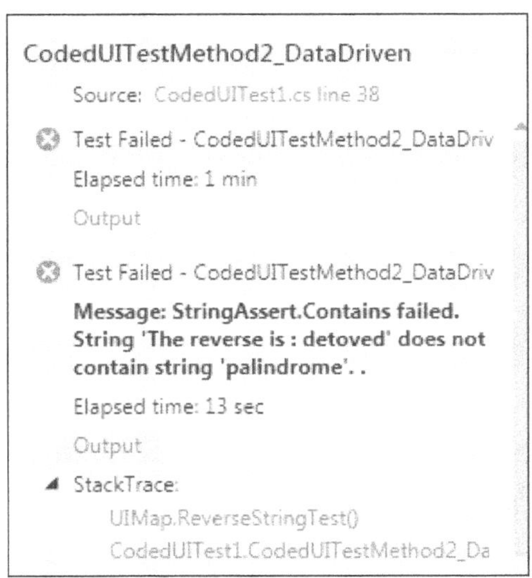

When a test fails in Test Explorer, there is a link that says **Output can be clicked to see the detailed logs available for that particular test**. You will see a screenshot being taken before the test runs.

These logs can be presented in some other format to identify debugging issues. To do this, we need to change `QTAgent32.exe.config`. This is the file that sets the configuration of the Coded UI Logs. The default location of the file is `C:\Program Files (x86)\ Microsoft Visual Studio 12.0\Common7\IDE`.

You can change the value of `EqtTraceLevel` of the file to include more verbose logging. If you set `EqtTraceLevel = 1` or higher, it will produce HTML logfiles too.

If you set `EqtTraceLevel = 3` or higher, screenshots will be taken for each action of the test.

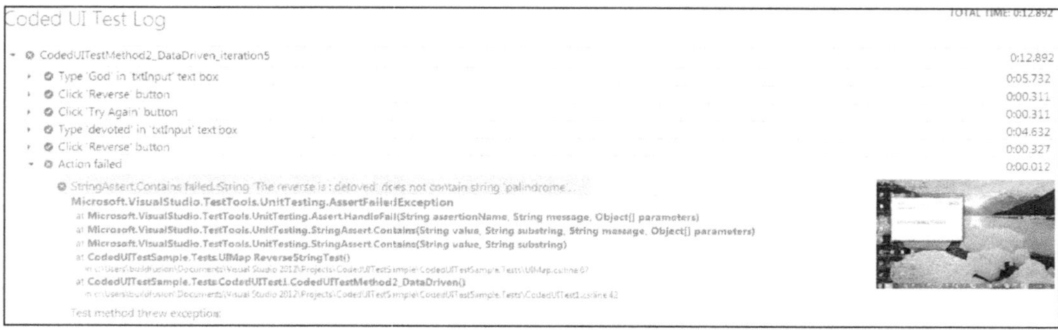

Here, the `EqtTraceLevel` is set to 2 and hence the application will produce HTML logs. If you run the project again, it will show HTML logs for each test.

In the preceding case, the word `devoted` has failed, which is seen in the HTML logs of the test output.

See also

> ▸ To learn more about working with Coded UI Tests in Visual Studio, refer to `http://bit.ly/CodedUITest`

Extending the Visual Studio IDE

In this chapter, we will cover the following recipes:

- Working with T4 templates in Visual Studio
- Working with Managed Extensibility Framework to write editor extensions
- Creating Visual Studio Package for tool windows and editor menus

Introduction

Visual Studio 2013 being the day-to-day tool for many developers gives rich user experiences such that it eases the development and debugging process. We have discussed a lot of functionalities in Visual Studio that enhance the power of the tool and also come in handy while working with code. Some of the features might help in sharing code from the tool itself while some are entirely regarding team activities. However, even though there are so many features prebuilt with the system, the community has always supported more features for advanced users. Visual Studio 2013 provides a wide ecosystem of extensibility so that people who want to customize the feel of Visual Studio can implement an environment of their own, rather than using the existing default environment supported by Visual Studio.

In this chapter, we are going to cover some of the extensibility points that can be used to enhance Visual Studio and also to enhance or customize the overall experience of the IDE best suited for a particular individual or organization.

 Visual Studio Extensibility requires you to install the Visual Studio SDK. The SDK provides a wide range of tools, project templates, and reference assemblies that are required to build extensions in Visual Studio 2013. If you haven't installed the SDK yet, try installing it from `http://www.microsoft.com/en-in/download/details.aspx?id=40758`.

The following are the different ways to build extensions in Visual Studio:

- For a new programming language or a new project system, you can use Visual Studio Package to create an entire package and install it in the client machine

- For applications that require Visual Studio to be integrated, you can use the **Visual Studio Isolated Shell** extensions

- For editor and other components, you can use the **Managed Extensibility Framework** (**MEF**) components to plug in your components to Visual Studio

- You can use **T4 templating** in Visual Studio to help/enhance the code generation in Visual Studio

Working with T4 templates in Visual Studio

Visual Studio supports a number of extension techniques that help in customizing an application or application parts. It is an integrated IDE that provides various ways of tooling, which may often be required by the application developer while creating and/or debugging an application. Many of the features that exist in Visual Studio are merely related to working with Visual Studio or its debugging capabilities. With the versatility of Visual Studio, people use it to develop tools that require two to three lines of .NET code for an application that could spread over one hundred thousand lines of code or even more. People write so much code inside the IDE that many of the IDE features are solely related to writing code in Visual Studio. However, when working with big projects, there are some parts of code that could be automatically generated with a fixed set of data. We often need to rely on external tools that can generate files with source code or write our own. These extensions help in writing iterative code, generating a class from XML/JSON or other data formats, or even writing database-driven classes. Code generation is an important part of day-to-day coding as a large portion of the application may be autogenerated. To customize the code generation process of generating code inside Visual Studio, you have the following two options:

- Write your own customized tool using `ResXFileCodeGenerator` and install it in Visual Studio

- Use T4 templates

We are going to cover T4 templates in this section and create some classes on the fly. Let's take a look at the benefits of T4 templates:

- T4 templates are raw text files (with a `.tt` extension) that can be directly included inside Visual Studio Solutions
- `TextTemplatingFileGenerator` parses the file automatically
- They can work on several project files at a time
- Changes in T4 templates automatically recreates/updates the generated code
- Visual Studio automatically lists the generated file inside the T4 template file
- They can be written in any .NET language (VB.NET or C#)

In this recipe, we are going to create a T4 template inside the Visual Studio IDE and generate some runtime code based on a static XML file.

Getting ready

Although it is worth noting that T4 templates are very easy to write and pretty straightforward, the only catch is to identify the code generation blocks and logic around the generated code. We use a combination of `<#` and `#>` inside a `.tt` file to add logic around a generated file, and directly write the text content to get them printed in the file.

Let's add a console application, for the time being, and a `FirstTemplate.tt` file to the solution. Once the file is added, it will display a warning message, **Running the text template can potentially harm your computer.....** At any time the `.tt` file is saved again, this generation process is executed and the same message is displayed. You can get rid of this warning by clicking on the **Don't show this message** checkbox.

How to do it...

In this recipe, we are going to create a number of classes dynamically from the database by logging in to the SQL Server and getting the schema details such that every table is mapped with a `model` class.

1. Remove all the content from the file and add the following content in place of the first and second lines of the code:

   ```
   <#@ template debug="false" hostspecific="false" language="C#" #>
   <#@ output extension=".cs" #>
   ```

   The first line of the preceding code defines the template header. The template header defines whether the template is created as `hostspecific`. When `hostspecific` turns `true`, you can query through the solution and files. The `hostspecific` flag defines the language that has been used to write the logic. The output defines the output file. The `extension=".cs"` value denotes whether the file that will be generated by the system has a `.cs` extension.

2. As you already know that we can directly write content to the file, let's add some text using it:

```
// This file is autogenerated from the T4 template
// Generated on <# Write(DateTime.Now.ToString()); #>
```

If you save the file now, you will see the generated file that contains the comments with the date of creation.

3. The `Write` and `WriteLine` methods can be used inside `<# -- #>` to write the code in the file. Here, the `Write` method is used to write the content directly in the generated file. You can use `PushIndent` and `PopIndent` to indent your code and use the `Error` and `Warning` methods to indicate an error or a warning message when compiling:

```
<# PushIndent("      "); #>
//The file is created by Abhishek Sur
<# PopIndent(); #>
<# Warning("The application automatically includes all the T4
generated classes."); #>
```

In the preceding code, a `PushIndent` method is invoked, which places `tabstop` in the editor, such that any line created after that will be tabbed accordingly. The `PopIndent` method helps in clearing the indent. Just to show a use case scenario, we added a warning message that will display a message in the **Error** window of the project.

4. Let's now create a database connection and class files for each table where the column names will act as properties:

```
CREATE DATABASE Test
GO

Create Table Country
(
    CountryId NVARCHAR(50) PRIMARY KEY,
    CountryName NVARCHAR(100),
    Capital NVARCHAR(100)
)
GO
CREATE TAble States
(
    StateId      NVARCHAR(50) PRIMARY KEY,
    CountryId    NVARCHAR(50),
    StateName    NVARCHAR(100)
)
```

5. Here, we created a `Test` database with two tables, a country, and states. To create `Table` objects that map with those tables, we create a connection to the database and search `sys.tables` for tables that will be later mapped with a class, and `sys.columns` is used to search the columns present on the table to map the properties. To do such thing, we write the following code:

```
<#@ template debug="false" hostspecific="true" language="C#" #>
<#@ assembly name="System.Core" #>
<#@ assembly name="System.Data" #>
<#@ import namespace="System.Data.SqlClient" #>
<#@ output extension=".cs" #>
// This file is autogenerated from the T4 template
// Generated on <# WriteLine(DateTime.Now.ToString()); #>
<# PushIndent("        "); #>
//The file is created by Abhishek Sur
<# PopIndent(); #>
<# Warning("The application automatically includes all the T4
generated classes."); #>


<#
string connectionstring = "data source=192.168.1.201;Database=Test
;User ID=sa;Password=p@ssword;Trusted_Connection=False;Encrypt=Tru
e;Connection Timeout=30;";
var strcommandText = "select name, object_id from sys.tables where
type = 'U' and name not like 'sys%'";
SqlConnection scon = new SqlConnection(connectionstring);
scon.Open();
SqlCommand scmd = new SqlCommand(strcommandText, scon);
var reader = scmd.ExecuteReader();
while(reader.Read())
{
PushIndent(" ");
string name = reader.GetString(0);
int objectid = reader.GetInt32(1);
WriteLine("public class " + name);
WriteLine("{");
PushIndent(" ");

    string propCmd = "select name from sys.columns where object_id
= " + objectid.ToString();
   SqlConnection pscon = new SqlConnection(connectionstring);
   pscon.Open();
    SqlCommand pscmd = new SqlCommand(propCmd, pscon);
```

```
    var preader = pscmd.ExecuteReader();

  while(preader.Read())
  {
     string pname = preader.GetString(0);
     WriteLine("public string " + pname + " { get; set; }");
  }

  preader.Dispose();

  pscmd.Dispose();
PopIndent();
WriteLine("}");
PopIndent();
}
#>
```

In the preceding code, we imported the `System.Core` and `System.Data` assemblies. The assembly instructions on the header will load the assembly. The import statement imports the `System.Data.SqlClient` namespace. The following screenshot shows how the classes **Country** and **States** are created using the preceding template:

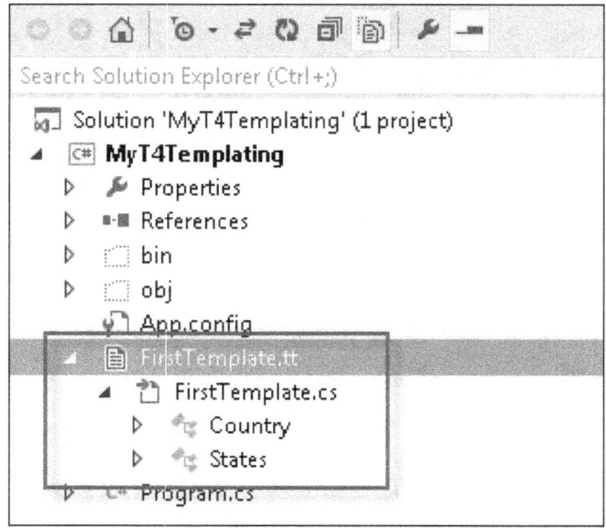

6. We then open a new connection to query the `sys.tables` database where the type is `U`, which indicates the tables in the database, and we neglect the system tables by omitting the tables that start with `sys`. We then open `DataReader` using `ExecuteReader` to recursively call the `sys.tables` and `sys.columns` databases to search for the properties and classes. When you save the `.tt` file, Visual Studio will create two classes, `Country` and `States`, as shown in the following code:

```
// This file is autogenerated from the T4 template
// Generated on 2/10/2014 1:14:36 AM
   //The file is created by Abhishek Sur

   public class Country
   {
      public string CountryId { get; set; }
      public string CountryName { get; set; }
      public string Capital { get; set; }
   }
   public class States
   {
      public string StateId { get; set; }
      public string CountryId { get; set; }
      public string StateName { get; set; }
   }
```

Now, you can use the preceding code to create the table objects directly within your project without rewriting the same schema repeatedly.

7. You can now go ahead and change the class definitions according to your requirements, such as adding a constructor to the class, adding additional methods, and creating base classes.

How it works...

The architecture of a T4 template is very simple. Every line of code that you write in a T4 template automatically inherits from a `Template` class, which has a `TransformText` method that allows you to convert the text into a valid output file.

Every T4 environment maintains a `StringBuilder` object, which acts as a writer to write lines in the output files. The `<# -- #>` combination is used to invoke the `Write` operation in the T4 template. The `StringBuilder` object can be referenced anywhere using `this.GenerationEnvironment` inside the T4 template file. The `GenerationEnvironment` property will allow you to get the content already written in the output file using the tool. When you save the `.tt` file, Visual Studio automatically calls the `TransformText` method, which writes the output data to the file.

In the preceding recipe, we made a connection to the database to get the schema and created the classes that could map the schema using normal ADO.NET classes.

There's more...

Even though we understand the basics of T4 templates, let's consider some more complex scenarios that we generally come across while creating templates.

Creating multiple output files using T4 templates

T4 templates generally support a single output file, so whatever you write in the templates is copied into a single output file. This makes the T4 templating system unusable as most of the time we may be required to create multiple files and add them to the solution.

As I have already explained that you can use `GenerationEnvironment` to get a reference to the already written text on the buffer, you can use a normal file writer object to write the files to the location:

```
<#@ template debug="false" hostspecific="true" language="C#" #>
<#@ import namespace="System.IO" #>
<#@ output extension=".txt" #>
<#
string templateDirectory = Path.GetDirectoryName(Host.TemplateFile);
string outputFilePath = Path.Combine(templateDirectory, "1.txt");
Write("This goes to file1");
File.WriteAllText(outputFilePath, this.GenerationEnvironment.
ToString());

this.GenerationEnvironment.Clear();

outputFilePath = Path.Combine(templateDirectory, "2.txt");
Write("This goes to file2");
File.WriteAllText(outputFilePath, this.GenerationEnvironment.
ToString());
#>
```

The preceding code uses `Host.TemplateFile` to get the directory location path, where the template file exists and write files directly in the same folder. The `File.WriteAllText` method writes all the output text to the output files `1.txt` and `2.txt`. Once all the file content is written, we need to remove the content by calling `Clear` on the `StringBuilder` object.

To use the `Host` object, you need to make the `hostspecific` flag in the `Template` header `true`.

After saving the preceding code, if you look at the **Solution Explorer** pane, as shown in the following screenshot, you will see that two files `1.txt` and `2.txt` have been created, but the problem is that they are not included in the solution:

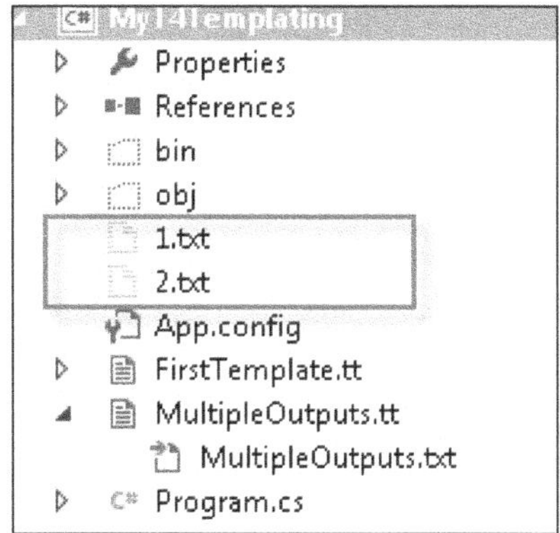

Now to include the file in the solution, we need to use multiple template files so that we can pass a parameter to a template file to write the content repeatedly. Thus, the files are generated from another template each time with a new filename.

Let's create a template file, name it `FileManager.tt`, and add the following code to it:

```
<#@ template debug="false" hostspecific="true" language="C#" #>
<#@ import namespace="System.IO" #>
<#@ output extension=".txt" #>
<#+
void CreateFile(string fileName)
{
    string templateDirectory = Path.GetDirectoryName(Host.
TemplateFile);
    string outputFilePath = Path.Combine(templateDirectory, fileName);
    File.WriteAllText(outputFilePath, this.GenerationEnvironment.
ToString());
    this.GenerationEnvironment.Clear();
}
#>
```

The preceding code looks exactly the same as before. We just created a file with the `helper` method. The `CreateFile` function takes a filename as the input, writes the `GenerationEnvironment` property buffer to the file, and clears the content after writing it.

It is worth noting that `<# -- #>` is used to write content directly to the output file or `<#= -- #>` to write a single line, while `<#+ -- #>` is used to list the helper methods. These short keywords can be ignored using `\` (backslash). Thus, if you want to write `<#` as the content, you can do so by using the `\<#` or `\#>` syntaxes.

Now to include the file in the project, we need to use the EnvDTE objects for the host project. Let's add the EnvDTE assembly and other Visual Studio Interop assemblies, as shown in the following code:

```
<#@ assembly name="System.Xml" #>
<#@ assembly name="EnvDTE" #>
<#@ assembly name="Microsoft.VisualStudio.OLE.Interop" #>
<#@ assembly name="Microsoft.VisualStudio.Shell" #>
<#@ assembly name="Microsoft.VisualStudio.Shell.Interop" #>
<#@ assembly name="Microsoft.VisualStudio.Shell.Interop.8.0" #>
<#@ import namespace="System.Collections.Generic" #>
<#@ import namespace="System.Diagnostics" #>
<#@ import namespace="System.IO" #>
<#@ import namespace="System.Text" #>
<#@ import namespace="System.Xml" #>
<#@ import namespace="Microsoft.VisualStudio.Shell" #>
<#@ import namespace="Microsoft.VisualStudio.Shell.Interop" #>
<#@ import namespace="Microsoft.VisualStudio.TextTempating" #>
```

The following assemblies and imports are added to `FileManager.tt`. Then, we add two lines at the end of the `CreateFile` method, as shown in the following code:

```
void CreateFile(string fileName)
{
    string templateDirectory = Path.GetDirectoryName(Host.
TemplateFile);
    string outputFilePath = Path.Combine(templateDirectory, fileName);
    File.WriteAllText(outputFilePath, this.GenerationEnvironment.
ToString());
    this.GenerationEnvironment.Clear();
    EnvDTE.ProjectItem templateProjectItem = __
getTemplateProjectItem();
    templateProjectItem.ProjectItems.AddFromFile(outputFilePath);
}
```

Here, we create the `ProjectItem` object for the currently created file and write the following file inside the project:

```
IServiceProvider hostServiceProvider = (IServiceProvider)Host;
EnvDTE.DTE dte = (EnvDTE.DTE)hostServiceProvider.
GetService(typeof(EnvDTE.DTE));
```

The `hostService` method is used to get the `ItempContext` DTE service and add the file to the project. We have used the article from `http://www.codeproject.com/Articles/16515/Creating-a-Custom-Tool-to-Generate-Multiple-Files` for reference.

The `__getTemplateProjectItem()` method is a method that creates the DTE `ProjectItem` object for a particular project and returns the object reference. Once the `ProjectItem` object is created, we can use a `AddFromFile` method to add the item to the project.

Now to test the file, let's add a new template and include the preceding file in the project:

```
<#@ template debug="false" hostspecific="true" language="C#" #>
<#@ output extension=".txt" #>
<#@ include file="FileManager.tt" #>

<#
    Write("File1");
    CreateFile("1.txt");
    Write("File2");
    CreateFile("2.txt");
#>
```

The preceding code creates two files and adds them to the project. This can be verified from the following screenshot:

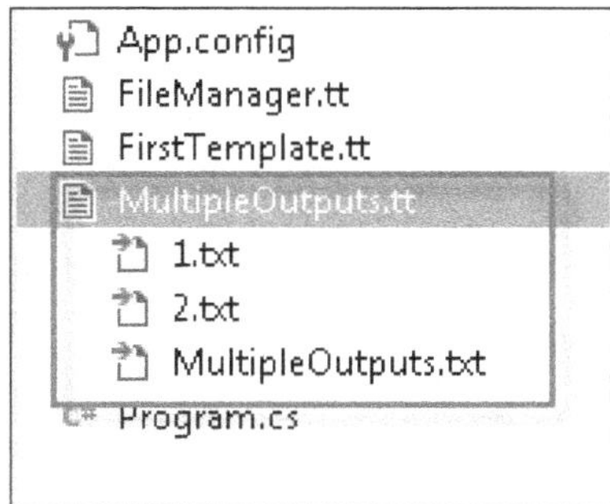

In the preceding screenshot, you can see the files that are already added to the **Solution Explorer** pane and even listed inside the template file.

The `__getTemplateProjectItem()` method can be found inside the source code `FileManager.tt` in the `MyT4Templating` project source.

Optimizing code generation using T4 templates and its easy syntaxes

As you are already habituated with T4 templates, let me show you another example to demonstrate the power of the templating code generation. Let's take a look at the following code:

```
<#
    var logVariants = new []
        {
            new { Variant = "Bright"    , Color = "White"    },
            new { Variant = "Normal"    , Color = "Gray"     },
            new { Variant = "Url"       , Color = "Cyan"     },
        };
#>
    using System;

     static partial class MyLogClass
      {
<#
    foreach (var logVariant in logVariants)
    {
#>
        static void Write<#=logVariant.Variant#>Line (string message)
        {
            var color = Console.ForegroundColor;
            Console.ForegroundColor = ConsoleColor.<#=logVariant.
Color#>;
            try
            {
                Console.WriteLine (message ?? "");
            }
            finally
            {
                Console.ForegroundColor = color;
            }
        }

<#
    }
#>

    }
```

You can see that the template generates a `Variant` method directly inside the code. The variants are created as an array while the methods are created on the fly such that each method will have a separate color to write on the console.

The important thing to understand here is how the code is laid out. You can see that rather than using the template methods `Write` or `WriteLine`, we can directly write content to the file outside the `<#` and `#>` tags such that the data is written directly to the file.

See also

> ▸ You can read more about T4 templates from the official blog at `http://bit.ly/msdnt4`. Visual Studio does not provide features such as Syntax Highlighting and IntelliSense for T4 editors.

> ▸ You can install the Devart T4 editor from `http://bit.ly/t4editor`.

Working with Managed Extensibility Framework to write editor extensions

Visual Studio uses Managed Extensibility Framework (MEF) to extend most of the code instead of writing `VSPackage`. MEF is an extensibility framework built inside the framework to support the plugin function of the application. The plugin model has been used by the IDE itself to ensure that we can hook in some of the code inside the IDE as an MEF component so that when the IDE loads up, it can compose elements directly as extensions.

Before we get started with MEF, let's try to understand what it is and how it works.

MEF is a framework that is built on top of the reflection API that addresses one special kind of requirement, which most of the current developers are into. Modularizing an application is one of the biggest concerns for any software giant. When we try to implement a pluggable model, we generally look for some sort of a plugin-based modularization for our respective application and ultimately end up doing in the same way we did before. Finally, this does not solve the problem as someone else might end up doing the same thing in a different manner and eventually we may face a "my plugins cannot go into your application" kind of a situation. Hence, we need some sort of standardization to address this situation such that every plugin-based application can work together. MEF addresses this situation by giving you a sleek way to define your modules as plugins and your application as a standard host for any plugins.

MEF allows defining imports and exports for classes such that it can allow you to plug-in classes to import the host automatically. Visual Studio has defined a number of imports as hooks inside the IDE, while you need to write their corresponding exports inside the plugin to hook into it.

You can read a lot more about MEF from the posts at `http://bit.ly/mefch6` and `http://bit.ly/meftipch6`.

In this recipe, we will create an editor extension using MEF to plug in our code inside Visual Studio Editor.

The Visual Studio Editor UI is built using **Windows Presentation Foundation** (**WPF**), which provides a rich visual experience and consistent programming model that separates the presentation layer with the business logic.

Getting ready

There are a number of editor extension points that you can use to extend the editor. A few of them are as follows:

- Content types
- Classification types and formats
- Margins and scrollbars
- Tags
- Adornments
- Mouse processors
- Drop handlers
- Options
- IntelliSense

These extensions can be handled using MEF. In this recipe, we will be extending the editor using the MEF endpoint to show how this works inside the IDE. To do this, you need to install the Visual Studio SDK from `http://bit.ly/vssdk`.

Once the SDK is installed, Open Visual Studio and click on **Extensibility**. There are a number of project templates that you will see, as shown in the following screenshot:

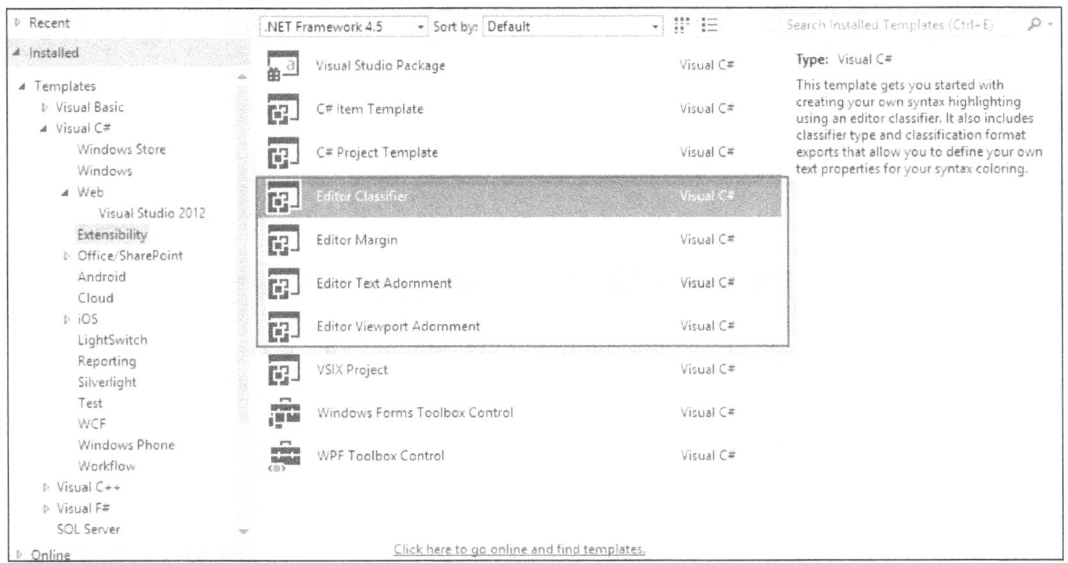

In the preceding screenshot, you can see **C# Item Template**, **Project Template packages**, **The Visual Studio Package**, and some of the editor extensions too. The **Editor Classifier**, **Editor Margins**, **Editor Text Adornment**, and **Editor Viewport Adornment** extensions are the project types that are associated with MEF extensibility.

In this recipe, we are going to create a statement completion extension, which is triggered when certain characters are typed inside the IDE like the one you see in IntelliSense. This recipe will show you how to implement a statement completion for a hardcoded set of strings appearing in the IntelliSense menu.

How to do it...

Now, let's build an editor classifier using MEF to see how it behaves inside the IDE:

1. Create a project with **Editor Classifier** and name it `StatementCompletionAdorner`.

2. Open the VSIX manifest file and check whether the `Microsoft.VisualStudio.MEF` component is added as a content type in the **Asset** section. Add your name as the publisher, and then save and close the file. Delete all the existing files created and add the following references:

    - `Microsoft.VisualStudio.Editor`

    - `Microsoft.VisualStudio.Language.IntelliSense`

    - `Microsoft.VisualStiudio.Shell.12.0`

- `Microsoft.VisualStudio.Shell.Immutable.10.0`

- `Microsoft.VisualStudio.OLE.Interop`

- `Microsoft.VisualStudio.TextManager.Interop`

Once the references are added, we can start creating the project. You can find the files in the `C:\Program Files (x86)\Microsoft Visual Studio 12.0\VSSDK\VisualStudioIntegration\Common\Assemblies\v4.0\` folder.

3. Now to create the completion IntelliSense editor, we need to implement the following four components:

    - `CompletionSource`: This class is responsible for collecting the identifiers that you type into the IDE and creating the content for the **Completion** window. We use a static source for our completion texts for the time being.

    - `CompletionSourceProvider`: This is an MEF component that instantiates the `Source` class.

    - `CommandHandler`: This is the main command completion handler, which is implemented from `IOleCommandTarget` and can trigger, commit, or dismiss the process.

    - `CommandHandlerProvider`: This is an MEF component that instantiates the `CommandHandler` interface.

So, basically, there are two classes: one to create the identifier component and one to handle keystrokes over the `CompletionSource` class.

4. Now, let's add the `CompletionSource` class to the project. This class should implement the `IComletionSource` interface. The `AugmentCompletionSession` method allows you to create `completionSets` and add a `ITrackingSpan` element directly in the current caret's position, as shown in the following code:

```
private CompletionSourceProvider sourceProvider;
        private ITextBuffer txtBuffer;
        private List<Completion> lstCompletion;
public CompletionSource(CompletionSourceProvider sourceProvider,
ITextBuffer textBuffer)
{
    this.sourceProvider = sourceProvider;
    this.txtBuffer = textBuffer;
}
void ICompletionSource.AugmentCompletionSession(ICompletionSession
session, IList<CompletionSet> completionSets)
{
    List<string> elList = new List<string> { ".NET", ".COM",
"Microsoft", "PacktPub", "Visual Studio", "Managed Extensibility
Framework",
```

```
                    "Windows Presentation Foundation", "Packt
    Publications"};     lstCompletion = new List<Completion>();
        foreach (string el in elList)
            lstCompletion.Add(new Completion(el, el, el, null, null));

        completionSets.Add(new CompletionSet(
            "Tokens",
            "Tokens",
            FindTokenSpanAtPosition(session.
    GetTriggerPoint(txtBuffer), session),
            lstCompletion,
            null));
    }
    private ITrackingSpan FindTokenSpanAtPosition(ITrackingPoint
    point, ICompletionSession session)
    {
        SnapshotPoint currentPoint = (session.TextView.Caret.Position.
    BufferPosition) - 1;
        ITextStructureNavigator navigator = sourceProvider.
    NavigatorService.GetTextStructureNavigator(txtBuffer);
        TextExtent extent = navigator.GetExtentOfWord(currentPoint);
        return currentPoint.Snapshot.CreateTrackingSpan(extent.Span,
    SpanTrackingMode.EdgeInclusive);
    }
```

In the preceding code, we can see that we implemented the
`AugmentCompletionSession` method of the interface `ICompletionSource`,
so that we can handle the tokens. We have used a standalone token list and added
it to the `CompletionSource` class. Once the `CompletionSet` class is created,
we add that to `completionSets` passed into the method just next to the caret's
position. The `FindTokenSpanAtPosition` method will create a `TextExtent`
class just next to the caret to show a menu of options to the user.

5. The `CompletionHandler` class, on the other hand, helps in adding the handler,
   which will run when the `CompletionSource` class is picked or dismissed by the
   user. Let's now add a class called `CompletionCommandHandler` and implement
   it from `IOleCommandTarget`. The two methods that need to be implemented are
   `QueryStatus` and `Exec` respectively, where the `Exec` method is the method that
   actually processes the request. Let's see what the `Exec` method looks like:

```
public int Exec(ref Guid pguidCmdGroup, uint nCmdID, uint
nCmdexecopt, IntPtr pvaIn, IntPtr pvaOut)
{
    if (VsShellUtilities.IsInAutomationFunction(handlerProvider.
ServiceProvider))
    {
```

```csharp
            return nextCommandHandler.Exec(ref pguidCmdGroup, nCmdID,
nCmdexecopt, pvaIn, pvaOut);
        }


    uint commandID = nCmdID;
    char typedChar = char.MinValue;
    if (pguidCmdGroup == VSConstants.VSStd2K && nCmdID == (uint)
VSConstants.VSStd2KCmdID.TYPECHAR)
    {
        typedChar = (char)(ushort)Marshal.GetObjectForNativeVarian
t(pvaIn);
    }
    if (nCmdID == (uint)VSConstants.VSStd2KCmdID.RETURN
        || nCmdID == (uint)VSConstants.VSStd2KCmdID.TAB
        || (char.IsWhiteSpace(typedChar) || char.
IsPunctuation(typedChar)))
    {
        if (completionSession != null && !completionSession.
IsDismissed)
        {
            if (completionSession.SelectedCompletionSet.
SelectionStatus.IsSelected)
            {
                completionSession.Commit();
                return VSConstants.S_OK;
            }
            else
            {
                completionSession.Dismiss();
            }
        }
    }


    int retVal = nextCommandHandler.Exec(ref pguidCmdGroup,
nCmdID, nCmdexecopt, pvaIn, pvaOut);
    bool handled = false;
    if (!typedChar.Equals(char.MinValue) && char.
IsLetterOrDigit(typedChar))
    {
        if (completionSession == null || completionSession.
IsDismissed)
        {
            this.TriggerCompletion();
            completionSession.Filter();
        }
        else
        {
```

```
            completionSession.Filter();
        }
        handled = true;
    }
    else if (commandID == (uint)VSConstants.VSStd2KCmdID.BACKSPACE
        || commandID == (uint)VSConstants.VSStd2KCmdID.DELETE)
    {
        if (completionSession != null && !completionSession.
IsDismissed)
            completionSession.Filter();
        handled = true;
    }
    if (handled) return VSConstants.S_OK;
    return retVal;
}
```

The preceding code first checks the input to be a character before handling it. Once it ensures that it has received a character, it checks whether it is due to a return key hit, a *Tab* press, a white space, or a punctuation mark. If this is the case, it will treat as a `Commit` operation. It commits the `selectedStatus` class and statements. On the other hand, if the command is `Backspace` or `Delete`, it will redo the filter. The commit on `completionSession` inserts the text into the buffer, and ultimately when closing the IntelliSense menu, it will pick the element. The `Dismiss` operation, on the other hand, will unpick the element and dismiss the IntelliSense menu or the presenter to be destroyed.

6. The `TriggerCompletion` method creates a dismissal on the current IntelliSense menu for the current caret's position, which is invoked when something outside the range is typed in:

```
private bool TriggerCompletion()
{
    //the caret must be in a non-projection location
    SnapshotPoint? caretPoint =
    txtView.Caret.Position.Point.GetPoint(
    textBuffer => (!textBuffer.ContentType.
IsOfType("projection")), PositionAffinity.Predecessor);
    if (!caretPoint.HasValue)
    {
        return false;
    }

    completionSession = handlerProvider.CompletionBroker.
CreateCompletionSession
    (txtView,
```

```
            caretPoint.Value.Snapshot.CreateTrackingPoint(caretPoint.
        Value.Position, PointTrackingMode.Positive),
            true);

        //subscribe to the Dismissed event on the session
        completionSession.Dismissed += this.OnSessionDismissed;
        completionSession.Start();

        return true;
    }
```

The preceding code retrieves `currentCompletionSession` and calls its `Start` method, which will invoke the completion and ultimately the dismissal of the menu.

7. To implement the providers, we first export the `ICompletionSourceProvider` class that we need to be created as an MEF composable component, as shown in the following code:

```
[Export(typeof(ICompletionSourceProvider))]
[ContentType("plaintext")]
[Name("token completion")]
public class CompletionSourceProvider : ICompletionSourceProvider
{
    [Import]
    internal ITextStructureNavigatorSelectorService
NavigatorService { get; set; }
    public ICompletionSource TryCreateCompletionSource(ITextBuffer
textBuffer)
    {
        return new CompletionSource(this, textBuffer);
    }
}
```

In the preceding code, the `CompletionSourceProvider` class is implemented from `ICompeletionSource`. The `Export` attribute on the header exports the component to the corresponding import defined inside Visual Studio. You might have also noticed that the `ICompletionSource` class has a `TryCreateCompletionSource` method, which needs to return the `CompletionSource` object. The `ContentType` property is defined as plain text, thus the completion will work on text files.

8. Similar to `ICompletionSourceProvider`, there is another export that we need to implement, which can connect `CompletionHandler`. Let's create a `CompletionHandlerProvider` class and type in the following content:

```
[Export(typeof(IVsTextViewCreationListener))]
[Name("token completion handler")]
```

```
[ContentType("plaintext")]
[TextViewRole(PredefinedTextViewRoles.Editable)]
public class CompletionHandlerProvider :
IVsTextViewCreationListener
{
    [Import]
    internal IVsEditorAdaptersFactoryService AdapterService =
null;
    [Import]
    internal ICompletionBroker CompletionBroker { get; set; }
    [Import]
    internal SVsServiceProvider ServiceProvider { get; set; }
    public void VsTextViewCreated(IVsTextView textViewAdapter)
    {
        ITextView textView = AdapterService.GetWpfTextView(textVie
wAdapter);
        if (textView == null)
            return;

        Func<CompletionCommandHandler> createCommandHandler =
delegate() { return new CompletionCommandHandler(textViewAdapter,
textView, this); };
        textView.Properties.GetOrCreateSingletonProperty(createCom
mandHandler);
    }
}
```

9. The preceding code implements `IVsTextViewCreationListener`, which will allow you to listen to the keystrokes pressed in the IDE. The `VSTextViewCreated` method will be called whenever the `TextViewCompletionSource` class is created. We add a delegate to `textView` such that the handler gets called whenever a key is pressed. Here, the export will be mapped to the appropriate import inside Visual Studio and your code will be called.

10. Now, let's compile the code and see if there are any problems. When everything is successful, you can run the code to open Visual Studio Experimental Instance (We intentionally selected the black theme here). Open a text file and type M; it will list **Microsoft** and **Managed Extensibility Framework**. You can start typing to filter the content or press *Enter, Tab, Space bar*, or any punctuation to select the content.

In the following screenshot, you can see that when we first pressed M, it opens the IntelliSense menu in the text file, where we can either choose the option or continue typing:

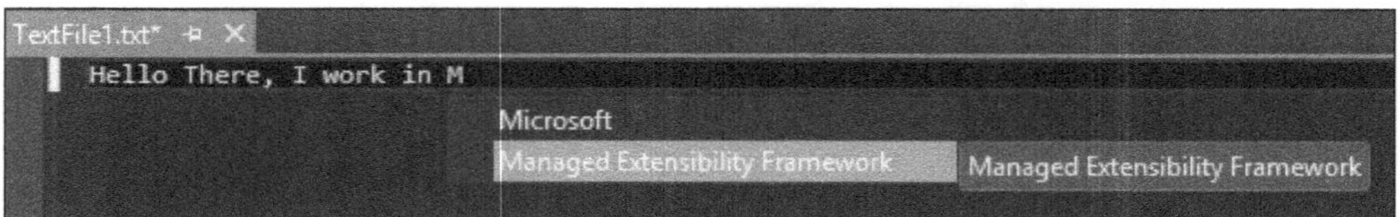

How it works...

Visual Studio Editor is built using WPF such that the model and the UI remain separated. It also extensively uses MEF to control plugins or extensions to it. The various interfaces that are built into it allows the developer to export their respective logic in the form of classes, such that it seamlessly plugs in to the IDE.

The preceding code adds a key listener to the `PlainText` content type IDE editor, so whenever something is typed in, certain words pop up in the menu, which could be either picked in or continued typing in.

The `ICompletionSource` interface works on data blocks where you provide the dictionary of texts as `CompletionSet`, and the `IOleCommandTarget` interface provides the command to target for. The objects are exported using `ICompletionSourceProvider` and `IVsTextViewCreationListener`. The listener allows you to hook the handler, which needs to be executed when a certain key is pressed on the editor.

There's more...

Building Editor Extension is a vast topic. There are a lot of hooks that you could use to implement extensions to Visual Studio. Let's look at some more examples in this section.

Creating a SmartTag extender using MEF

Smart tags are a common way of providing additional options for text inside the IDE. There are a lot of endpoints that can handle the smart tags so that you can define some additional options to the text. Some classes that are worth noting to define a smart tag are `ITagger`, `SmartTags`, `TagProvider`, and `SmartTagActions`. Let's create a project and name it `SmartTaggingText`.

Create a class and implement it from `SmartTag`. We add a constructor to pass `ActionSet`. It is important to note that `SmartTagType` is factoid when a blue line appears and ephemeral when a red line appears on the IDE:

```
public class SmartTagText : SmartTag
{
    public SmartTagText(ReadOnlyCollection<SmartTagActionSet>
actionSets) :
        base(SmartTagType.Factoid, actionSets) { }
}
```

We defined `SmartTag` as `Factoid` so it will allow us to open the smart tag even though the word is not complete.

Let's create another class and implement it from `ITagger`, as shown in the following code:

```
public class SmartTaggerText : ITagger<SmartTagText>
    {
public IEnumerable<ITagSpan<SmartTagText>> GetTags(NormalizedSnapshotS
panCollection spans)
        {
            ITextSnapshot snapshot = buffer.CurrentSnapshot;
            if (snapshot.Length == 0)
                yield break;
            ITextStructureNavigator navigator = provider.
NavigatorService.GetTextStructureNavigator(buffer);

            foreach (var span in spans)
            {
                ITextCaret caret = view.Caret;
                SnapshotPoint point;

                if (caret.Position.BufferPosition > 0)
                    point = caret.Position.BufferPosition - 1;
                else
                    yield break;

                TextExtent extent = navigator.GetExtentOfWord(point);
                if (extent.IsSignificant)
                    yield return new TagSpan<SmartTagText>(extent.
Span, new SmartTagText(GetSmartTagActions(extent.Span)));
                else yield break;
            }
        }

        private ReadOnlyCollection<SmartTagActionSet>
GetSmartTagActions(SnapshotSpan span)
        {
```

```
            List<SmartTagActionSet> actionSetList = new
List<SmartTagActionSet>();
            List<ISmartTagAction> actionList = new
List<ISmartTagAction>();

            ITrackingSpan trackingSpan = span.Snapshot.
CreateTrackingSpan(span, SpanTrackingMode.EdgeInclusive);
            actionList.Add(new UpperCaseSmartTagAction(trackingSpan));
            actionList.Add(new LowerCaseSmartTagAction(trackingSpan));
            SmartTagActionSet actionSet = new
SmartTagActionSet(actionList.AsReadOnly());
            actionSetList.Add(actionSet);
            return actionSetList.AsReadOnly();
        }
    }
```

In the preceding code, we have created Smart Tags. The `GetTags` function will be automatically called when the blue arrow for the smart tag is hit on the editor and the menu is opened. We created `SmartTags` for the current text using `GetSmartTagAction`. Based on the current text, we can also create actions here.

The actions are classes derived from `ISmartTagAction`, which have an `Invoke` method. The `Invoke` method is called when an action is chosen from the list:

```
public class LowerCaseSmartTagAction : ISmartTagAction
    {
public LowerCaseSmartTagAction(ITrackingSpan span)
        {
            this.span = span;
            tsnapshot = span.TextBuffer.CurrentSnapshot;
            lower = span.GetText(tsnapshot).ToLower();
            display = "Convert to lower case";
        }
public void Invoke()
        {
            span.TextBuffer.Replace(span.GetSpan(tsnapshot), lower);
        }
    }
```

Here, the text that has been passed to `SmartTagAction` is changed to lowercase. Finally, to hook `SmartTag` to the IDE, we need a provider. The `IViewTaggerProvider` interface allows you to export the type to the IDE as `SmartTagger`. Let's see the following code:

```
[Export(typeof(IViewTaggerProvider))]
    [ContentType("plaintext")]
    [Order(Before = "default")]
```

```csharp
    [TagType(typeof(SmartTag))]
    public class SmartTaggerProviderText : IViewTaggerProvider
    {
        [Import(typeof(ITextStructureNavigatorSelectorService))]
        internal ITextStructureNavigatorSelectorService
NavigatorService { get; set; }

        public ITagger<T> CreateTagger<T>(ITextView textView,
ITextBuffer buffer) where T : ITag
        {
            if (buffer == null || textView == null)
            {
                return null;
            }

            //make sure we are tagging only the top buffer
            if (buffer == textView.TextBuffer)
            {
                return new SmartTaggerText(buffer, textView, this) as
ITagger<T>;
            }
            else return null;
        }
    }
```

In the preceding code, the `CreateTagger` method checks whether the `TextBuffer` class has data and based on `CreateTagger` creates an object of `SmartTaggerText` with the buffer value. The object is exported to the `IViewTaggerProvider` import and defined within the IDE. Thus, we do not need to handle anything manually.

When you run the project and type something in the text editor on the experimental instance of Visual Studio, a blue line appears on the first character. When it is clicked, you will see the tagger, as shown in the following code:

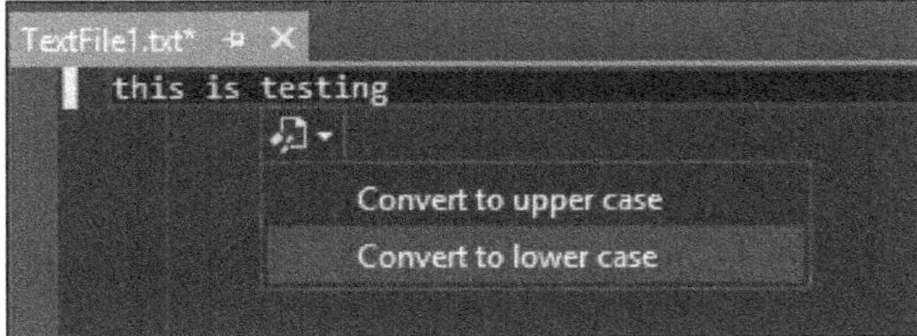

The tagger allows you to change the case of the underlying text.

Creating Visual Studio Package for tool windows and editor menus

Sometimes when the requirements are too high and not related to the editor itself, there is also an option to create a Visual Studio Package for the project. The Visual Studio Package project creates a basic `VSPackage`. The template has the written code ready to implement a `MenuItem` class or a tool window.

 As we already know that the editor is built using WPF, we also need to know the basics of WPF to implement the tool window inside the IDE.

Getting ready

Open Visual Studio and create a project from Visual Studio Package. Visual Studio Package is a complete installation of Visual Studio, which is signed with a valid key. We name the project `VSPackageSample`.

Once you select the project type, you will be provided with a wizard, as shown in the following screenshot:

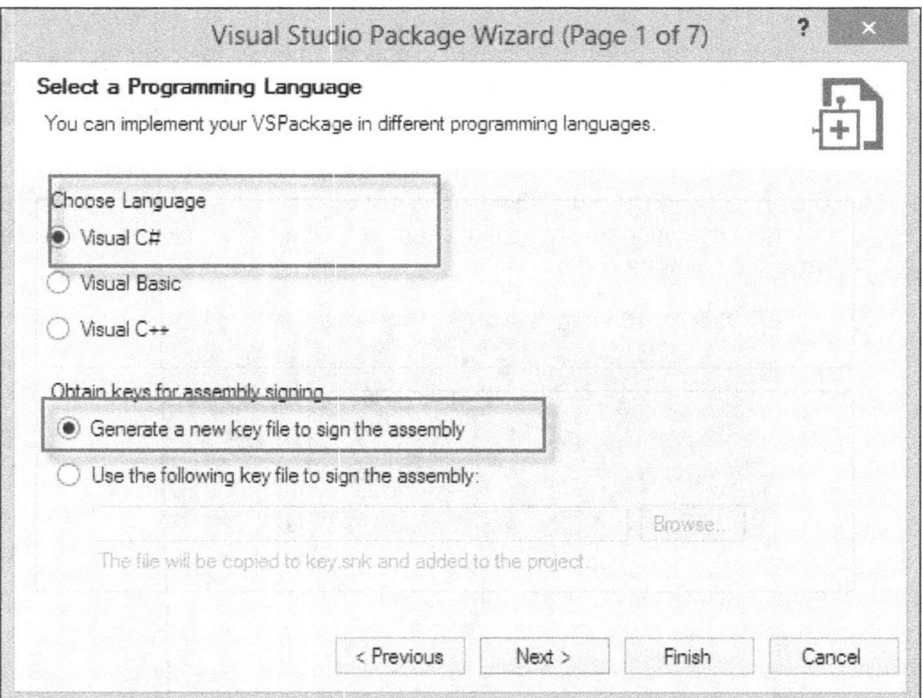

As we know, the Visual Studio Package is a complete install for Visual Studio, so it needs a singing assembly. We choose **Generate a new key file to sign the assembly** to move forward. You can even select a key for yourself using the **Use the following key file** option, as shown in the following screenshot:

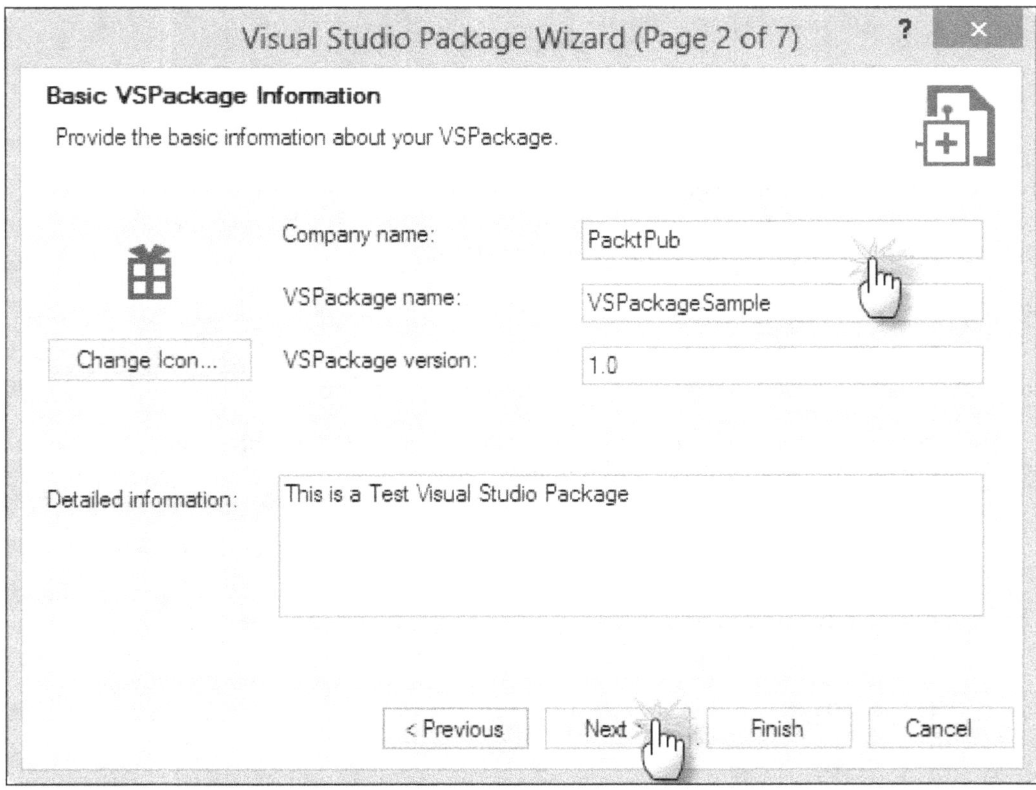

The next screenshot asks for the company name and basic package configuration. You can pick the icon here for the project and also provide a detailed description.

Here, we also need to choose what type of extensions we want to include.

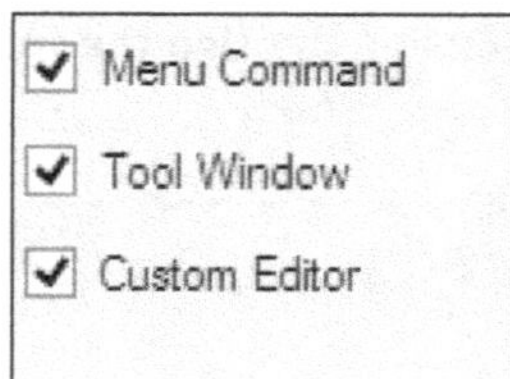

There are three options. One is **Menu Command**, which will add a menu to the tools menu and can be invoked to call a method you specify. You can also choose **Tool Window** to open a window and **Custom Editor** to edit something inside the IDE. The tool window is a WPF control, while the custom editor is Windows Forms Control.

How to do it...

Now, let's create a `VSPackage` extension to implement such an editor:

1. After you finish the wizard, the entire project is created. There are a number of files to work on. The very entry point of the project is the `VSPackageSamplePackage.cs` file. Open the file and you will see a class that inherits from the `Package` class.

2. In the **Package Members** section, you will see how the menu and the command are initialized:

```
// Add our command handlers for menu (commands must exist in the
.vsct file)
OleMenuCommandService mcs = GetService(typeof(IMenuCommandServi
ce)) as OleMenuCommandService;
if ( null != mcs )
{
    // Create the command for the menu item.
    CommandID menuCommandID = new CommandID(GuidList.
guidVSPackageSampleCmdSet, (int)PkgCmdIDList.cmdidMyCommand);
    MenuCommand menuItem = new MenuCommand(MenuItemCallback,
menuCommandID );
    mcs.AddCommand( menuItem );
    // Create the command for the tool window
    CommandID toolwndCommandID = new CommandID(GuidList.
guidVSPackageSampleCmdSet, (int)PkgCmdIDList.cmdidMyTool);
    MenuCommand menuToolWin = new MenuCommand(ShowToolWindow,
toolwndCommandID);
    mcs.AddCommand( menuToolWin );
}
```

In the preceding code, a `MenuCommand` class is created for `menuItem` and `ToolWindow`. Both are added to the `OleMenuCommandService` class. The `MenuCommandService` class lets you define the menu for the commands.

3. When the menu is clicked, `ShellMessage` is invoked to show `MessageBox` on the IDE. The menu will appear in the **Tools** menu. The `MenuItemCallback` class uses `uiShell.ShowMessageBox` to show the message:

```
Microsoft.VisualStudio.ErrorHandler.ThrowOnFailure(uiShell.
ShowMessageBox(
                    0,
                    ref clsid,
                    "VSPackageSample",
                    string.Format(CultureInfo.CurrentCulture,
"Inside {0}.MenuItemCallback()", this.ToString()),
                    string.Empty,
                    0,
                    OLEMSGBUTTON.OLEMSGBUTTON_OK,
                    OLEMSGDEFBUTTON.OLEMSGDEFBUTTON_FIRST,
                    OLEMSGICON.OLEMSGICON_INFO,
                    0,          // false
                    out result));
```

You can write your custom code to invoke selection of the menu.

4. On the contrary, `ToolWindow` opens up the `MyControl.xaml` file. You can design `ToolWindow` using XAML and show the content directly inside Visual Studio:

```
ToolWindowPane window = this.FindToolWindow(typeof(MyToolWindow),
0, true);
                if ((null == window) || (null == window.Frame))
                {
                    throw new NotSupportedException(Resources.
CanNotCreateWindow);
                }
                IVsWindowFrame windowFrame = (IVsWindowFrame)window.
Frame;
                Microsoft.VisualStudio.ErrorHandler.
ThrowOnFailure(windowFrame.Show());
```

The window frame is created and the control gets loaded inside the frame to ensure there is a consistent feel to the IDE.

5. Open the `MyControl.xaml` file and you will see a button placed inside the IDE, so that when the control is invoked, `MessageBox` will be shown. You can open `ToolWindow` by navigating to **View | OtherWindow | CommandExplorer**.

The window currently does nothing. It has a button, which can be clicked to open a `MessageBox`.

6. There are some additional files such as `EditorFactory`. This is the main editor class that handles the instance creation and destruction of the editor. The `EditorFactory` class is registered to the extension and automatically called whenever any component of the editor is called.

7. Finally, when your package is built successfully, you can double-click on the `vsix` file on the debug screen to run and install the extension to Visual Studio.

How it works...

The VS Package is the main packager for Visual Studio extensions. Visual Studio packager allows you to add UI elements to the IDE to provide a better experience for the user. You can deploy any package, either distributing manually or through the Visual Studio gallery, such that developers can download and use the extension that you have created.

The main criterion for the package to execute is written inside the `VSPackageSamplePackage` file. Here, the `ProvideToolWindow` function registers the extension tool window for the package. The `EditorFactory` class is registered for additional extension components and the `VSPackageSamplePackage` class itself creates the menu items.

After you compile the project, a VSIX file gets created. This file is nothing but a zipped archive with all the deployable components. Rename the file to a `.zip` extension, and you will see the following content:

The `pkgdef` file is the package definition file, which stores all the metadata associated with the extension. The `extension.manifest` file is the manifest file for the extension. The manifest file includes the name of the extension, details, description, and so on. The main code is compiled as a `.dll` file, which represents the actual extension.

The Visual Studio extensions can be deployed and/or uploaded directly to the Visual Studio gallery at `http://visualstudiogallery.msdn.microsoft.com/`.

7
Understanding Cloud Computing with Windows Azure

In this chapter, we will cover the following topics:

- ▶ Working with various storage options in Windows Azure
- ▶ Creating, updating, and deploying a cloud service in Windows Azure
- ▶ Working with SQL Azure
- ▶ Working with HDInsight (Hadoop) for Big Data processing
- ▶ Working with Mobile Services in Windows Azure

Introduction

Cloud computing is now one of the major metaphors for the Internet after Web 2.0 was deprecated. A cloud means the server, and when it is combined with computing, it means real-time computing on the server, scalability of infrastructure on the fly, adding a new infrastructure without changing the environment or without investing in new infrastructures, and training new personnel or licensing new software. Cloud computing encompasses a subscription-based pay per use service that in real time is capable of extending the existing capabilities.

Cloud computing comprises four service models:

- **Software as a Service (SaaS)**: In this type of environment, a single piece of software is delivered to a thousand clients through web browsers in a multi-tenant architecture. From a customer's point of view, this means no upfront investment in servers or software licensing. On the contrary, the provider also needs minimum investment as there is one more application to maintain with almost no additional cost as such.

- **Platform as a Service (PaaS)**: Another variant of SaaS is PaaS or Platform as a Service, which provides the basic computing platform and a solution stack as a service. In the case of Platform as a Service, the consumer creates software using tools and libraries from the provider. The provider here gives partial access to the platform using a portal, which the consumer needs to maintain.

- **Infrastructure as a Service (IaaS)**: In the case of IaaS or Infrastructure as a Service, the whole machine is provided as a service. The virtual machines are created on the cloud, and the consumer needs to access it and configure everything on their own. The provider, on the other hand, creates a virtual machine and gives the user access to it with no maintenance on their side whatsoever.

- **Network as a Service (NaaS)**: A variant of a service model called NaaS provides network/transport connectivity services between two intercloud networks. NaaS bridges two or more networks in a unified network as a whole; for example, NaaS services could be a **Virtual Private Network (VPN)**, which bridges two geographically separate locations into a single local area network without compromising on security.

Cloud computing could be implemented using any of the preceding models; each of these differs with regards to the overall structure of the cloud, but each of them follows some basic characteristics and principles. They are as follows:

- **Agility**: This provides an agile-based infrastructure and resources.

- **Application Programming Interface (API)**: This provides access to APIs to maintain, scale, and interact with the cloud environment.

- **Elasticity and flexibility of the system**: The main importance of cloud computing is scalability of the Web. Cloud provides a flexible system to deploy and maintain software with the support of elasticity that is based on the traffic.

- **Measurable service**: This is the payment per use.

- **Individual use of resources**: A user can use a resource anytime he or she desires. These resources include server space or server time, and they can be accessed without the need for human intervention from a client.

Working with various storage options in Windows Azure

A number of components of the Windows Azure platform are exposed using Internet protocols. There are a number of storage components exposed with Windows Azure Platform. Hence, these components need to be secured behind a valid authentication. Windows Azure Storage Service manages the storage of blobs, queues, and tables. Each storage account has an account name and an access key that are used to authenticate to access the storage service.

The storage service supports **Hash-based Message Authentication** (**HMAC**) in which the storage operation request is hashed with the access key such that upon receiving the request, the storage service validates it and either accepts or denies it. The Windows Azure storage client library provides several classes that support various ways to create HMAC, which hides the complexity of creating and using messages.

The Windows Azure SDK provides a compute and storage emulator. It points to the `localhost (127.0.0.1)` service and hence uses a hardcoded account name and access key. This hardcoded value will be treated differently to ensure that a proper local emulator gets connected.

There are three types of storages supported by Storage Service:

- **Blobs**: These are used to store the static content of the Web. The static content could be images, videos, audios, and so on, or anything that does not change over time.

- **Queues**: These are special objects that support the FIFO algorithm and can handle objects in a sequence. The queue-based object gets objects from one point, while the objects are inserted at the other end. A Queue supports 8 KB of data to be put as messages.

- **Tables**: These provide NoSQL data objects where data is stored in a key/value pair. These Tables support transaction and locking on data without SQL support.

The storage emulator has a hardcoded account name and access keys. The storage service uses different subdomains to indicate each storage accounts, while the storage emulator uses different ports to differentiate the different subdomains. The different ports are as follows:

- Blobs: `127.0.0.1:10000/devstoreaccount1`

- Queues: `127.0.0.1:10001/devstoreaccount1`

- Tables: `127.0.0.1:10002/devstoreaccount1`

In this recipe, we'll create Blobs, Queues, and Tables inside the project so that at a later stage we can use them in real environments.

Getting ready

Open Visual Studio, create a Windows Azure project, and add a worker role to it. We name it `MyWorkerRole`, as shown in the following screenshot:

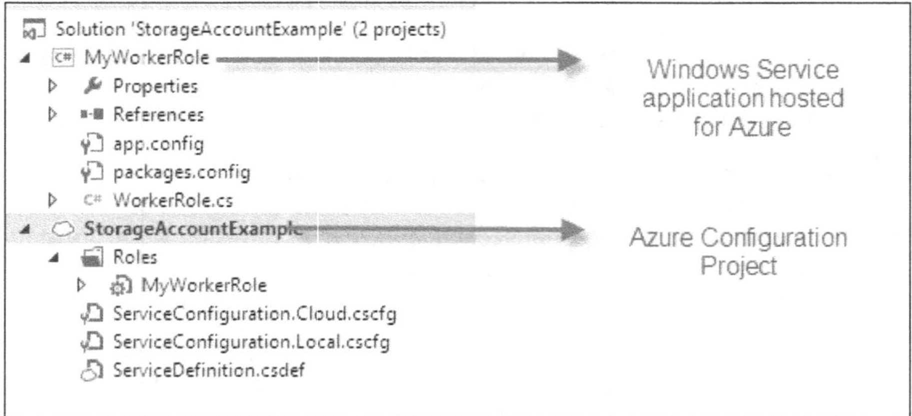

After adding the `MyWorkerRole` project to the Azure project, Visual Studio creates two nodes in the **Solution Explorer** window. There is a cloud project that stores all the configurations about the cloud projects. Here, it is named `StorageAccountExample`, which is same as the project name we specified while creating a cloud solution, and another is the `WorkerRole` project we created. As we are going to create different storage classes, let's create some classes in the `MyWorkerRole` project to demonstrate the working principles of the storage objects.

How to do it...

Now, let's consider creating a storage-based cloud service, which can have a front-facing web application and a connecting background service such that both can seamlessly talk to each other.

1. Add a new class to the `MyWorkerRole` project and name it `BlobExample`.

2. Add the following constructor to create a Blob connection:

```
private CloudBlobContainer cloudBlobContainer;

public BlobExample(string containerName)
{
    CloudStorageAccount cloudStorageAccount =
CloudStorageAccount.DevelopmentStorageAccount;
    CloudBlobClient cloudBlobClient = cloudStorageAccount.
CreateCloudBlobClient();
    cloudBlobContainer = cloudBlobClient.GetContainerReference(co
ntainerName);
}
```

In the preceding code, we created `CloudStorageAccount` in connection to the Development account. If you want to switch to production, you can put it inside the configuration, use `CloudStorageAccount.Parse`, and send the connection string. We then create `CloudBlobClient`. The `clientBlobClient` method is used to create a connection between the Blob account and the storage. Using the client, you can get a reference to the Blob account.

3. Now, add the following method:

```
private void CreateBlob(String blobName)
        {
            using (MemoryStream stream = new
              MemoryStream())
            {
                StreamWriter writer = new
                  StreamWriter(stream);
                writer.WriteLine(blobName);
                writer.Flush();

                CloudBlockBlob cloudBlockBlob =
cloudBlobContainer.GetBlockBlobReference(blobName);

                //Write data to the stream and upload it to
                  the storage blob
                cloudBlockBlob.UploadFromStream(stream);

                writer.Dispose();
            }
            this.TakeSnapshot(blobName);
        }
```

The `UploadFromStream` method takes a stream as an argument and uploads the data into the stream. Once the stream source is specified, in our case it is only the Blob name, it uploads the data to the Blob storage.

4. The `TakeSnapshot` method is used to take a backup of the Blob. As an Azure account does not charge for storage, it charges for uploads and downloads; you can take as many backups of data as required:

```
private DateTimeOffset TakeSnapshot(string blobName)
        {
            CloudBlockBlob cloudBlockBlob = cloudBlobContainer.Get
BlockBlobReference(blobName);
            CloudBlockBlob snapshot = cloudBlockBlob.
CreateSnapshot(); //Backs up the blob
            return (DateTimeOffset)snapshot.SnapshotTime;
        }
```

5. Now to create Blobs based on a URL, you can call the `CreateBlob` method as many times to create specified Blobs:

```
private void CreateBlobs()
        {
            cloudBlobContainer.CreateIfNotExists();
            CreateBlob("Abhishek/FirstBlob");
            CreateBlob("Abhishek/SecondBlob");
        }
```

Here, two Blobs are created inside the `Abhishek` directory of the Blob container. The data stored inside the Blobs would be the path of the Blob name.

6. To traverse the Blob directories inside the container, you can pass a `directoryname` string and all the Blobs inside the directory would be listed using the following code:

```
private void TraverseDirectoryTree(String directoryName)
{
    CloudBlobDirectory cloudBlobDirectory =
cloudBlobContainer.GetDirectoryReference(directoryName);
    IEnumerable<IListBlobItem> blobItems = cloudBlobDirectory.
ListBlobs();
    foreach (CloudBlobDirectory cloudBlobDirectoryItem in
blobItems.OfType<CloudBlobDirectory>())
        {
        Uri uri = cloudBlobDirectoryItem.Uri;
        Trace.WriteLine(uri.ToString());
        IEnumerable<CloudBlockBlob> leafBlobs =
cloudBlobDirectoryItem.ListBlobs().OfType<CloudBlockBlob>()
;
        foreach (CloudBlockBlob leafBlockBlob in leafBlobs)
        {
            Uri leafUri = leafBlockBlob.Uri;
            Trace.WriteLine(leafUri.ToString());
        }
    }
}
```

The preceding code writes the URLs in a debugger. The `GetDirectoryReference` method gets the reference of a directory under the Blob container and `ListBlobs` on it gets all the items present in the directory. It is worth noting that the Blob inside a directory can also represent `CloudBlobDirectory`. Hence, a nested loop is required.

7. Similar to Blob, let's create another class for Tables; we'll name it `TableExample.cs`. Now, add the following code:

```
private CloudTableClient cloudTableClient;
        public TableExample()
        {
```

```
            CloudStorageAccount cloudStorageAccount =
CloudStorageAccount.Parse(CloudConfigurationManager.GetSetting("St
orageConnectionString"));
            cloudTableClient = cloudStorageAccount.
CreateCloudTableClient();
        }
```

8. To create a Table, we either call `Create` or `CreateIfNotExists` on the `CloudTable` reference using the following code:

```
public void CreateTable(string tableName)
{
    CloudTable table = cloudTableClient.
GetTableReference(tableName);
    table.CreateIfNotExists();
}
```

9. Similar to this, `DeleteIfExists` could be called to delete the table if it exists, as follows:

```
public void DeleteTable(string tableName)
{
    CloudTable table =
cloudTableClient.GetTableReference(tableName);
    table.DeleteIfExists();
}
```

10. To list all the tables in a client, we use the following code:

```
public void ListTables(string tablePrefix)
{
    var listTable = cloudTableClient.ListTables(tablePrefix);
    foreach (var table in listTable)
        Trace.WriteLine(table.Name);
```

11. Now, to add an entry to the table, we can either use `TableEntity` or create a class and inherit from `TableEntity` to add additional columns. There are two fixed columns for each `TableEntity`, `PartitionKey`, and `RowKey` object. `PartitionKey` is used to group rows and `RowKey` represents the unique identifier for each partition. Let's take a look at the following code:

```
public class TableData : TableEntity
    {
        public TableData(string partition, string row)
        {
            this.PartitionKey = partition;
            this.RowKey = row;
        }

        public int Age { get; set; }
```

```
    }
public void AddEntryToTable(string tableName, TableData
   customData)
        {
            CloudTable table = cloudTableClient.
GetTableReference(tableName);
            table.CreateIfNotExists();
            var insertOperation =
               TableOperation.Insert(customData);
            table.Execute(insertOperation);
        }
```

Here, `AddEntryToTable` takes a reference of `TableData`. The `TableData` class inherits from `TableEntity` and adds a new property called `Age`. We use a constructor to specify `PartitionKey` and `RowKey` because these values need not be left blank. When `TableOperation.Insert` gets executed, the data object is embedded into a `TableOperation` object, which could later be executed on `CloudTable`.

12. We can also use the following `BatchOperation` method instead of a single operation to ensure all the entries on the Batch are executed at a time:

```
public void AddEntryToTable(string tableName)
{
    CloudTable table = cloudTableClient.
GetTableReference(tableName);
    table.CreateIfNotExists();
    TableBatchOperation batch = new TableBatchOperation();
    batch.Add(TableOperation.Insert(new TableEntity {
RowKey = "Abhishek", PartitionKey = "Kolkata" }));
    batch.Add(TableOperation.Insert(new TableEntity {
RowKey = "Abhijit", PartitionKey = "Kolkata" }));
    table.ExecuteBatch(batch);
}
```

Here, in the preceding code, the `TableOperation` objects are added to `TableBatchOperation`, and all of them are executed using the `ExecuteBatch` method API.

13. Let's add the following code:

```
public void UpdateEntryToTable(string tableName, TableData
   customData)
{
    CloudTable table =
      cloudTableClient.GetTableReference(tableName);
    table.CreateIfNotExists();
    var replaceOperation =
      TableOperation.Replace(customData);
    table.Execute(replaceOperation);
}
```

The `Replace` method automatically compares the `TableEntity` object using the `PartitionKey` and `RowKey` attributes and determines which object needs to be replaced. Similarly, to delete an entry, you can use the `Delete` method and pass the reference of the `TableEntity` object.

14. You can also query a Table using either `PartitionKey` and `RowKey` or anything. To query a Table, we use LINQ, as follows:

```
public void QueryTable(string tableName, string partitionKey,
string rowKey)
{
    CloudTable table = cloudTableClient.
GetTableReference(tableName);
    TableQuery<TableData> tableQuery = new
TableQuery<TableData>().Where(TableQuery.CombineFilters(
        TableQuery.GenerateFilterCondition("PartitionKey",
         QueryComparisons.Equal, partitionKey),
        TableOperators.And,
        TableQuery.GenerateFilterCondition("RowKey",
         QueryComparisons.Equals, rowKey)));

    foreach (TableData data in table.ExecuteQuery(tableQuery))
        Trace.WriteLine(data.ToString());
}
```

The preceding code creates a filter for a specific `PartitionKey` and `RowKey` combination such that it gives you an entry that is unique in the Table.

15. Similar to Blobs and Tables, Queues follow the same type of development approach. The only difference with Queues is that a Queue follows FIFO logic and, hence, the message that goes in first will come out first. Let's take a look at how to work on Queues:

```
private CloudQueueClient cloudQueueClient;
        public QueueExample()
        {
            CloudStorageAccount cloudStorageAccount =
CloudStorageAccount.DevelopmentStorageAccount;
            cloudQueueClient =
cloudStorageAccount.CreateCloudQueueClient();
        }
```

16. To create a Queue, we use the following code:

```
public void CreateQueue(string queueName)
{
    CloudQueue cloudQueue = cloudQueueClient.
GetQueueReference(queueName);
    cloudQueue.CreateIfNotExists();
}
```

The `GetQueueReference` method gets a reference of the Queue present in the cloud, which is the main repository for Queue messages. The `CreateIfNotExists` method will create the Queue if it is not present.

17. To add a message to the Queue, we use the following code:

```
public vcid Enqueue(string queueName, string message)
{
    CloudQueue cloudQueue =
cloudQueueClient.GetQueueReference(queueName);
    CloudQueueMessage cmessage = new
CloudQueueMessage(message);

    cloudQueue.AddMessage(cmessage);
}
```

Here, `CloudQueueMessage` can take a message as an argument, and you can use the `AddMessage` method to add that message to the Queue.

18. To dequeue a message, you can use the following code:

```
public void Dequeue(string queueName)
{
    CloudQueue cloudQueue =
cloudQueueClient.GetQueueReference(queueName);
    CloudQueueMessage cmessage = cloudQueue.PeekMessage();
//Gets message without removing it

    Trace.WriteLine(cmessage.AsString);

    cmessage = cloudQueue.GetMessage(); //Gets message and
makes it invisible for 30 sec
    cloudQueue.DeleteMessage(cmessage); //deletes the
      message
}
```

In the preceding code, we can either use `PeekMessage`, which will get the message without altering or removing the first item from the queue, or you can use `GetMessage`, which will get the message and make the same message invisible on the Queue for 30 seconds. In between, if the process invokes `DeleteMesssage` on the message, the Queue message will be removed. So `Dequeue` is a two-step process to call `GetMessage` with `DeleteMessage`.

19. The `UpdateMessage` method can be performed when the message is available:

```
public void UpdateMessage(string queueName, string message)
{
    CloudQueue cloudQueue = cloudQueueClient.
GetQueueReference(queueName);
    CloudQueueMessage cmessage = cloudQueue.GetMessage();
    cmessage.SetMessageContent(message);
```

```
    cloudQueue.UpdateMessage(cmessage, TimeSpan.FromSeconds(0d),
MessageUpdateFields.Content |
MessageUpdateFields.Visibility);
}
```

The preceding code invokes `GetMessage`, which will get the first message from the Queue and make it invisible. The `SetMessageContent` method will change the content and finally `UpdateMessage` will update the message in the Queue after a specified time. In the preceding code, the message gets updated on the Queue and immediately becomes visible to the Queue.

20. Blobs, Tables, and Queues form the basic storage units of Azure storage, and based on the requirement of the situation, any type of storage could be used.

How it works...

In the Azure environment, three types of Azure storages are found: **Blobs**, **Tables**, and **Queues**. Each of these forms a REST-based URI approach to store and retrieve data, as shown in the following figure:

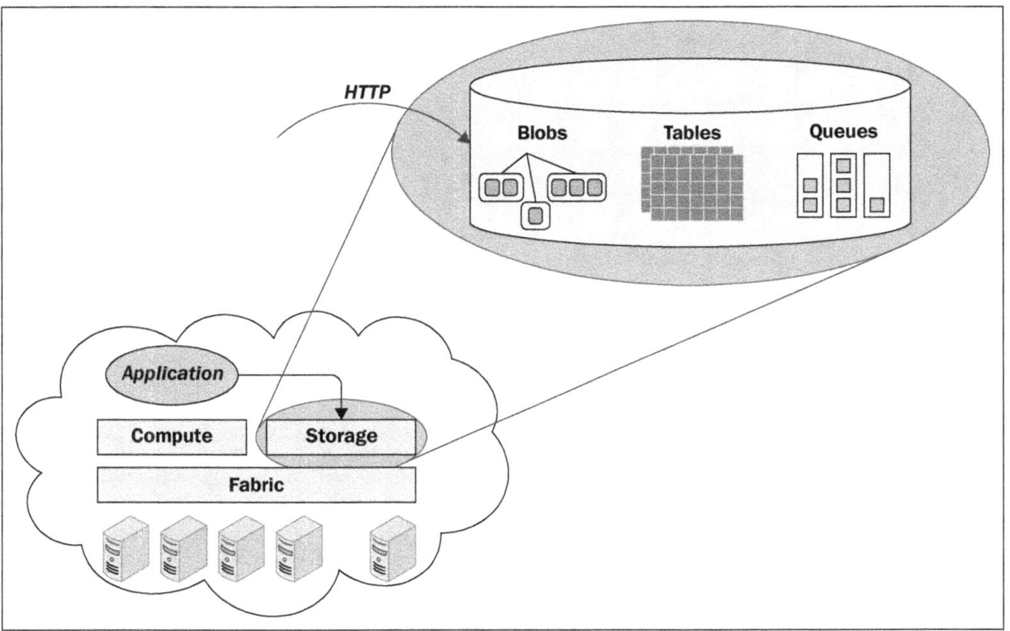

In the main Azure Storage, storage components are exposed as HTTP objects over a network. Blobs are used to store large unstructured data, which does not change over time. Tables are used to store key/value pair objects with a special capability of performing a query over the data based on keys and Queue, which mainly stores messages following the FIFO algorithm.

When dealing with Azure Storage, the following three components are present:

- **Account**: This is mapped to a client.
- **Container**: This is mapped to the reference container for Blob, Tables, or Queues. One account can hold a number of containers, each of which is named with an identifier.
- **Objects**: These are the main storage blocks that are placed inside a container.

Account can point to a `CloudStorageAccount` reference object. Here, you can either use `CloudStorageAccount.DevelopmentStorageAccount` to point the client to a local emulator, or you can parse a connection string from the portal and add it back here.

To find the actual `connectionstring` from the portal, open the Azure portal (`https://manage.windowsazure.com`); navigate to **NEW | STORAGE | QUICK CREATE**; and enter the unique **URL**, **LOCATION**, and **SUBSCRIPTION**, as shown in the following screenshot:

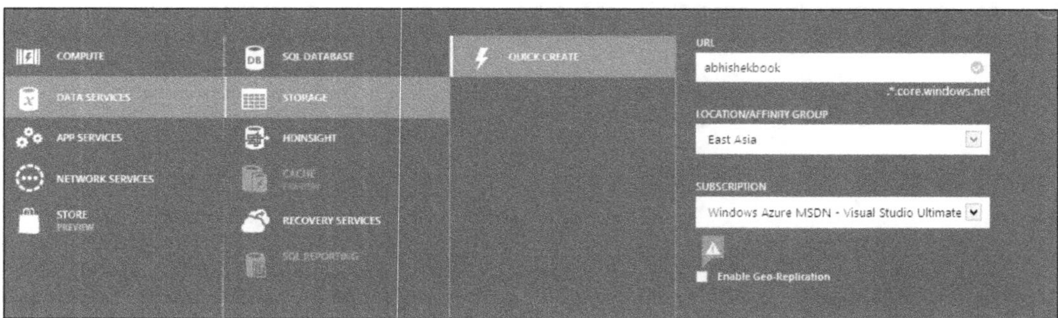

Here, we created a storage account called `abhishekbook.core.windows.net`. When you create the service, it will create the storage client for you where you can store data. Once the storage account has been created, you will find the storage links from the dashboard, as shown in the following screenshot:

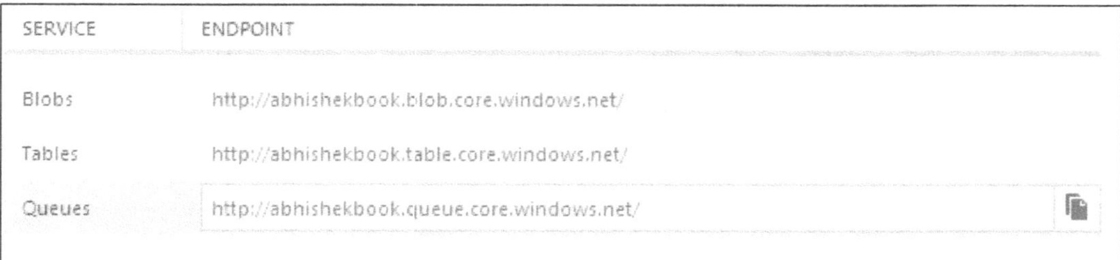

SERVICE	ENDPOINT
Blobs	http://abhishekbook.blob.core.windows.net/
Tables	http://abhishekbook.table.core.windows.net/
Queues	http://abhishekbook.queue.core.windows.net/

Each of the links points to the development storage account. Now, let's specify `StorageAccountName` and a key to `ConnectionString` to create a valid connection.

The name of the account would be `abhishekbook`, and there will be two access keys that can be accessed via the **Manage Access Key** button when **Storage** is clicked on the left-hand pane.

Now, go to properties of the **Worker Role** project and select **Settings** to add a new settings key. You can go to the alias in the connection string to access the window to configure the keys for the connection; you can name it `StorageConnectionString`. You can directly connect to the Azure portal to get the entire `connectionstring` from the superior tool of Visual Studio, as shown in the following screenshot:

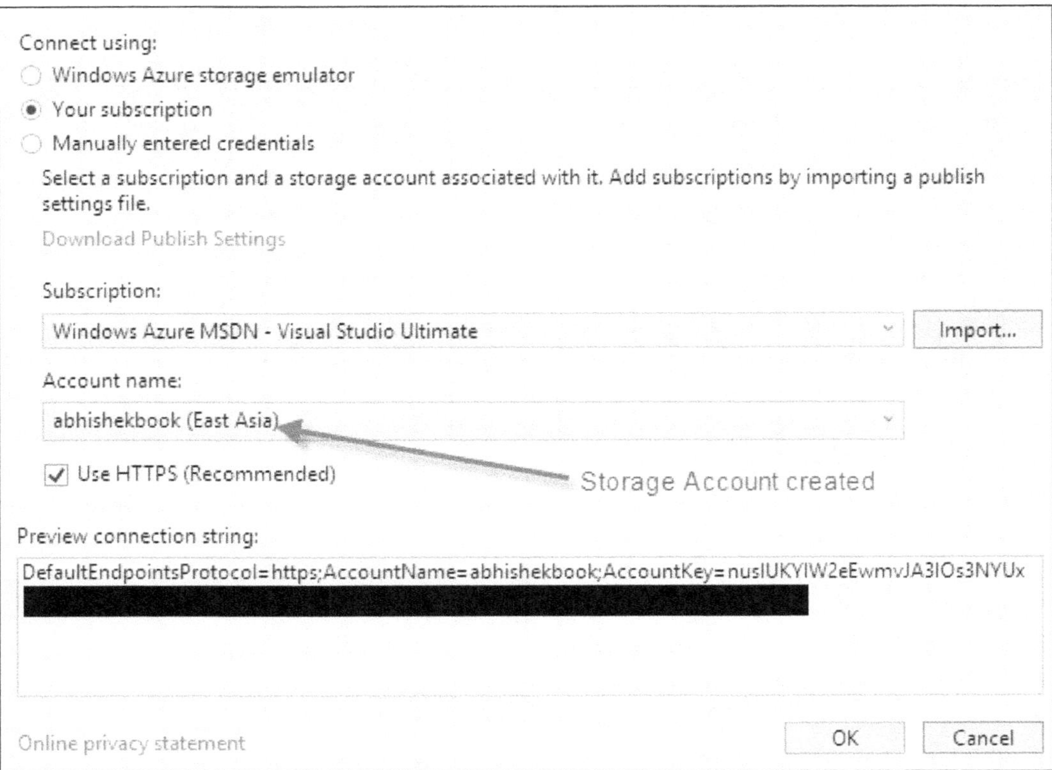

Once you get the connection, you can access the connection using the following code:

```
CloudStorageAccount cloudStorageAccount =
CloudStorageAccount.Parse(CloudConfigurationManager.GetSetting("St
orageConnectionString"));
```

The first step for any client is to connect to an appropriate storage account. Once the storage account object is created, we need to set up a client with an appropriate storage type. The client can be created using `CreateCloudBlobClient`, `CreateCloudTableClient`, or `CreateCloudQueueClient`.

The client can access the container that can be accessed with a unique identifier. In the steps defined earlier, each storage is accessed by following these simple steps. Once the container is retrieved, individual methods are used to manipulate the data inside it.

There's more...

Above simple storage usages, there are a number of additional things that are worth noticing. The following sections present some of them.

Combining Blobs and Queues for Big Data sequential processing

A Queue can store up to 8 KB of messages. This limitation is very small when dealing with real-world scenarios. It is often required to access a large storage file from another process. A Queue is used to communicate with two processes, but if you need to send data that is larger than the maximum size of the Queue, it makes it impossible to use such a data structure.

In addition to a queue, a Blob storage is used to communicate large data between the processes. The data is stored inside a Blob instead of a Queue, and the URL that uniquely identifies the Blob is stored in the queue. We access the data through the Queues sequentially getting the blob URL and fetching the data from the Blob storage.

Say, for instance, we want to process large files on a service. To deal with large files, we will create a Blob storage, as follows:

```csharp
public void UploadFileForProcessing(string path, string fileName)
{
    CloudStorageAccount storageAccount = CloudStorageAccount.
Parse(ConfigurationManager.ConnectionStrings["
StorageConnectionString"].ConnectionString);
    CloudBlobClient blobClient = storageAccount.
CreateCloudBlobClient();
    CloudBlobContainer container = blobClient.GetContainerReference("la
rgeDatafolder");
    container.CreateIfNotExists();
    container.SetPermissions(new BlobContainerPermissions {
PublicAccess = BlobContainerPublicAccessType.Blob });

    CloudBlockBlob blockBlob = container.GetBlockBlobReference(fileNa
me);

    //Create the Queue reference
    CloudQueueClient queueClient = storageAccount.
CreateCloudQueueClient();
```

```
   CloudQueue queue = queueClient.GetQueueReference("fileProcessingQu
eue");
   queue.CreateIfNotExists();

   using (var fileStream = System.IO.File.OpenRead(path))
   {
       blockBlob.UploadFromStream(fileStream);
       //Once upload finished, add the message to the Queue
       CloudQueueMessage newBlobAddress = new
CloudQueueMessage(blockBlog.Uri);
       queue.AddMessage(newBlobAddress);
   }
}
```

Here, the Queue `fileProcessingQueue` is used to send a message between two processes. Once the message has been added to the Queue, the other process will receive it via the `GetMessage` method from the Queue and process the Blob from its URL, as follows:

```
public void ProcessFileFromQueue(string downloadfilePath)
{
    CloudStorageAccount storageAccount =
CloudStorageAccount.Parse(ConfigurationManager.ConnectionStrings["
StorageConnectionString"].ConnectionString);

    //Create the Queue reference
    CloudQueueClient queueClient = storageAccount.
CreateCloudQueueClient();
    CloudQueue queue = queueClient.GetQueueReference("fileProcessingQu
eue");
    queue.CreateIfNotExists();

    CloudQueueMessage blobAddress = queue.GetMessage();
    if(blobAddress != null)
    {
        CloudBlobClient blobClient = storageAccount.
CreateCloudBlobClient();
        CloudBlobContainer container = blobClient.GetContainerReference
("largeDatafolder");

        CloudBlockBlob blockBlob = container.GetBlockBlobReference(blob
Address.AsString);
        using (var fileStream = System.IO.File.
OpenWrite(downloadfilePath))
        {
            blockBlob.DownloadToStream(fileStream);
        }
        queue.DeleteMessage(blobAddress);
    }
}
```

The preceding code downloads the files one by one from the Blob storage, which is uploaded by another process and notified using a request that comes from the Queue. Being the medium for exchanging information, the Queue cannot hold the whole file; instead, the requested URL could be sent through Queue, and the process that is subscribed to the same Queue can access it in real time. Thus, the files sent from a process using `UploadFileForProcessing` are eventually sent to another process shown in the `ProcessFileFromQueue` method.

Choosing the best Azure Storage based on the type of use

As we move forward, you might think about which Azure Storage to use when there are a number of storage types available in Windows Azure. The storage types are as follows:

- Blobs
- Tables
- Queues
- Azure Drive
- SQL Azure

Windows Azure Blobs support two types of Blobs: one that supports blocks for streamed access and another that supports a page for random read-write access. The maximum size of a block Blob is 200 GB and the maximum size of a page blob is 1 TB. The primary use of block Blobs is to have streaming content on websites, while the primary use of page blobs is to store VHDs.

The Table gives a structured `NoSql` data to store a collection of entities where each entity has a primary key of `PartitionKey` and `RowKey` as well as a `Timestamp` property. The Table does not support indexes as of now. However, it supports the transaction when the input is in batches.

Queues store messages up to 8 KB of message size and return messages based on FIFO. The messages in Queue remain there until they get deleted or remain there for a maximum of 7 days.

The Azure drive allows an instance to be mounted as an NTFS drive, a VHD stored as a page Blob. Once mounted, VHD has full access to perform the read/write function.

SQL Azure is a relational database with full transactional capabilities of SQL Server running on Windows Azure data centers. The Azure database in the portal initially has a maximum size of 50 GB, but it can be subsequently changed using an alternate database statement up to 150 GB or even up to 500 GB as per the latest news. The following command changes the maximum size of the database to 100 GB:

```
ALTER DATABASE MyDatabase MODIFY (EDITION='BUSINESS', MAXSIZE=100GB)
```

Refer to the following list:

- We choose Blobs if we want to have large data content streamed on websites (block Blob) or perform random read/write access to a large file (page Blob)
- We choose Azure Tables if we need a cost-effective, highly scalable storage of entities that accept the limitations of a query
- We choose SQL Azure if we want relational databases
- We choose Queues when we need to implement disconnected communication between processes
- We choose Azure Drive if we need NTFS Access to a durable disk

See also

- Refer to the Azure Storage documentation at `http://bit.ly/azurestoragech7`

Creating, updating, and deploying a cloud service in Windows Azure

When you create an application and run it in Windows Azure, the configuration file along with the code that constitutes the package together is called a Windows Azure cloud service. With a cloud service, you can host a multi-tier application in a single host and combine one or more cloud services together with the Web role and/or worker roles, each with its own application files and configurations with the support of autoscaling. A cloud infrastructure maintains the services for you by maintaining virtual copies of the software, patching operating systems and attempting to recover hardware failures. A cloud service is recommended to have at least two instances running to qualify Windows Azure Level Agreement that states 99.95 percent guaranteed connectivity.

Cloud service roles that constitute application and configuration files are of two types:

- **Web role**: This is a frontend application hosted in IIS
- **Worker role**: This is a long-running service that runs in the background without any frontend interactions

There are three types of files present in each package. They are as follows:

- **Service definition file** (`.csdef`): This file defines the service model and the number of roles
- **Service configuration file** (`.cscfg`): This file provides configuration settings for the cloud service as well as individual roles, including the number of instances per role
- **Service package** (`.cspkg`): This is a zipped archive with the application code and service definition file

Now, let's create a service with one Web role and one worker role and host them into a cloud.

Getting ready

Open Visual Studio and create a Windows Cloud Service application; we name it `CloudServiceSample`. On the next screen that is presented, we add `WebRole` and `WorkerRole`. The project adds two projects in addition to the Service Configuration project in the **Solution Explorer** window. `WebRole` is actually a `WebForms` application (if you have chosen `WebForm` from a template), and `WorkerRole` represents a mere Windows service.

If you run the project, `WebRole` pops up a new Internet Explorer, and the default template is good enough for our deployment.

After you compile, you will get two files: one that is produced with a `.cspkg` extension, which represents a zipped archive holding the whole package with application files and service definition files, and the other is a `.cscfg` file for configurations.

How to do it...

Let's deploy the small project that comes with the template and configure it to the Azure portal using the following steps:

1. Open the Windows Azure portal (`www.manage.windowsazure.com`).
2. Create a new **CLOUD SERVICE**, as shown in the following screenshot, and name it as something you want:

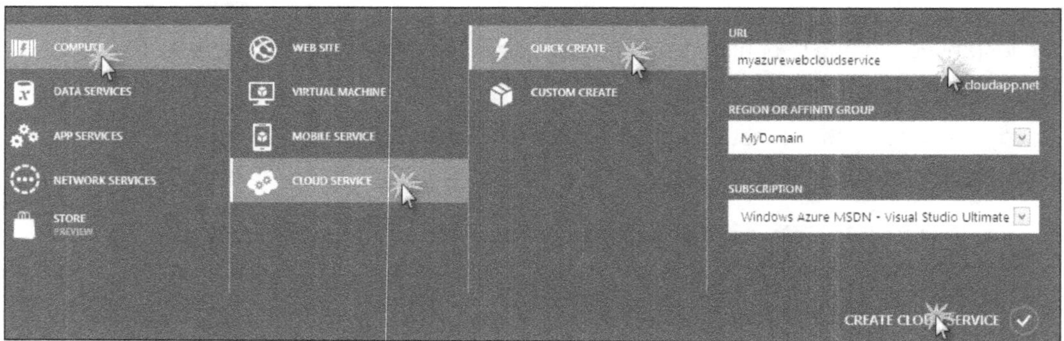

3. The `myazurecloudservice` name would have already been assigned to you, but change this name to something that suits you.

4. Once the service is created and ready, we need to upload the created package to the service. When you open the service, you will see there are two options to upload the package. The production environment will automatically put the URL to production, while staging is used for testing purposes with a temporary URL.

5. Let's upload the package file here. To upload, select the **Upload** option at the bottom of the page on the **Staging** tab.

6. Select **DEPLOYMENT LABEL** for the application and choose the **PACKAGE** file and the **CONFIGURATION** file from the `app.publish` folder where the package has been created from Visual Studio:

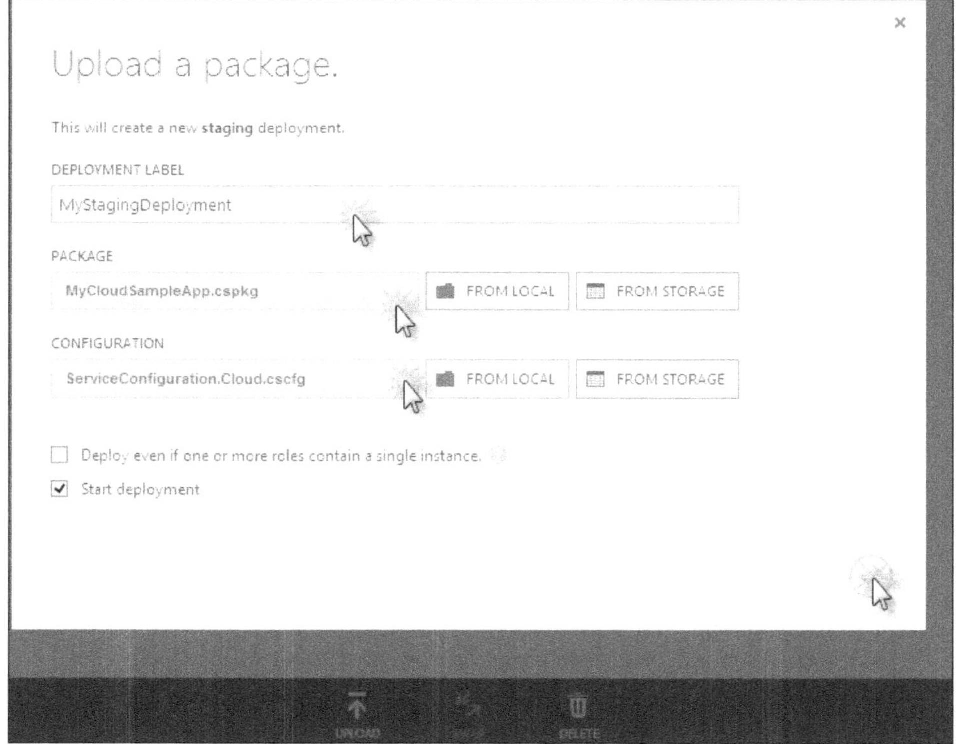

> If the **Start deployment** option is checked, it means the application will be automatically deployed after it is uploaded.

7. Let's choose these settings; after the application is uploaded, you will see the application is listed on the websites section as a deployed website. The dashboard allows you to configure different options of the website.

8. To configure the IIS Server, you can use the **Configuration** option on the website. The **Configuration** option allows you to handle the .NET Framework version for the website, the platform type, the application settings, connection strings, default pages, HTTP handler mappings, and so on. All the things that you may have been doing in IIS would be available through this tab.

9. On the other hand, the **Scaling** tab, as shown in the following screenshot, allows you to scale the application's performance. With scaling, you can increase the number of parallel instances that the same website will run on, the size of the machine where it is deployed, and so on.

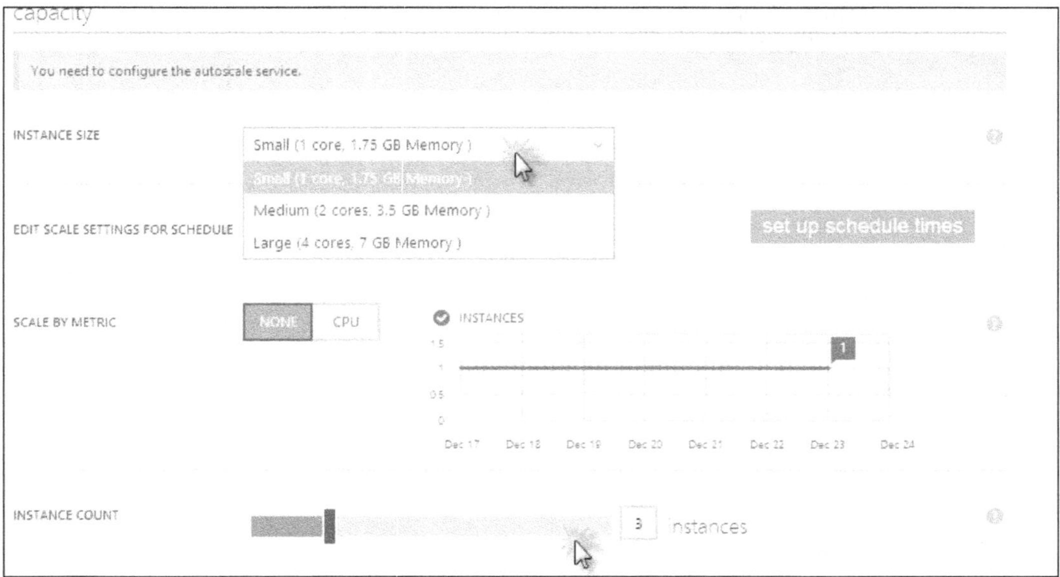

Here, you can see the capacity is configured to run on a small instance machine with one core and 1.75 GB of memory and scaled to three instances.

10. You can also link resources to automatically add firewall settings or other features that are required to access the resources from Windows Azure websites.

How it works...

An Azure service application runs IIS over a cloud environment as a distributed application. The application developed in Visual Studio can be deployed to the cloud server without changing any code. Everything that is required to configure the application could be done inside Visual Studio, and finally, it can be deployed to the server using a management portal.

In the preceding recipe, we tried to deploy a website to the staging environment, and the same technique can be used to deploy the application to production.

There's more...

Deploying data into Windows Azure is very important. There are a few more things that can be worth noting.

Using DataMarkets for your applications

Windows Azure runs in cloud platforms. The main advantage of deploying applications to the cloud is to enable data and services to be consumed by external applications. The Windows Azure Marketplace is a global online market where ISVs and data publishers can publish the data and make money.

Start a web browser and enter `http://datamarket.azure.com`. Sign in using a live account, and you can then browse the datasets available. Once you are in the portal, you can access any dataset available in the marketplace. Some of the data is free, while some is paid. The free dataset could be accessed without the use of credit cards.

If you go to your account using the **My Account** link, there are some additional tabs that you might look at. The **MY DATA** tab in the following screenshot shows all the data services that this account is subscribed to. The account key is used by a third-party application to access your subscription. It is important to note that the account key is sensitive, and you shouldn't give the same key to multiple vendors.

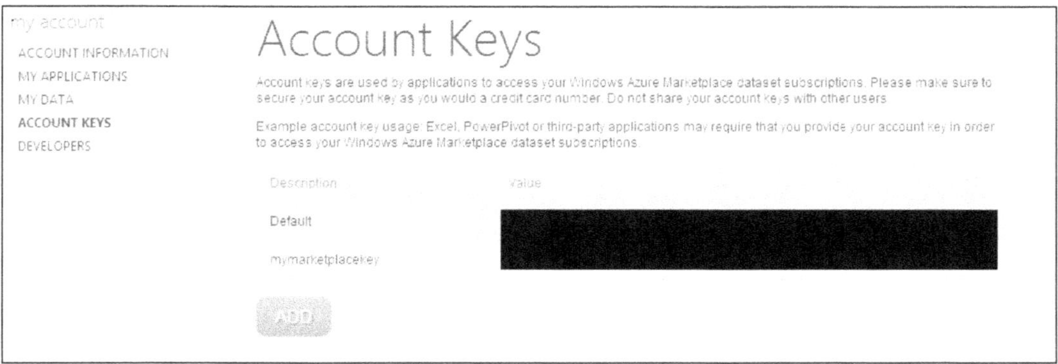

There is a remove link to remove the account keys once they are not in use. To subscribe to a data service, you need to simply go to the service and subscribe. There is also an option to autorefill a service after the subscribed value is over. For example, the **STATS Sports Database** service gives access to **50 Transaction/month** for **$12.00**, as shown in the following screenshot:

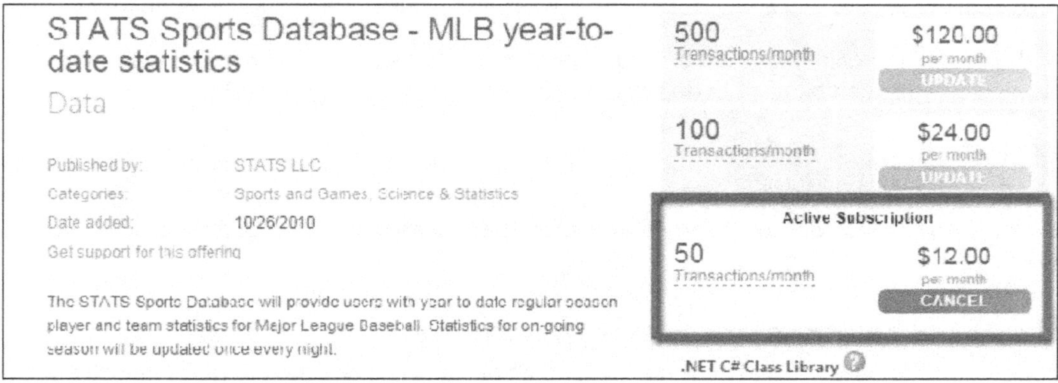

You can navigate to the **MY DATA** tab in the **My Account** link to enable the autorefill option after the number of transactions are already consumed. For paid subscriptions, there is a small link that says **Enable Auto refill**, which will enable you to select the autorefill option for the dataset.

Now, to use the dataset, you can go to **MY DATA** and select **Use**. The dataset can also support downloading in CSV or Power Pivot formats.

Finally, to publish the dataset to the marketplace, you need to register for data publishing. You can use the **Publish** link to register for publishing. This is a paid enrollment, so you might need to put your credit card information while registering. Once you are registered, you will see the following **Publisher** home page:

On this page, you can either add a dataset or add an app service. When selecting **Add DataSet**, you will be redirected to **Add DataSource**. There are two ways to add a data source:

- Connecting to SQL Server or the SQL Azure database
- Connecting to an existing web service

Choosing **Connecting to an existing web service** allows us to connect to the data source and the type of service and finally connect to the service.

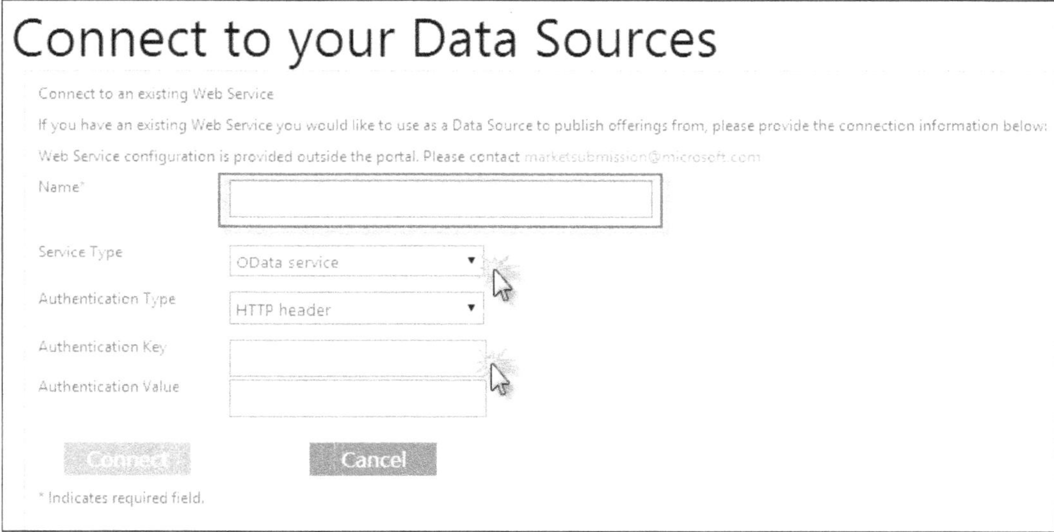

It is worth mentioning that web service is a better way to expose data rather than going for full database sharing. You can also use a SQL database and provide a SQL connection to the marketplace.

Once the service gets connected, the deployed database tables/dataset can be configured from the **Publisher** page. You can configure the data-offering credentials from the page for a particular dataset and finally select **Publish**.

Once it is successfully published, people will start finding the dataset to the Windows Azure marketplace.

Working with SQL Azure

SQL Azure adds relational databases to the Windows Azure platform. It is essentially an SQL Server running on Azure servers. Microsoft keeps the management of the SQL Server to themselves at the physical level. SQL Azure helps in provisioning and deploying relational database solutions to the cloud with the automatic benefit of scalability, availability, security, replication, and so on. This brings all the benefits of cloud computing to SQL Server.

SQL Azure supports the SQL relational database model in contrast to Table storage, which provides a NoSQL-styled database. SQL Azure is highly available. With high availability, it means it is fault tolerant, replicated, and has an automatic failover. This means when data is written to the database, the same data is replicated into multiple storages such that during disaster recovery, the data could be easily recovered. SQL Azure automatically handles high availability thus, when one instance of the database is not available, SQL Azure will automatically put another instance online rather than making the database server go down. Microsoft guarantees that there is less than 43 minutes of downtime per month for the database, which means they are 99.9 percent available.

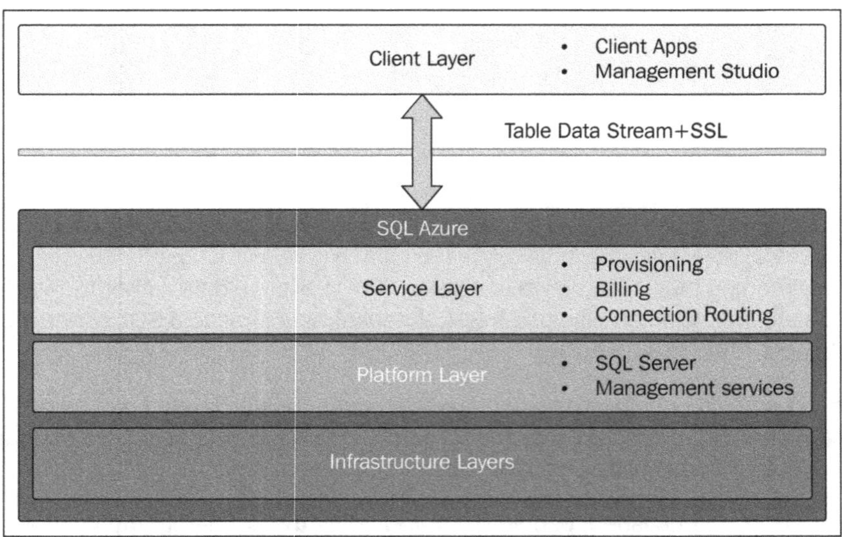

SQL Azure communicates with the Azure service following the preceding architecture. Client apps communicate the SQL Azure via **Table Data Stream** using the SSL communication channel and connects it to the service layer. The service layer consumes the data and passes it to the platform layer, which has the actual SQL Server instance. This is like communicating with a web service using SSL. The service layer redirects the data to the SQL Server with the support of provisioning. The service also deals with billing of data and connection routing.

The platform layer communicates with the cloud infrastructure for physical storage. The infrastructure also allows the database to be distributed over the cloud environment so that it becomes easier to handle instances over large number of servers, and Microsoft also does not need to handle each individual server manually.

SQL Azure does not support Windows authentication, but supports SQL's username and password to communicate between machines. However, it has a security firewall, which allows you to access SQL Servers only from a fixed number of machines. SQL Azure uses port number 1433 to communicate data. Thus, when the service layer receives a request to log in, the layer maintains a table of all the clients that have access to that particular instance which have been called for. For instance, if SQL Azure is accessed from Windows Azure, the IP address of 0.0.0.0 needs to be allowed to the SQL Azure instance to prevent the firewall from passing through the login process from Windows Azure.

Getting ready

To get started with SQL Azure, lets open `https://manage.windowsazure.com`, go to **NEW | DATA SERVICES | SQL DATABASE**, select **QUICK CREATE**, and enter `MyAzureDatabase` in the **DATABASE NAME** field for the time being. Then, click on **CREATE SQL DATABASE**, as shown in the following screenshot:

Once the database has been created, you can select the database from the list to open the dashboard. The dashboard not only allows you to monitor and scale like other services, but also allows you to configure the database.

You can add the allowed IP addresses as I mentioned before. The portal will automatically suggest the IP address of the system you are browsing with. Click on **DashBoard** and select **Manage IP Addresses**. You will see the following screen:

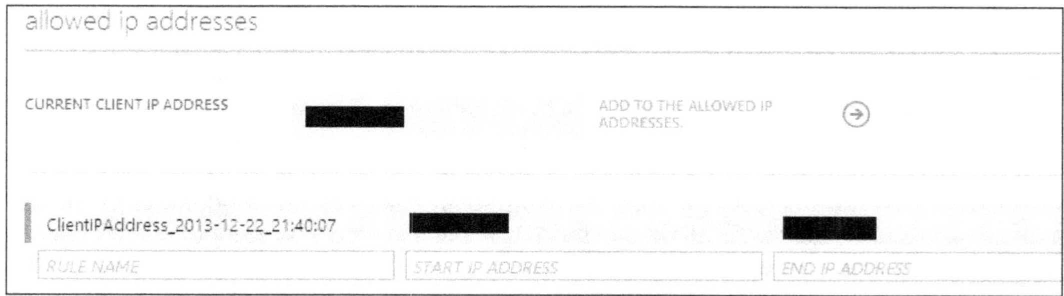

Now this IP firewall is applied to the server that you might have created before. For instance, if you go to the dashboard of your service, you can click on the **Reset Administrator Password** option that you might have created before:

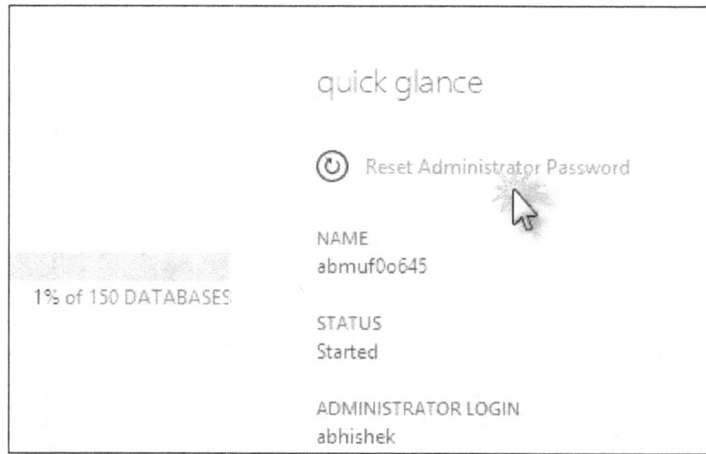

Each database service instance allows 150 databases inside it and gives a unique URL to access the service and databases inside it. The database server can be thought as a service that runs as an instance on your machine where SQL server is installed.

Once the configuration is done, open **Management Studio** and enter the unique URL for the database server that is created and use its username and password. Your server name would be `xxxx.database.windows.net`, and the port that it need to access is 1433.

In addition to this, the portal also supports a management studio inside the web browser, which allows you to to access the database, create tables, and everything that you might be doing in the SQL Server management studio.

In the dashboard section, you can click on **Design your SQL Database** to access the management studio. The various connection strings to access the database server is also available at the hyperlink, **View SQL Database connection strings for ADO.NET, ODBC, PHP, and JDBC**, as shown in the following screenshot. You can use them to access the database server from the applications.

In the following section, let's implement an OData service using SQL Azure.

How to do it...

OData is a web protocol to query and update data using HTTM, ATOM publishing protocol, and/or JSON. The OData protocol is released under Open Specification Promise. OData provides generic CRUD interfaces to access data on the server using normal HTTP protocols. SQL Azure supports SQL databases to be exposed over OData. The entire security model will act behind the scene, and even you can allow read-only access to OData to be safe. Now, let's create an OData service through steps that will use SQL Azure tables and host it over HTTP:

1. Open **Management Studio** and connect to the database with appropriate credentials.

2. Open the **Security** node and create new login credentials. Logging in will execute the `CREATE LOGIN` statement on the master database, as follows:

```
CREATE LOGIN odataLogin
    WITH PASSWORD = 'OD@t@l0g1n'
GO
```

   The preceding code creates a login for the database service.

3. Once this is done, we need to create a user that will use the same login credentials. To do that, we open the `MyAzureDatabase` node, and under the **Security** node, we add a new user. This will open up the script pane, where we add the following code:

```
CREATE User odatalogin
    FOR LOGIN odatalogin
    WITH DEFAULT_SCHEMA = MyAzureDatabase
GO
```

   This will add the `odatalogin` user with `odatalogin` and default database access to the database.

4. We also need to provide a role to the user so that it can access certain privileges of the database. As we wanted to use read-only data access, we need to add the `db_datareader` role to the user:

```
EXEC sp_addrolemember N'db_datareader', N'odatalogin'
GO
```

5. Now, we open Visual Studio and create a cloud service application and select an ASP. NET web role. As you already know, a web role is just an ASP.NET web application. Name it `MyODataService` and select **Web Forms**.

6. Add the ADO.NET Entity data model and use the **Generate From Database** option. Select the connection to the Azure database using the `odatalogin` user with an appropriate password and click on **Next**.

7. From the listed tables, select the tables that you need to add. We created two tables, `Customers` and `Orders`, to test our OData service.

8. Add a new item to the solution and select **WCF Data service**. Name it `MyAzureData.svc`.

9. In `InitializeService` of the WCF data service, we add the following lines:

```
config.DataServiceBehavior.MaxProtocolVersion =
    DataServiceProtocolVersion.V3;

config.SetEntitySetAccessRule("*", EntitySetRights.All);

config.SetServiceOperationAccessRule("*",
    ServiceOperationRights.All);
```

The preceding lines will set access to all the tables, and as we are using the user who has only read-only access to the database, the server data will be safe from external updates.

10. Finally, package the service and deploy it to Windows Azure. You can access the service using the `yourserver/MyAzureData.svc/{tableName}` link.

How it works...

OData uses open data specification published by Open Data Protocol, which is a REST-based protocol standard that enables accessing database objects and updating the database objects using open standards such as HTTP and using common standard formats of data such as JSON or XML. In the preceding application, we created an OData service application, consuming the SQL Azure database. We configured the SQL Azure database, put a service layer over it, and provided easy access to the objects inside the SQL Azure database. We can host the service either in Azure or any other server as standalone and consume the data from the service.

The WCF service automatically enumerates the entity objects from the database and provides the formatted data to the consumer.

SQL Azure provides a number of important features that are worth noting. Let's take a look at some more advantages of using SQL Azure.

Running transactional queries from the portal

Even though it is recommended that you access the SQL server through the management portal, there is also an option to run the management tools directly from the browser itself. The Windows Azure management portal gives an option to design the database schema or relationships. To open the database in the online management portal, go to the database and use the **Design your SQL Database** link, as shown in the following screenshot:

Once you open the portal, you need to feed in the appropriate username and password of the database instance to open the management portal for the database. When you open the portal, it gives a summary of the database portal, as shown in the following screenshot:

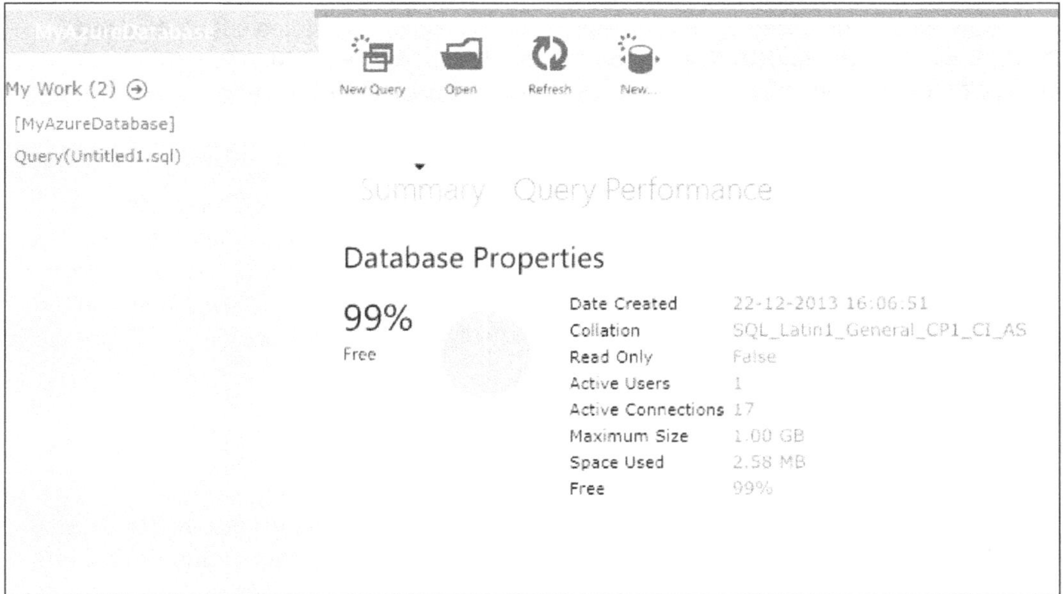

One can select **New Query** to start writing a query in the query window, and the query will be listed on the left-hand side pane.

You can also use the **Design** tab at the bottom-left corner of the screen to open the designer for Tables. This option is absent for Azure databases when they use **Management Studio**. The portal can even list the estimated and actual execution plans while running a query on the database.

See also

▸ Refer to the MSDN documentation of SQL Azure at `http://bit.ly/sqlazurechdoc`

Working with HDInsight (Hadoop) for Big Data processing

SQL Azure provides a relational database technology to the Windows Azure platform. However, sometimes the data becomes so vast that it could not be handled using a relational database. Even sometimes, the data that needs to be analyzed is not relational at all. Hadoop is a new technology that has been introduced recently to help in analyzing Big Data problems.

Hadoop is an Apache-based open source project. This technology stores data in **Hadoop Distributed File System** (**HDFS**) and then lets the developers create MapReduce jobs to analyze that data. The main advantages of a Hadoop filesystem is that it stores data in multiple servers, and then allows to run chunks of MapReduce jobs, letting Big Data be processed in parallel.

HDInsight is the name of the Windows Azure Apache Hadoop-based service. HDInsight lets HDFS to store data in clusters and distribute it across multiple virtual machines. It also spreads the MapReduce job across VMs. HDInsight uses Windows Azure Storage Vault to store data in Blobs. The use of ASV allows you to save money, as you can delete your HDInsight cluster when not in use and still have data in the cloud in the form of Blob storage.

Getting ready

To get ready to use HDInsight, let's understand a few basic concepts:

▸ **Pig**: This is a high-level platform for processing data in Hadoop clusters. Pig consists of a data-flow language called Pig Latin, which supports queries over large datasets. The Pig Latin program consists of a dataset transformation series that is converted to a MapReduce program series under the covers.

- **Hive**: This is a Hadoop query engine built for data warehouse summarization queries. Hive is used for analysis and gives a SQL-like interface and a relational data model. Hive uses a language called HiveQL, a dialect for SQL. Just like Pig, Hive is also an abstraction on top of MapReduce.

- **Sqoop**: This transfers data from Hadoop to relational, structured data storages such as SQL as efficiently as possible.

To run this sample, you need to install Azure PowerShell as well.

How to do it...

Now let's try to see how you can leverage the Azure portal to create a Hadoop job to count the number of occurrences of the words with parallel nodes running on files:

1. Open the Windows Azure management portal and create a storage account. Take a note of the credentials to access it.

2. Create an HDInsight data service with four nodes and a password to access the service. You also need to specify a storage account information that you have just created.

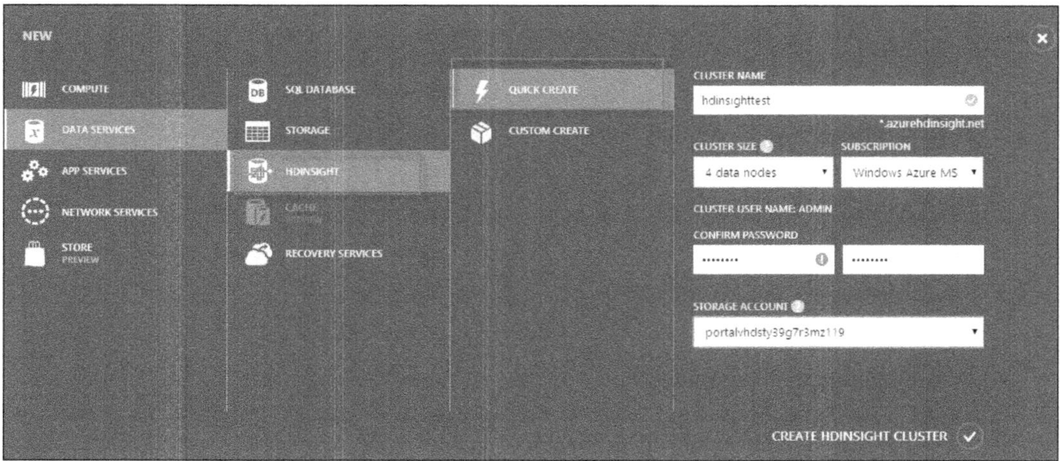

3. This will create an HDInsight node with four clusters. The storage account once selected cannot be changed later, and if the storage account is removed, the clusters would no longer be available for use.

4. Once the HDInsight nodes are created, it will be time to run some sample code to demonstrate MapReduce algorithms. Let's try to run the MapReduce job on `WordCount`.

5. Open Windows Azure PowerShell and run the following command:

```
$subscriptionName = "<YourSubscriptionName>"

$clusterName = "<YourHDInsightClusterName>"
```

6. The following command creates a MapReduce job description. The `hadoop-examples.jar` file comes with an HDInsight cluster distribution and can be used for testing MapReduce on the clusters:

```
$wordCountJobDefinition = New-AzureHDInsightMapReduceJobDefiniti
on -JarFile "wasb:///example/jars/hadoop-examples.jar" -ClassName
"wordcount" -Arguments "wasb:///example/data/gutenberg/davinci.
txt", "wasb:///example/data/WordCountOutput"
```

7. Once the MapReduce job is created from the `hadoop-examples.jar` file, you can start running the job. To submit the job, run the following command:

```
Select-AzureSubscription $subscriptionName

$wordCountJob = Start-AzureHDInsightJob -Cluster $clusterName
-JobDefinition $wordCountJobDefinition
```

   Here, you can see that in addition to `SubscriptionName`, you also need to pass in `Clustername` where the MapReduce operation needs to run.

8. You can ask the portal to check the completion of a MapReduce job using the `Wait-AzureHDInsightJob` command, as follows:

```
Wait-AzureHDInsightJob -Job $wordCountJob -WaitTimeoutInSeconds
3600
```

   This command will wait with a timeout of 60 minutes. To see the job output, you can use the following command:

```
Get-AzureHDInsightJobOutput -Cluster $clusterName -JobId
$wordCountJob.JobId -StandardError
```

9. When the job is finished, Windows Azure stores the result in the Blob storage. So, to retrieve the storage, you need a container name for the reference. Let's create another variable for `$containerName`.

10. We run the following command to create the Windows Azure context object:

```
Select-AzureSubscription $subscriptionName

$storageAccountKey = Get-AzureStorageKey $storageAccountName | %{
$_.Primary }

$storageContext = New-AzureStorageContext -StorageAccountName
$storageAccountName -StorageAccountKey $storageAccountKey
```

   The `Select-AzureSubscription` command is used to set the default subscription for the entire command.

11. Once the context is set up, you can download the job result from the Blob storage. We can use `Get-AzureStorageBlobContent` and pass in the container name to get the Blob content, as follows:

```
Get-AzureStorageBlobContent -Container $ContainerName -Blob
example/data/WordCountOutput/part-r-00000 -Context $storageContext
-Force
```

The default filename for the MapReduce job is `part-r-00000`, and in this example, the file gets downloaded to the `c:\example\data\WordCountOutput` folder.

12. Finally, to print the MapReduce job, you can run the following command in the PowerShell window:

```
cat ./example/data/WordCountOutput/part-r-00000 | findstr "there"
```

The preceding command will list all the words that have the word `there` in it with the count of number of occurrences of each word.

How it works...

Hadoop is a technology that allows you to process Big Data into multiple machines simultaneously and thereby solve the problem of Big Data. The Hadoop for `WordCount` parses the document in parts in different clusters and provides a key value collection where the key specifies the word and the value specifies the total number of occurrences.

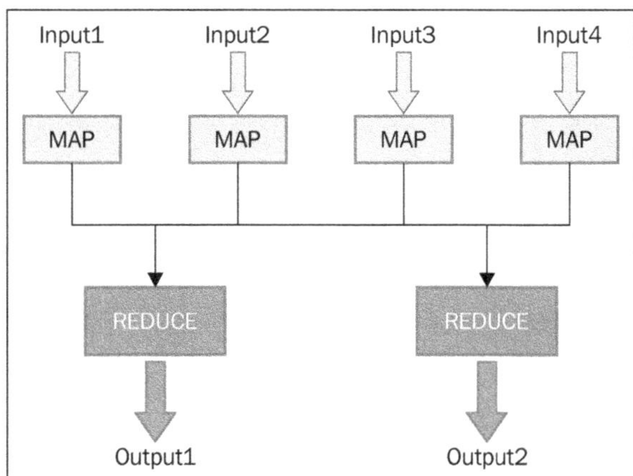

In the preceding diagram, you can see the input divided into four parts, and each of them is sent to an individual cluster to invoke mapping. Following the `WordCount` example, the mapper takes each line from the input text and breaks it into words; it then breaks each word into a `KeyValue` pair and follows it up by 1. The reducer then sums up the individual counters for each word and emits a single `KeyValue` pair containing the word, followed by the sum of occurrences.

Let's see what the WordCount Java code looks like:

```java
public class WordCount {

  public static class TokenizerMapper
       extends Mapper<Object, Text, Text, IntWritable>{

    private final static IntWritable one = new IntWritable(1);
    private Text word = new Text();

    public void map(Object key, Text value, Context context
                    ) throws IOException, InterruptedException {
      StringTokenizer st = new StringTokenizer(value.toString());
      while (st.hasMoreTokens()) {
        word.set(st.nextToken());
        context.write(word, one);
      }
    }
  }

  public static class IntSumReducer
       extends Reducer<Text,IntWritable,Text,IntWritable> {
    private IntWritable result = new IntWritable();

    public void reduce(Text key, Iterable<IntWritable> values,
                       Context context
                       ) throws IOException, InterruptedException {
      int sum = 0;
      for (IntWritable val : values) {
        sum += val.get();
      }
      result.set(sum);
      context.write(key, result);
    }
  }

  public static void main(String[] args) throws Exception {
    Configuration conf = new Configuration();
    String[] otherArgs = new GenericOptionsParser(conf, args).
getRemainingArgs();
    if (otherArgs.length != 2) {
      System.err.println("Usage: wordcount argument mismatch");
      System.exit(2);
    }
    Job job = new Job(conf, "word count");
    job.setJarByClass(WordCount.class);
    job.setMapperClass(TokenizerMapper.class);
    job.setCombinerClass(IntSumReducer.class);
    job.setReducerClass(IntSumReducer.class);
    job.setOutputKeyClass(Text.class);
```

```
        job.setOutputValueClass(IntWritable.class);
        FileInputFormat.addInputPath(job, new Path(otherArgs[0]));
        FileOutputFormat.setOutputPath(job, new Path(otherArgs[1]));
        System.exit(job.waitForCompletion(true) ? 0 : 1);
    }
}
```

In the preceding code, you can see that there are two methods: one is `map` and another is `reduce`. The `map` method breaks each word into a set and initializes the output with `1`, while the `reduce` method sums up all the similar words and increases the counter. From the **Main** page, the job is created and the classes are set. Finally, the job result is sent to the output path.

The `New-AzureHDInsightMapReduceJobDefinition` method takes a classname and runs the class from the `.jar` file with the arguments specified:

```
$wordCountJobDefinition = New-AzureHDInsightMapReduceJobDefiniti
on -JarFile "wasb:///example/jars/hadoop-examples.jar" -ClassName
"wordcount" -Arguments "wasb:///example/data/gutenberg/davinci.txt",
"wasb:///example/data/WordCountOutput"
```

The preceding code calls the `WordCount` class with the argument `davinci.txt` and the output file to be written to `WordCountOutput`.

See also

► Refer to the HDInsight tutorials at `http://bit.ly/hdinsightch7`

Working with Mobile Services in Windows Azure

With the growing number of mobile developments around the world, there is a constant need for a server system to closely interact with the mobile environment. The server needs to handle scalability and allow advanced features such as Push Technology and Scheduling to the server. Windows Azure Mobile Services are a solution to this problem. Windows Azure Mobile Services provide some benefits that include the following:

► Stores data in a SQL Server database

► Secures and supports multiple authentication modes (Live authentication and Facebook authentication)

► Provides the Push messaging service

► Provides the ability to schedule recurring jobs

From an application developer's point of view, Mobile services provide a complete solution to all the problems that need to be handled as a server for an app.

Getting ready

Open the management portal and create a Mobile Service.

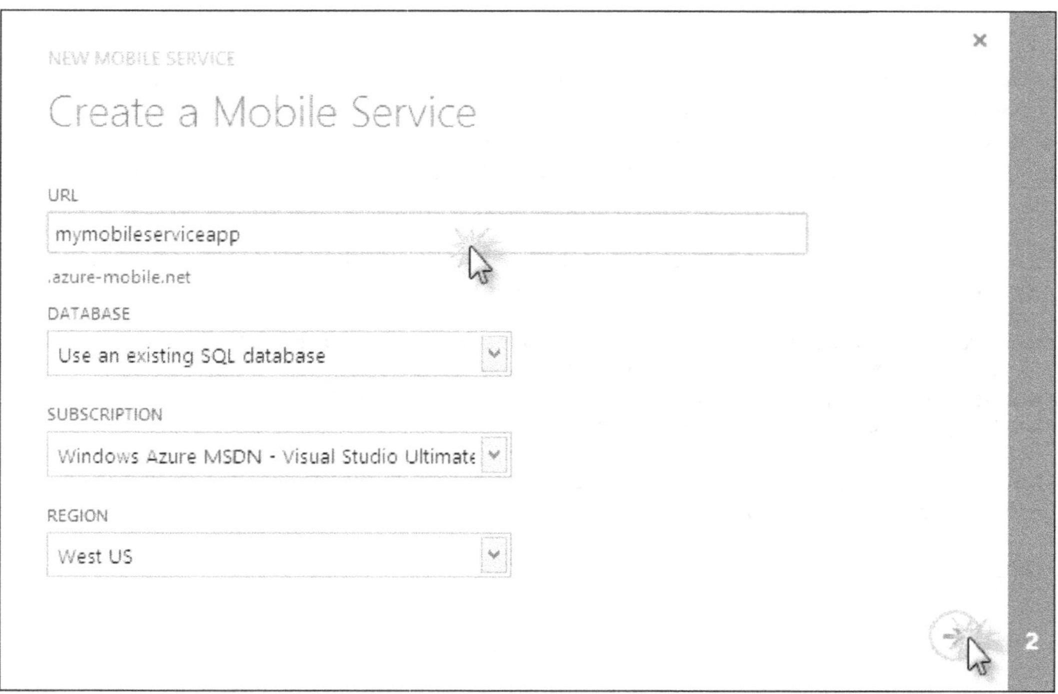

We name it `mymobileserviceapp`. Once the service is ready and in the running state, you can configure it to provide authentication, push notification, scheduling, and so on.

How to do it...

Now let's create a Mobile Service and use it for the server-side app for devices.

1. Open **Mobile Service** and navigate to **Identity**.
2. Enter the details of the client ID and client secret for various settings that you want to enable.

3. Now, create a table and select the option to provide permission to access for only authenticated users.

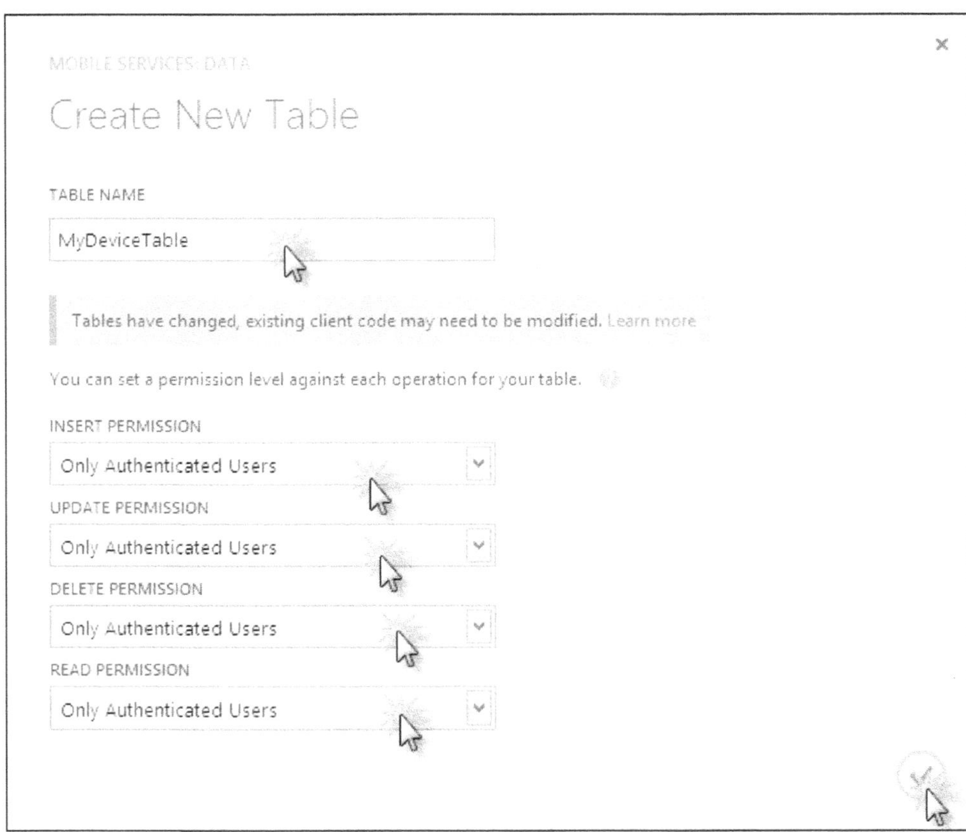

The table then created will only be accessed by an authenticated user from the app.

4. Now, once you navigate to the dashboard, download the Windows 8 App for C# with the `ToDoItems` table included.

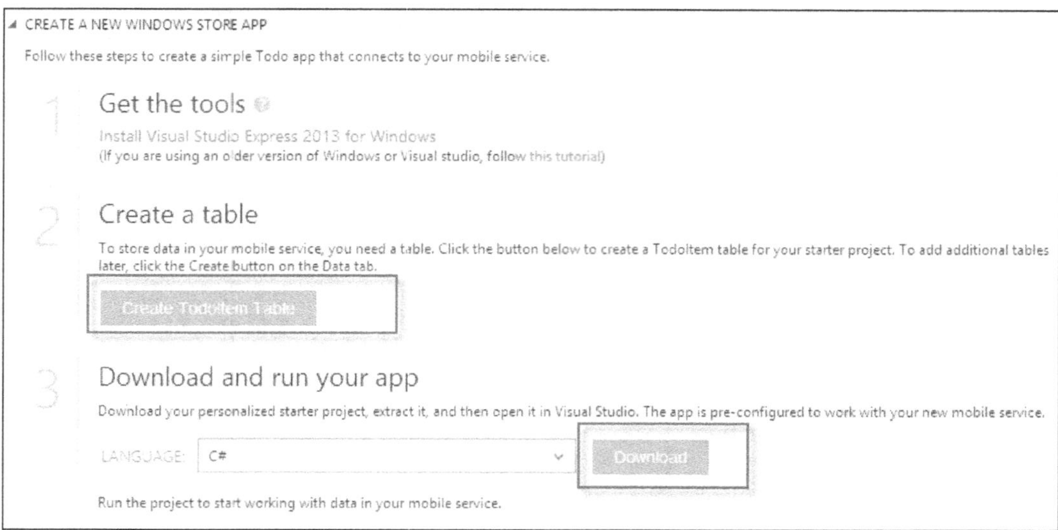

If you open the project, you will see that `MobileServiceClient` is already referenced for the current Mobile Service and configured appropriately.

5. Now, to authenticate the application using credentials, we use the following code:

```
var user = await App.MobileService.LoginAsync(MobileServiceAuthent
icationProvider.Facebook);
```

The preceding code will authenticate the service using the Facebook authentication for the current device. Now, if you call it `OnNavigatedTo` of the main page, the application will authenticate on startup.

6. To add a schedule update script to the application, go to the **Scheduler** tab of the Mobile Service and add a scheduler job. Let's name it `getupdateavailablescript`:

```
getupdatesavailablescript

CONFIGURE    SCRIPT

1  var updatesTable = tables.getTable('Updates');
2
3  function getUpdatesAvailableScript() {
4      updatesTable.insert({
5          date : new Date()
6      });
7      console.warn("You are running an empty scheduled job. Update the script for
8  }
```

7. Here, `getTable` gets a table called `Updates` and inserts a date into the table. After every scheduled time is elapsed, data is inserted into the `Updates` table with the current date and time. Note that the `Updates` table has a column date. You can use a scheduler to push data to the clients at an interval.

8. Open the Windows store app and add a push notification to the application. The application opens up with a **Register name** dialog. Register the app name here and finish the wizard. The app is now registered for notifications.

9. To send the push notification, we use the following code:

```
function sendNotifications(uri) {
    console.log("Uri: ", uri);
    push.wns.sendToastText01(uri, {
        text1: "Sample toast from sample insert"
    }, {
        success: function (pushResponse) {
            console.log("Sent push:", pushResponse);
        }
    });
}
```

The preceding code sends the push notification with the `Sample toast from sample insert` text to the app.

How it works...

Mobile Services act as a backbone for any mobile app. Windows Azure built Mobile Services to ensure the scalability of Azure is easily available to mobile apps. The server supports scheduling and allows access to push notification services; it also allows the app to use an existing technology to easily add features that might be commonly needed for an app to run.

Mobile Services handle authentication and security so that only authenticated users can access the service.

Mobile applications have been widely becoming popular nowadays. With the increase in app development, Mobile Services are widely been favored as they are pluggable and support ready code for various mobile platforms. Let's look at some other things that might be worth noting about Mobile Services.

Calling a custom API from Mobile Services

Mobile Services support the addition of a custom API such that mobile devices can call the API to get the data or run specified batch requests. A custom API gives the ability to send a single POST request and sets a defined task.

We open the Windows Azure management portal and add a new API with the name MyCustomAPI. As we require POST messages to be accessed by this API, we set **POST PERMISSION** to **Everyone** to avoid security of the application:

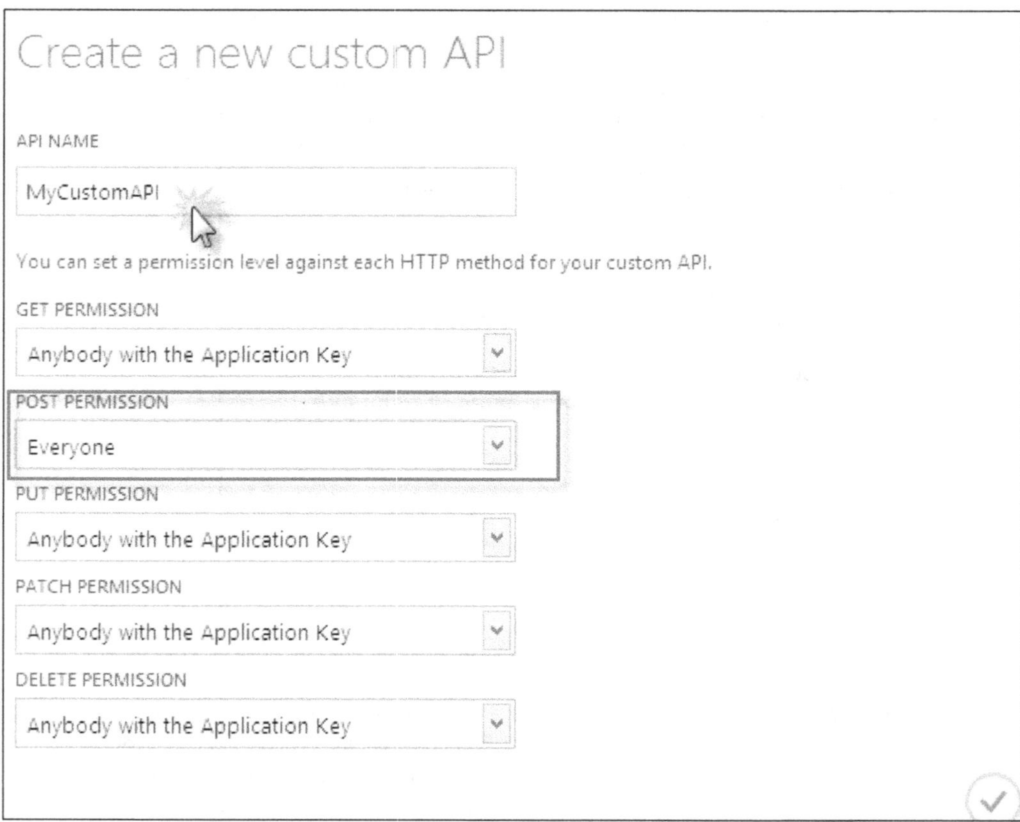

Once the custom API is created, you need to add some code to it so that when the API is called from the client, the server is updated:

```
exports.post = function(request, response) {
    var mssql = request.service.mssql;
    var sql = "insert into Updates (data) values (GetDate())"
    mssql.query(sql, {
        success: function(results) {
            if(results.length == 1)
                response.send(200, results[0]);
        }
    })
};
```

Here, the preceding code inserts a new row to the table `Updates` when it is called from the client. To call the API from the client application, we use the following code:

```
var result = await App.MobileService.InvokeApiAsync<MarkAllResult>("m
ycustomapi",
            System.Net.Http.HttpMethod.Post, null);
    message =  result.Count + " rows updated.";
```

Here, the Mobile Service calls the `mycustomapi` method created on the server to run the `Post` script and get the result from the query.

Uploading big files to Mobile Services

Uploading and saving large files on transactional databases is not a good practice. Windows Azure supports Blob storage to store data files that are big enough to store in transactional databases. Mobile Service supports relational databases, but occasionally, with a trick. You can also store files that are large in size to Blob storage and reference them using the URL rather than actual data being stored in the database. To configure this, create a storage account and update the credentials to the app settings of Mobile Service:

Once the storage account name and access key is added to the app settings of Mobile Services, then by taking the credentials from the Blob storage account, let's try to add some data to the Blob storage:

```csharp
private async void InsertData(MyDeviceTable deviceTable)
{
    string errorString = string.Empty;

    if (media != null)
    {
        deviceTable.ContainerName = "myimages";
        deviceTable.ResourceName = media.Name;
    }


    await deviceTable.InsertAsync(deviceTable);


    if (!string.IsNullOrEmpty(deviceTable.SasQueryString))
    {
        // Get the new image as a stream.
        using (var fileStream = await media.OpenStreamForReadAsync())
        {

            StorageCredentials cred = new StorageCredentials(deviceTable.
SasQueryString);
            var imageUri = new Uri(deviceTable.ImageUri);


            // Instantiate a Blob store container based on the information
in the returned item.
            CloudBlobContainer container = new CloudBlobContainer(
                new Uri(string.Format("https://{0}/{1}",
                    imageUri.Host, todoItem.ContainerName)), cred);


            // Upload the new image as a BLOB from the stream.
            CloudBlockBlob blobFromSASCredential =
                container.GetBlockBlobReference(deviceTable.ResourceName);
            await blobFromSASCredential.UploadFromStreamAsync(fileStream.
AsInputStream());
        }
    }


    // Add the new item to the collection.
    items.Add(deviceTable);


}
```

Here, when the `insert` operation on the Table is performed, it generates a SAS request that waits for the application to upload the data to the Blob storage. Here, you can see during the insertion of data to a `deviceTable` storage on the cloud. The large data file is being uploaded to the server using SAS credentials. Now, to enable the service to receive SAS credentials from the server such that the appropriate Blob storage container is used, we change the code of the `insert` statement of `MyDeviceTable` on the Azure portal to support the `SASString` response:

```
var azure = require('azure');
var qs = require('querystring');
var appSettings = require('mobileservice-config').appSettings;


function insert(item, user, request) {
    // Get storage account settings from app settings.
    var accountName = appSettings.STORAGE_ACCOUNT_NAME;
    var accountKey = appSettings.STORAGE_ACCOUNT_ACCESS_KEY;
    var host = accountName + '.blob.core.windows.net';


if ((typeof item.containerName !== "undefined") &&
   (item.containerName !== null)) {
     item.containerName = item.containerName.toLowerCase();

     var blobService = azure.createBlobService(accountName,
        accountKey, host);
     blobService.createContainerIfNotExists(item.containerName, {
         publicAccessLevel: 'blob'
     }, function(error) {
         if (!error) {
             var sharedAccessPolicy = {
                 AccessPolicy: {
                     Permissions:
azure.Constants.BlobConstants.SharedAccessPermissions.WRITE,
                     Expiry: new Date(new Date().getTime() + 5 * 60 *
1000)
                 }
             };


             // Generate the upload URL with SAS for the new image.
             var sasQueryUrl =
             blobService.generateSharedAccessSignature(item.
containerName,
             item.resourceName, sharedAccessPolicy);


             // Set the query string.
```

```
            item.sasQueryString = qs.stringify(sasQueryUrl.
queryString);

            item.imageUri = sasQueryUrl.baseUrl +
sasQueryUrl.path;


        } else {
            console.error(error);
        }
        request.execute();
    });
} else {
    request.execute();
}


}
```

The preceding code modifies the `insert` operation on `mydevicetable` such that it provides a window of 5 minutes to upload large data to the secured Blob storage. It generates the SASString URI for the Blob container, which is later used by the client to upload the files.

Index

Q

Queues
about 245, 253
combining, with Blobs 256-258

R

raw notification 143
relational databases
about 126
working with 126-137
reminder 120
Representational State Transfer (REST)
about 67
advantages 68
Request object 45
REST-based WCF service
writing 67-75
REST service
reference link 78

S

Select-AzureSubscription command 274
Server Application 165
service configuration file (.cscfg) 260
service definition file (.csdef) 260
service extensibility 92
ServiceHost class 48-50
service package (.cspkg) 260
shims 192
Simple Object Access Protocol (SOAP) 42
SmartTag extender
creating, MEF used 232-235
Software as a Service (SaaS) 244
solution 161
source code
debugging, breakpoints used 9-11
source code sharing 171
SQL Azure
about 266
cloud computing, benefits 266
transactional queries, running from
portal 271, 272
URL, for MSDN documentation 272
working with 266-270

SQLite
URL 137
Sqoop 273
storage account
creating 254, 255
Storage Service, Windows Azure
about 245
Blobs 245
Queues 245
Tables 245
stubs 192
SubmitChanges method 133
Suspended state 112
Suspending state 112
svcutil tool
about 55
used, for generating proxy classes 55, 56

T

T4 templates
reference link 223
used, for creating multiple
output files 218-220
used, for optimizing code
generation 222, 223
working with 212-217
TableAttribute 129
Table Data Stream 266
Tables 245, 253
Team Foundation Server. *See* **TFS**
team project 161
team project collection 161
Terminal Services 40
test-driven development
dealing with, in Visual Studio 189-191
Test Explorer 180
TFS
about 157-180
branching 170
merging 170
TFS Background Job Agent
reference link 177
TFS branching
checking, by inspecting visualizer 172
TFS scheduled jobs
creating 174-177

Thank you for buying
Visual Studio 2013 and .NET 4.5 Expert Cookbook

About Packt Publishing

Packt, pronounced 'packed', published its first book "*Mastering phpMyAdmin for Effective MySQL Management*" in April 2004 and subsequently continued to specialize in publishing highly focused books on specific technologies and solutions.

Our books and publications share the experiences of your fellow IT professionals in adapting and customizing today's systems, applications, and frameworks. Our solution-based books give you the knowledge and power to customize the software and technologies you're using to get the job done. Packt books are more specific and less general than the IT books you have seen in the past. Our unique business model allows us to bring you more focused information, giving you more of what you need to know, and less of what you don't.

Packt is a modern, yet unique publishing company, which focuses on producing quality, cutting-edge books for communities of developers, administrators, and newbies alike. For more information, please visit our website: `www.PacktPub.com`.

About Packt Enterprise

In 2010, Packt launched two new brands, Packt Enterprise and Packt Open Source, in order to continue its focus on specialization. This book is part of the Packt Enterprise brand, home to books published on enterprise software – software created by major vendors, including (but not limited to) IBM, Microsoft and Oracle, often for use in other corporations. Its titles will offer information relevant to a range of users of this software, including administrators, developers, architects, and end users.

Writing for Packt

We welcome all inquiries from people who are interested in authoring. Book proposals should be sent to `author@packtpub.com`. If your book idea is still at an early stage and you would like to discuss it first before writing a formal book proposal, contact us; one of our commissioning editors will get in touch with you.

We're not just looking for published authors; if you have strong technical skills but no writing experience, our experienced editors can help you develop a writing career, or simply get some additional reward for your expertise.

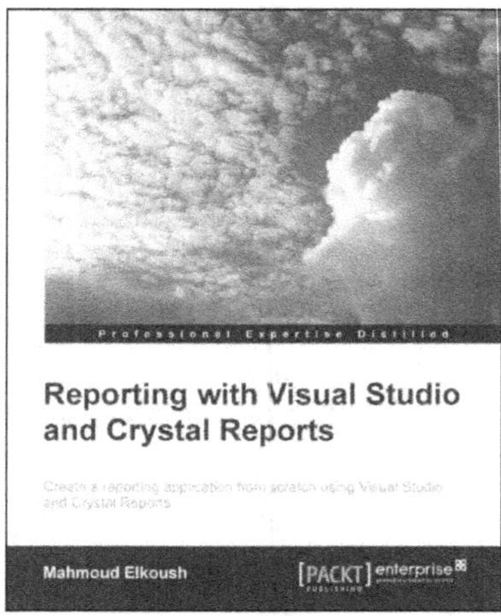

Reporting with Visual Studio and Crystal Reports

ISBN: 978-1-78217-802-6   Paperback: 148 pages

Create a reporting application from scratch using Visual Studio and Crystal Reports

1. A step-by-step guide that goes beyond theory, letting you get hands-on experience.

2. Utilize a dataset and table adapter as data sources for your report.

3. Learn how to add reports to forms and pass parameters dynamically.

Visual Studio 2012 Cookbook

ISBN: 9781-84968-652-5   Paperback: 272 pages

50 simple but incredibly effective recipes to immediately get you working with the exciting features of Visual Studio 2012

1. Take advantage of all of the new features of Visual Studio 2012, no matter what your programming language specialty is!

2. Get to grips with Windows 8 Store App development, .NET 4.5, asynchronous coding, and new team development changes in this book and e-book.

3. A concise and practical First Look Cookbook to immediately get you coding with Visual Studio 2012.

Please check **www.PacktPub.com** for information on our titles

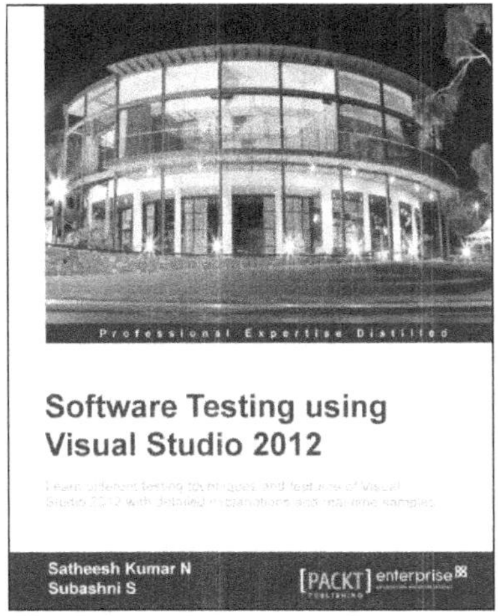

Software Testing using Visual Studio 2012

ISBN: 978-1-84968-954-0   Paperback: 444 pages

Learn different testing techniques and features of Visual Studio 2012 with detailed explanations and real-time samples

1. Using Test Manager and managing test cases and test scenarios.

2. Exploratory testing using Visual Studio 2012.

3. Learn unit testing features and coded user interface testing.

4. Advancement in web performance testing and recording of user scenarios.

.NET Framework 4.5 Expert Programming Cookbook

ISBN: 978-1-84968-742-3   Paperback: 276 pages

Over 50 engaging recipes for learning advanced concepts of .NET Framework 4.5

1. Explores the advanced features of core .NET concepts in step-by-step detail.

2. Understand great ways to enhance your website by securing against cross-site scripting attacks, enabling third-party authentications, and embedding maps.

3. Covers interesting real-world projects with ASP.NET, Silverlight, ADO.NET, and Entity Framework.

Please check **www.PacktPub.com** for information on our titles